"To study the Way is to study the self. To study the self is to forget the self. To forget the self is to be enlightened by all things."
~ Dogen, Buddhist scholar

"The Universe looks less and less like a big machine and more and more like a great thought."
~ Sir James Jeans, astronomer

The Wisdom Keys

A Channeler's Quest Reveals Four Steps to Your Highest Self

JUDI THOMASES

Copyright © 2014 Judi Thomases.

All rights reserved. No part of this book may be used or reproduced by any means, graphic, electronic, or mechanical, including photocopying, recording, taping or by any information storage retrieval system without the written permission of the publisher except in the case of brief quotations embodied in critical articles and reviews.

Illustrations from the Rider-Waite Tarot Deck® reproduced by permission of U.S. Games Systems, Inc., Stamford, CT 06902 USA. Copyright ©1971 by U.S. Games Systems, Inc. Further reproduction prohibited. The Rider-Waite Tarot Deck® is a registered trademark of U.S. Games Systems, Inc.

Balboa Press books may be ordered through booksellers or by contacting:

Balboa Press
A Division of Hay House
1663 Liberty Drive
Bloomington, IN 47403
www.balboapress.com
1 (877) 407-4847

Because of the dynamic nature of the Internet, any web addresses or links contained in this book may have changed since publication and may no longer be valid. The views expressed in this work are solely those of the author and do not necessarily reflect the views of the publisher, and the publisher hereby disclaims any responsibility for them.

The author of this book does not dispense medical advice or prescribe the use of any technique as a form of treatment for physical, emotional, or medical problems without the advice of a physician, either directly or indirectly. The intent of the author is only to offer information of a general nature to help you in your quest for emotional and spiritual well-being. In the event you use any of the information in this book for yourself, which is your constitutional right, the author and the publisher assume no responsibility for your actions.

Any people depicted in stock imagery provided by Thinkstock are models, and such images are being used for illustrative purposes only.
Certain stock imagery © Thinkstock.

Printed in the United States of America.

ISBN: 978-1-4525-1641-7 (sc)
ISBN: 978-1-4525-1643-1 (hc)
ISBN: 978-1-4525-1642-4 (e)

Library of Congress Control Number: 2014910402

Balboa Press rev. date: 7/1/2014

CONTENTS

Journeying ix
Introduction xi

The Four Advanced Worldviews of Awareness 3

At The Entrance: Everyday Life 15

**The First Worldview: Understanding The Fundamentals
Of The Soul's Wisdom Game** 21
   Keys Of Consciousness For The First Worldview 25

The Second Worldview: Mastering Creative Potential 53
   Keys Of Consciousness For The Second Worldview 58

The Third Worldview: Your True Relationship With The World ... 105
   Keys Of Consciousness For The Third Worldview 110

The Fourth Worldview: Truth Of You And God 157
   Keys Of Consciousness For The Fourth Worldview 162

Appendix A
   Techniques For The Quantum Shift 203

Appendix B
   The Cosmic Plan 205

Appendix C
   The Messages: Spiritual Guidance From The
      Brotherhood Of Light Workers 227

Appendix D
   Getting There... Arriving! 289

Works Consulted 295

ILLUSTRATIONS

- Floating Eye and Keys (cover)
- Continuum of Awareness
- The Four Worldviews: Getting From Here to There
- Before Awakening
- The First Worldview: The Wisdom Game ~ Inner Choices
- The Second Worldview: Empowerment & Joy
- Mandelbrot Set Patterns
- Breathing Box
- The Magician Tarot Card
- The Third Worldview: World & Connection
- A traveler puts his head under the edge of the firmament in the original (1888) printing of the Flammarion engraving.
- The High Priestess Tarot Card
- The Wheel of Fortune Tarot Card
- The Hanged Man Tarot Card
- The Fourth Worldview: Universe Awakening
- The Star Tarot Card
- The Strength Tarot Card
- The Dollar Bill
- Temperance Tarot Card
- Hubble Galaxy

JOURNEYING

What if one person's journey showed the way to your own enlightenment? What if my inner path could give you the key to solving your life?

There is no other way to tell this story than to begin with the personal "I". (However, as you'll see, that's just the route that will take *you* toward the greatest expansion of consciousness.)

I have been taken on a remarkable journey—a journey to infinity. Through visionary and mediumistic means, I have been taken out-of-body, contacted by wise entities (like teachers, or guides), and shown a perspective that transcends ego and form.

I have gone into a place where "I" was changed into *us*, and then into *them*, and finally into a merging of identity that is beyond the universe! I have been guided over a divide until I completely lost the sense of self, found a new realm (which I'll call The M Field), and then returned to the everyday experience with a zeal and a mandate to share the adventure with you, gentle reader. Everyone can make this journey; I can only report it, and show all my steps.

Because of my background in metaphysics and spiritual philosophies, once I reached that realm the pieces of a great puzzle came together… a hidden mystery that explains "I Am" (a key phrase in all metaphysical teachings) and reveals a Great Plan for mankind.

Some others who have attained this awareness over the centuries have been able to remain in it full-time. We call them saints or Realized Masters. But I couldn't. I was "sent back" into the lower, mundane consciousness in order to tell the story in a no-frills sort of way. Functioning as a reporter, and nothing else, I can now lay out a map of myriad clues to solving that great cloaked puzzle—a new way of viewing life so that all hidden symbols are but mystic markers along the same path and all prophecies are but pointers to the same goal.

By explaining where I've been led, I hope to help you too discover your way from *Here* to *There*.

Judi Thomases
Magnolia, DE
2014

INTRODUCTION

There is a journey that can only be taken inwardly. It is a journey that the self takes in finding its truth and its nature. Though it is different from person to person, nevertheless the milestones of the journey can be delineated, and the general steps conveyed to another self, another soul...to you.

For me the journey began in 2005 in a time when I couldn't sleep. I would sit in a rocking chair near my bedroom, half dozing, half in trance. In this fashion I began to receive a series of messages that seemed to come from a source beyond me. It wasn't the first time I had experienced this kind of altered awareness; since my youth I had recognized a connection to other planes of consciousness (memories?) of what could only be past lives, and at about age 30 I had had an out-of-body experience that opened my "third eye" of inner vision for good. Nor was it the first time I had encountered channeled messages of this type; just four years earlier than the journey's start I had received teachings from my spirit guides, The Brotherhood of Light Workers, that became the basis of a book called *Wisdom's Game*.

Suffice it to say, the gist of *Wisdom's Game* was that life truly *is* a game—one that Allness chooses to play *with Itself*, taking on individual forms (that's *us*) in order to experience contrast and thus gain wisdom. The opening gambit is to accept limitation and thus know anguish, and the winning strategy is to learn to master emotion and control the thought process to transcend suffering.

The book had just barely been released, but now more of these messages were "coming through," unbidden. There it was again, the demand to open up a space in the daily flow of life and be the conduit once more. The Brotherhood had more to say, and they weren't going to let me relax.

"No," I pushed back. "I'm too busy."

"Make time!" was all they said. *Funny!*, I groused silently, then griped aloud, *"Taskmaster!"* But in the wee hours, with my pen scribbling on a yellow pad and the letters trailing off in almost indecipherable scrawl, I complied and the messages came through—22 in all, over a period of 24 months—eventually taking shape as the book you're now holding.

WHERE "I" CEASES AND "ALL" BEGINS

As the messages continued, I was going on with my life, promoting *Wisdom's Game*, working with clients in my astrology and spiritual counseling practice, and even going through a big house renovation project. All the while, the content of these messages kept percolating through my psyche, subtly transforming me at great depths, and slowly entering my client sessions and my writings. I kept questioning who *they* were: Were *they* wise elders? Were *they* God? Were they just an aspect of me, inventing and imagining this process? I really didn't have a clear answer in my own mind. I only knew that the material coming through was definitely not from my own brain because I'd been getting that *"ah-ha!"* experience, the sense that what was just spoken/written/received was a new thought, a new concept, a piece of new information that was both surprising and awakening. But where it came from had been a confusing mystery.

It wasn't until several months had elapsed since the new book was initiated that the impact of the accumulated wisdom words hit me. My early dry analysis of the messages became steeped with meaningful life experiences, and I began having profound visions. It led me to the realization that I was being presented with nothing less than an entirely new view of life and of the world. In fact, you could say my entire notion of who *they* were, and consequently who I was, was being transformed and reconfigured.

Here, the nature of thought itself, and how thought is the constructor of the universe, was being examined and dissected. Elaborating upon the *Wisdom's Game* concept of spirit's play in human form, a new theorem dawned: the world of matter is built by inner thought-construction, and in fact *thought* is all that exists. There is no *self* without thought; there is no division. By pursuing the notion of delimited personal identity (ego) to its conclusion, I was brought full circle to No-Limitation, or Allness.

In order that this understanding would sink in, I was being "carried over a divide"... *shown*, not just told, how Self tells its story to itself, and how the contrast between the lower and higher aspects of consciousness (or inner and outer, or ego and God) can be realized simply as a flowing continuum of awareness. Suddenly, I saw and could comprehend how the world of appearance is constructed, and how to move easily between poles of awareness. I could see the role of emotion, and I could see more clearly than ever the marvelous soul's wisdom game that the universe is playing when "I" switches back and forth with "All", especially in moments of crisis or challenge when wise choice is paramount. Bottom line, the revelation dawned that there was no set point where I ended and *they* began; that there was a *sliding continuum of awareness* that defined me and *them*, and that that same infinite ladder also defined where I stopped and the world began. In other words, there was no definite division or separation at all, and the entire soul game of consciousness was simply a way that Creation (God) talked to itself, or Source conversed with Source; and in its need for infinite divine play and infinite creativity it created the illusion of you and me, which at the same moment was the illusion of me and the world, or the illusion of time and space.

Everything began to make sense. All the teachings of the mystics, all the philosophy of the East, all the wisdom of Kabala and of numerology and of astrology and of tarot, all of the Buddhist koans, all the gurus' words suddenly held new meaning. It was as though a veil had been lifted and a piercing light of understanding had broken through.

After that moment of pure enlightenment, I saw that there was a way to take others on that same journey, or up that same infinite ladder of Me, and usher them as best as words would allow into a similar understanding, if not the very experience itself. That would be the next book – this very one.

This is what we're writing here. And it is "We." The effort is that of myself and my guides, but also of me and you, because ultimately the epiphany is that I am you, you are me, and we are one. We are Light itself.

THE JOURNEY: GETTING FROM HERE TO THERE

The amazing thing about this journey is that the more personal it is, the more universal it becomes. It is impossible, in other words, to discover your own deepest truths without simultaneously discovering everyone's deepest truths... because at bottom what one discovers is not just the deepest truth of self, but the universal truth of the nature of life itself, and the ultimate truth of what the self is, what life is, and even what God is. For these are all the same.

The deepest possible questions can be answered by the inward journey. *Know thyself.* When that journey is profound enough, these ultimate questions are answered very simply. All the mysteries of life and death, the afterlife, the beyond, and the purpose of it all, are suddenly resolved. Enlightenment dawns. An epiphany is reached. Realization becomes crystal clear. Yet, frustratingly, the Nirvanic experience is the hardest to describe. The word usually reverted to is "ineffable," because no words can convey it. Or ample words are used but don't do it justice.

Furthermore, in reaching this profound state, the mind also discovers related truths about the nature of the Present Moment and of current "reality" that give clarity to so much that is confusing and even agonizingly conflicting. Personal enlightenment, it turns out, is exactly the same as entering the Mind of God. It is equivalent to reaching full wisdom about the Self's great soul's wisdom game of life and of its willing participation in the illusion of duality. Personal enlightenment means penetrating the veil of illusion, seeing the structure of the universe, knowing your real power in it, and realizing oneness, joy, and lightness. The importance of understanding one's personal creative power can't be minimized. It's about becoming whole, holistic, and holy. All spiritual paths, and all mystical symbols, are the pointers to this destination.

The value of such realization becomes instantly obvious. Life looks like play. Experiences become subject to the new perspective in which even the concept of suffering can be conceived differently… joyously! Wisdom can represent the very solution to personal problems. The ponderous sense of "real life" is transmuted into a lightness of being. The identity is forever shifted from helpless pawn to empowered co-creator. Inner peacefulness is gained. An expansion of consciousness allows the self to permeate all realms, including the "paranormal". The boundaries of 3-D form are bridged. And the fear of death is removed forever.

The "pay-off", to the personal consciousness, is just this: the goal of ascension. But to the Universal Mind, the "pay-off" is something much larger. It's the development of "spiritualized matter" – a race of beings who are fully aware and blessedly good. It's the intention of this book to describe one person's inner journey as it arrives at a universal destination of clarity and understanding, simultaneously uncovering a grand plan of destiny for the human race.

So ultimately, as the great mystery comes clear, here's the nugget of the guidance that's been given: **You have the power to create your future as you improve your strategic efforts in your soul's wisdom game of life. You and I are really Oneness learning, evolving, and mastering choice. We are self, world, and God, all at once and all in one. We are waking up to this amazing revelation, and in so doing we are realizing that we create the universe as we go along.**

HOW TO USE THIS BOOK AS AN ACCELERATION TOOL FOR YOUR PERSONAL EVOLUTION

In this book, an ultimate journey is revealed: a map to reach your greatest self and additionally save our struggling world. Evolving consciousness is presented as four stages, or Worldviews. The journey leads through a continuum of awareness, from the illusion of duality to the awakening into Oneness. When you follow a path to understanding through these four stages, you arrive at a realization of this core truth: that there is only consciousness playing its game of duality. That's the "end" of the journey—the self realizing what Self really is.

Wisdom's Game had come through unbidden in the shape of clairaudient and fully-formed concepts, pretty much like taking dictation. Its core message is that we are infinite spirit, bored with endless bliss, playing a self-invented, completely realistic game – the soul game of life – in which we deliberately immerse our newly-minted separate identities into circumstances that entail suffering. The point of the soul's wisdom game is to gain wisdom, especially the wisdom of compassion. The game plan is to accept a dilemma, follow a passion, and thus create a life-task. Part of the soul's wisdom game is the ultimate awakening to its very existence – which is happening right now! – and the ensuing recreation of the game's terms in a fresh and conscious way. That's the current era called The Age of Aquarius.

Now The Brotherhood is presenting new messages that examine the nature of thought, elucidate the concept that the world is created by mind, and reveal that there is no real differentiation between the observer and the source. These **twenty-two channeled messages** that precipitated this journey and formed the basis for the epiphany that I want to share with you are presented as Appendix C.

The main body of this book outlines **The Four Worldviews of the Continuum of Awareness,** the "meat" of *The Wisdom Keys*. It turns out that each Worldview is a gateway into a new view of reality (a new paradigm), and each gate requires a key. Surprises await you as you grasp each key; murkiness falls away and you gain insights into the nature of reality that radically change your sense of who you are. Here then, you'll learn all about the following ground-breaking concepts: *The Quantum Shift, Capping the Point of Awareness, Realization of How You are the Creator of Your Reality, How the You Doesn't Exist,* and *How You Can Overcome the Fear of Death.* By the end of The Fourth

Worldview, the game-plan is transparent and you have much of the knowledge you need to begin applying understanding to your personal struggle—you're on the fast track to liberating wisdom.

The purpose of this book is to wake people up!
To work with the Law of Cause & Effect (Karma) as well as the Law of Attraction
To reach higher and deeper levels of inner awareness
To understand The Wisdom Game.
To *Know Thyself*

Game-player alert: this book has power! It has power to change you. It will *shift* you.

You might not be able to read it through at one sitting. It is never easy to work with the hidden mysteries. You may need to read a part, and then come back to it. The power to shift you is the means to change your view of the world and of yourself. Your mind and heart must open to accommodate these words. If you come to a point where you need to pause and lay down the book, do so for a while to let your mind adjust to the new vision.

Take heart. You are the universe waking up! And we're in this together.

THE FOUR WORLDVIEWS
OF
THE CONTINUUM OF AWARENESS

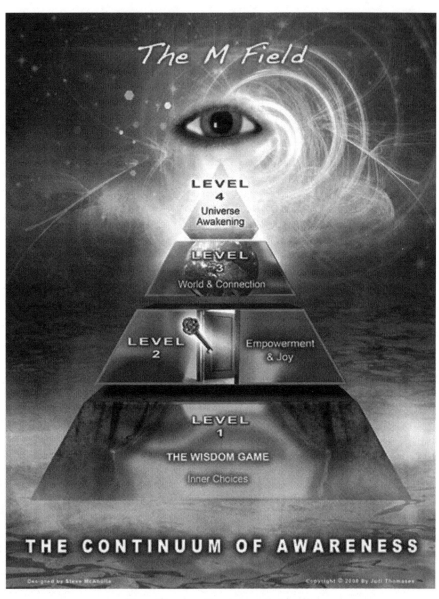

Graphics by Stephen McAnulla

THE FOUR ADVANCED WORLDVIEWS OF AWARENESS

I received the channelings mentioned over a period of twenty-four months (from January 12, 2005, to January 7, 2007). My first reaction was to ponder them deeply with reason and intellect. But digesting the teachings began a process that ushered me forward into new realizations. Questions arose about the process of channeling itself: Who is talking? Who is answering? Who am *I*? These in turn gave rise to musings filtered through a lifetime of studies and daily work in metaphysics, astrology and extrasensory perceptions. The ideas percolated within my consciousness, and I underwent a powerful psychological transformation as the concepts worked their magic on my psyche… whereupon odd notions, vision and mystical connections, and an amazing avenue of discovery unfurled. Only then was I able to put two and two together, and in a flash, "got" singularity! In no time (literally!), I *saw*. The riddle of the ages was solved – the same way it'll perhaps be for you.

Revelation came in stages as I distilled my new understandings into a four-level continuum of awareness—the path we'll trace together in this book.

The first revelation on my journey was that we are spiritual beings (energy) choosing to participate in a soul game; the soul's wisdom game has rules and strategies, and a way to "win". This is The First Worldview, the first stage of understanding – the notion that we are in a theater of life, playing our self-created roles in our self-created scripts.

The second revelation was that the higher beings who were "talking" to me were an aspect of my own self (or of any self), taking interior positions along a spectrum of consciousness – **a *continuum of awareness*** – in order to engage in a dialogue to question and explore "reality". There are no fixed points on this sliding scale, but there is always the sense of duality. Sometimes the voice seemed far wiser than I; sometimes only that of a next-door neighbor! Sometimes it was obvious that the answering voice had a larger perspective to access understanding that was beyond my current ken, but at other times it felt perplexingly like talking to myself. I realized that I was tracing the universal process of splitting the core self into Me & Other, or Do-er & Observer. Here, then, is also the point at which the notion of co-creation appears, wherein the world becomes malleable to one's will, and the hard facts of "reality" start to relax a little.

The third revelation was that the entire illusion of contrast, occurring only in the mind, and very fluid, defines the basis of the creation of all separate things: the world, the individual, God, reality. Conversely, all separate things are just the one consciousness – *"I Am"* – engaging in this terrifically creative and enlightening drama. Allness is just interacting with itself. At The Third Worldview, seeing this, I began to lose the sense of separateness as the bounds of hard reality loosened even more.

The fourth big revelation was that nothing exists, only the Mind of God; people are just projections, and the world and its myriad components are likewise just a projection. Similarly, time and space are not real, nor are "inner" and "outer"; this leaves only one thing existent: conscious awareness, continuously evolving (expanding) into its ever-increasing creative potential... that is to say, into wisdom. With this last realization at The Fourth Worldview, a paradox unfolds as the very meaning of the concept of "I" is altered. Suddenly, "I" am both Self and All. "I" (who am not what "I" think "I" am, but oh, so much greater, existing primarily to wake up to all this veiled truth), am left with only one option: to love. To love "my" self. To love "my" fellow beings (who are simply projections of "my"self, of Oneness reflected). To love the world and all creation. To love "my" past and future selves in all their guises. Then, the glory of realizing the true power of love becomes obvious. By stepping through the last gateway into The Fourth Worldview, only "I AM" exists – pure awareness – and you have merged fully with The Creator.

GOING THROUGH THE GATES

Once I got past the mode of receiving the new channelings, and became psychologically immersed in their embedded wisdom, an organizational process came to the forefront of my mind. I found that I could systematize the continuum of awareness into four Worldviews, based on these stages of revelation.

AT THE ENTRANCE: EVERYDAY LIFE
   Prior even to embarking on this inner mystical journey of awakening, it's plain to see that the everyday world of shared consensus reality and small separated ego identity is all that is presented to our minds. We have no other perspective, no broader viewpoint. Furthermore, our worldview is stubbornly resistant to anything else. And so we exist in a hapless fog, feeling like pawns of a greater power and victims of our fate. We pray to God for help and succor. The world is a scary place, and we're lost in it.

THE FIRST WORLDVIEW: UNDERSTANDING THE FUNDAMENTALS OF THE SOUL'S WISDOM GAME
   Life is a soul game that you enter into willingly, forgetting its essence until you are given understanding. After that, in flashes of insight, you arrive at a changed perspective which includes a fresh outlook on the difficulties of the human drama, the role of personal choice, the rules of engagement, and a new awareness that allows you to overcome entrapment in order to leap out of the old paradigm into a new one, to see how it works, and to begin to reframe your very own soul's wisdom game. This is known as The Quantum Shift. You accept your karmic

choice and learn how to better engage with your drama. Here, you're awakening to life's wisdom game and how best to play it. Insight and empowerment result.

THE SECOND WORLDVIEW: MASTERING CREATIVE POTENTIAL

As you understand that you accepted challenges, you begin to perceive, and then acknowledge, and ultimately **overcome your karmic predicament.** As you do so, you see that there is a correlation between what you *think* (inner) and what occurs (outer), so the rigid walls of reality begin to flicker. It follows that you begin to perceive a larger field of reference, an energy field, a quantum reality. And your mind becomes able to maneuver in this new paradigm. In doing so, you structure thoughts and pull toward you that which you desire. Now you are realizing the Art of Manifestation, and playing with the Law of Attraction. Synchronicity (those odd but meaningful coincidences) is your delight as you awaken to your own joy and empowerment. The world becomes safer as you see your role in your life's design.

THE THIRD WORLDVIEW: YOUR TRUE RELATIONSHIP WITH THE WORLD

Full self-realization is the same as the understanding that **the exterior and interior are one.** In other words, the world doesn't exist outside of consciousness so much as *within* it, and so you realize that there's no separation between "me and the world", or "me and others", and you begin to integrate both. You have lifted the Veil, your heart opens, your intuition leads and can now begin to follow **the greater good**, gaining the universe's support in personal efforts. At the same time, your very work or purpose becomes that of benefiting the world because the world is seen as yourself. Meanwhile, the fear of death is removed! You as the New Human are born, awakening to your place in the planetary story.

THE FOURTH WORLDVIEW: THE TRUTH OF YOU AND GOD

A very advanced state, here begins the understanding of the universal truth: that the *self* is <u>the same as</u> the *other*. That you, in working consciously with your own thoughts, perceive the entire basic illusion of the world: that **nothing is real outside of the mind**, or outside of consciousness. There is only The All… or the One Self, or Mind of God, playing the soul's wisdom game of contrast and discovery. Then a further shift occurs in which the separation or duality between the self and the other, or between me and you, disappears. And the true oneness is known. Now the Veil is completely removed. There is only "I", the one heart, playing its wisdom game. You've awakened to waking up the world.

PLAYING THE GAME

The notion of life as a game may at first seem to be trivializing people's struggles. Substituting the word *drama* may feel more seemly, especially in view of the painful circumstances of many people's lives. However, from the most advanced, or cosmic, perspective – which is the destination to be reached through the Four Advanced Worldviews of Awareness – it will be seen that *game* or *play* are perfectly appropriate descriptions of reality. In fact, in Eastern philosophy, there is a word for this truth: *layla*. Layla means "divine play". The entire universe is the divine play of God. And since, as will ultimately be revealed, you are none other than an aspect of God, you must therefore be unconsciously participating in the divine wisdom game of life.

The spirit guides who are our teachers – The Brotherhood of Light Workers – wish for this game metaphor to be disseminated, that we begin to see our pain and travails as play, drama, illusion, a self-created trial that can be mastered and transcended. Becoming enlightened to this understanding, after all, means becoming lighter, more playful, less entangled, wiser, and more in control of your destiny, and thus of the world's.

As there are levels of awareness, there are **levels to playing** the soul's wisdom game. As you evolve, you will be able to access higher levels of the soul's wisdom game and choose the worldview at which you want to participate. At the start, you may feel that you are lost in your karmic dilemmas, confused as to what your path is, groping for answers, struggling with challenges, dealing with the painful or even frightening prospects of your life and of the world, and having only a glimmer of light (i.e., an inkling of your dreams or hopes) to make your way towards. But you know that there is more, and you have become a seeker to find some answers.

As you gain wisdom you'll move to the next Worldview, but initially you'll have to help yourself. Before you can do anything greater, the first step will be to realize that you're in the game – life's soul's game – in order to bring your issues right up to the surface and get your energy flowing. And then, as you see evidence that you have succeeded in navigating your obstacles while nevertheless continuing to flow, you'll find yourself reaching your purpose and manifesting your potential. In doing so, your perception will change profoundly, probably several times.

Once you've realized (seen, perceived) that identity and reality keep **shifting** from denser and more limited constructs into lighter and more expansive notions simply through a process of inner awakening, it dawns on you that you are not in a severe and victimized life story but in a rather magical place where you have choice regarding where to situate your being. You can, in other words, travel *within consciousness* from The First Worldview's limitations to The Fourth Worldview's transcendence merely by awakening to each possibility and then exploring life (being-ness) at that viewpoint.

Once the path is fully revealed, you can play with the entire notion of self and identity (or non-ego, if you choose) as you move along the infinite **continuum** while determining which spot is best for you at any moment. Eventually, you'll just become the Flow, and will be able to play the soul's wisdom game effortlessly.

OPENING THE GATES WITH KEYS & TOOLS FOR THE JOURNEY

To move out of everyday reality, and then through a series of worldviews, requires a passage of some sort through a boundary. Since new awareness is needed in each instance, here's where we need to talk about a gate. A **gate** is a door that stands between two places. By its very existence, it implies some sort of barrier, or divide, that separates and defines the two. Since gates have latches or keys, it also implies a way to limit or open access. Somebody controls or owns the power implied by this: a gatekeeper.

When we speak of consciousness, what gate could we refer to if not the one that opens with an inner key between interior realms?

Personal reality constitutes a realm (worldview). Although we take it for granted, our daily minds dwell in this realm – **a worldview or landscape** to which we give certain characteristics. Our current worldview (notion of reality) contains propositions such as: everything is composed of small molecules of matter; the human psyche is comprised of a conscious ego and a subconscious alter ego; nobody can control the weather; time is linear; UFOs may be real; and so forth. Some scientists and philosophers question these tenets but for the most part we all agree to this consensus reality.

Contemporary "reality" was not always thus. Worldviews have shifted profoundly over the course of human history. Once upon a time, the stars dotted a sphere that encapsulated the earth, the panoply of gods were real, and it made perfect sense to make sacrifice to them in order to secure felicity. In those days, the wisest human minds advised this because it fit the paradigm best. The past, therefore, was truly "a different world".

A worldview can be seen as global and evolutionary. All humans in each era believe in its properties, and the world is formed in this fashion. But always there were some who, by accident or application of technique, or even by grace, moved out of and beyond its limitations into new and more advanced awareness. Certain saints, for instance, or Zen masters, even during the darkest of ages were able to transcend the superstitions or limiting beliefs of their eras, and awaken to rapturous bliss or full compassion. On the inner level, they journeyed through a gate that held most people in check. They found the key that was needed.

In today's world, never was **a key** more urgently needed to let us out of the limitations of an outworn and self-sabotaging reality and into a better world. A more peaceful soul and a more beneficent society are on the other side of the gate. Transforming the worldview swiftly is the gift that is being given to us so that the individual can more quickly awaken.

So how do we get there?

Paradigm shifts take place in the mind, for that's where reality is held. Once you realize that you are the owner of the gate and the master of the key, nothing can stop you from evolving quickly – not just from one worldview to another, but all the way "forward' until you reach full comprehension. This goal is called **Self-Realization or Enlightenment**, and can be delineated as a journey through four unfolding worldviews—the levels of awareness we've discussed—each with its own set of characteristics and metaphoric tools for navigating it.

Each of the following symbolic elements and descriptive terms have been chosen in order to aid your understanding of the changing worldviews and the differences that the mind perceives as it moves through each boundary and into more light.

Using **four keys** of **four different symbolic metals** to open **four gates** that each lead into **four different** worldviews, a path to true self-realization is given. The chart on page 14 can be used as a meditation tool to illuminate the experience of the journey-er at each different level. It contains keywords that tell of each realm's special ability, tool, and result.

Remember that each gateway is a passage point or doorway from one worldview to another. The four transition points are seen as: **A Curtain, A Door, A Bridge,** and **A Portal**. These are symbolic representations of each stage of the mind's awakening. These, in short, are the gates, and gates, if locked, need their keys. Key 1 is **choice**; Key 2 is **The Art of Manifestation** (a *power* key); Key 3 is **vision**; and Key 4 is **service.** They're tied directly to each Worldview, and they are what open each next gate, so they are true keys (and quite real behavior patterns to learn).

The four metals, or transformative materials, are portrayed as: iron, copper, silver, and gold, corresponding symbolically to the levels of wisdom (i.e., light) contained therein as well as the degree and type of usefulness of each new awareness. Iron is sturdy and supportive; copper is shiny and malleable; silver is ethereal and reflectively divine; and gold is pure, incorruptible, and radiant.

And the four worldviews, or landscapes, are described as: **The Game, The Art of Manifestation, The Continuum,** and **The Mind of God**. (These are not symbolic, but actual worldviews, at each stage of awareness.) The First Worldview (The Game) looks like a gameboard or stage, with players/actors; The Second Worldview (The Art of Manifestation) is a shimmering "magical" place where solid forms are dissolving and reforming; The Third Worldview (The Continuum) is a ladder or bridge of endless light; and The Fourth Worldview (The Mind of God) is a limitless energy realm, a place of no-form.

WHAT CAN YOU GET FROM THE WISDOM KEYS?

With these symbolic tools and metaphysical maps in hand, you're about to embark on a journey into greater awareness. It will take you in understanding step by step to a radically different but greatly and increasingly more empowered and happy mindset while altering your view of life, answering a lot of deep questions (e.g., why do bad things happen to good people?, what's the point of it all?), and sorting out many famous teachings and age-old symbology.

For those who allow their minds to be opened by these Four Worldviews of revolutionary concepts, and let their thoughts broaden beyond the limiting barriers of mere words, an inter-dimensional portal will appear through which only awareness (not logic) can pass; then a far-reaching shift in consciousness will occur that will transport them past a restrictive notion of ego-identity, and into a transcendent realm of truth and peace.

The Brotherhood of Light Workers' teachings, made accessible in this fashion, provide the clues and comprehension to carry you from where you may now reside in your psychological outlook, to a wholly new place of spiritual connectedness that can help you solve personal issues, and even reinvent your role in the improvement of the world.

LIVING THE MYSTERY

As I'm sitting here writing this material, I'm alone at a friend's house, using it as a kind of writer's retreat for quietude and minimal distractions. And because she's a lot taller than I am, she's got her teacups stored on a shelf that's too high for me to reach. She has given me a great gift – that is, the use of her beautiful home – and I'm here joyfully appreciating it. But at the same time, I'm realizing that I can't get the needed teacup! Round about this time, the phone rings and my host asks if I wouldn't mind letting a plumber in to fix a faucet. Of course, I assent, and when he shows up, I realize that he's just the right height to ask a favor! My need is thus easily met, and I recognize the unity of the practical desire and the almost immediate fulfillment of it.

In a broader sense as I labor, my everyday mind is appreciative of my friend's benefaction and of my good fortune in being given this wonderful opportunity to write the book and get my thoughts straight, and have some peace and quiet to do so. And a part of me wonders in earnest at this general stroke of luck. But then, another part of me – the evolved and enlightened wisdom part that is actually writing this book – comes to the forefront of my mind and says to me: You have created all this in perfect harmony with the needs of your spiritual task; you have manifested just what was required. Yes, your friend – the other you of the moment – has with an open heart offered her largesse, but at the very same moment so did you, co-creator of reality, bring it into manifestation, even to its particulars.

This then, is the story being told, the fundamental mystery that in every moment, whether the big ones that are life-changing, or the minutiae when you are picking up your dry cleaning – only "you" exist and only "you" create the experience "you" know as life and as the world. This will become clearer as you encounter and move through the Worldviews.

From here let's begin to unravel the mysteries and learn what is really taking place beneath the surface of things.

GETTING FROM HERE TO THERE

GATE/ WORLDVIEW	APPEARANCE	LANDSCAPE/ REALM	KEY	ABILITY	METAL	TOOL	RESULT
AT THE ENTRANCE	Everyday Life	Fog	Karmic Predicament	To live	Lead	Passion	Suffering
1	Curtain	The Wisdom Game	Choice (The Quantum Shift)	To switch out of negativity	Iron	Emotional Mastery, Control of Thought	Wisdom
2	Door	The Law of Attraction	Power (The Art of Manifestation)	To co-create what you desire	Copper	Conscious Co-creation	Joy
3	Bridge	Continuum	Vision (Capping the Point of Awareness)	To realize who you are and overcome the fear of death	Silver	Intuition & ESP	Light
4	Portal	Mind of God	Service (Merit)	To know truth and be the Way	Gold	No-Ego, Surrender	Bliss

###

AT THE ENTRANCE

EVERYDAY LIFE BEFORE AWAKENING

GATE// WORLDVIEW	APPEARANCE	LANDSCAPE/ REALM	KEY	ABILITY	METAL	TOOL	RESULT
AT THE ENTRANCE	Everyday Life	Fog	Karmic Predicament	To live	Lead	Passion	Suffering
1	Curtain	The Wisdom Game	Choice (The Quantum Shift)	To switch out of negativity	Iron	Emotional Mastery, Control of Thought	Wisdom
2	Door	The Law of Attraction	Power (The Art of Manifestation)	To co-create what you desire	Copper	Conscious Co-creation	Joy
3	Bridge	Continuum	Vision (Capping the Point of Awareness)	To realize who you are and overcome the fear of death	Silver	Intuition & ESP	Light
4	Portal	Mind of God	Service (Merit)	To know truth and be the Way	Gold	No-Ego, Surrender	Bliss

Where do you stand, and what is your relationship to the soul's wisdom game of life at this point? At this entry point, the existence of the first gate is unrecognized, the doorway unseen, and the great route into and through new and evolving worldviews exists only in potential. Not only is the path into and through new consciousness shrouded, but its potential is felt only vaguely as aspiration or intuition while its reality beckons only through dreams and myths. In a word, you simply don't know the game exists, or what its rules are, how to enter it, how to play it, where it leads, or even why it is desirable to go there. You have been plopped into a body, on a planet, your memory erased, and you are left to your own devices. You are a pawn of fate.

Before you set forth, you are in a foggy place of confusion, emotionality, and amnesia. The metal is LEAD, the basest material, a dense element that scarcely emits light. You see no path, no point. The landscape is AMORPHOUS – unclear, uncertain. You are lost within the story of yourself (ego), and though you may see a dim light on the horizon, or follow blindly toward a louder ego-voice than your own, in fact you have no KEY to pass through this place, and only one tool: PASSION. You have been following your passion and groping around. The world seems a scary place,

<u>GATE/WORLDVIEW: AT THE ENTRANCE</u>

APPEARANCE: Everyday life. Everything seems normal – that is to say, you feel buffeted by circumstances, and don't sense much control over destiny.

LANDSCAPE / REALM: Fog. Nothing's very clear to you, especially the future.

KEY: You are playing out your givens, coping as best you can with your karmic predicament.

ABILITY: Being alive is the gift and the challenge.

METAL: Lead. It weighs a lot. It's strong enough. It doesn't conduct or reflect any light. It can be harmful or shielding.

TOOL: Passion. No matter what you're living through, or what hand you've been dealt, you have a dream. You carry a desire. You'll keep forging ahead to realize it.

RESULT: Suffering. Life often feels like a "vale of tears", full of pain and struggle.

and from time to time you probably feel weak and small. This dark place is sometimes called Ignorance.

This is the typical experience of most people in the current era. The purpose of this book is to bring awareness to the path forward from here, to the advanced levels of conscious awakening that are available – indeed, beckoning – to us all..

EVERYDAY LIFE: NO KEYS, NO GATES, JUST THE USUAL

To be perfectly clear, there is nothing out of the ordinary to be at this stage. In fact, that's the point! The Entrance is daily life.

You go about your business feeling like an isolated personality interacting with other isolated personalities, doing your best to survive and thrive. You cope, and sometimes prevail. You play the hand you were dealt at birth, and try to maximize your luck and skills, but always feel at the mercy of larger forces beyond your control.

Even if you are one of the most fortunate people on the planet – for instance, the richest, most famous, most attractive, or most powerful – you still feel pretty impotent against nature, your own mortality, and usually a particular challenge that plagues you throughout your days. ("Everyone has Saturn somewhere in their chart," the astrologer would say.)

You talk to yourself all day long in your mind, weighing, planning, adjusting, and deciding. You learn from your mistakes; you relish your successes. You feel elated or thwarted depending on results. And you go about your daily business in this mind-set until the candle blows out.

There is nothing wrong with living your whole life in this limited mode of perception. Indeed, it's the history of mankind, with only very few people heretofore who ever discovered a path beyond it. But that's the wonderful thing about our current era, The Age of Aquarius: now the doors are opening, and all are invited through. The limited perception is called "darkness" or "ignorance" in spiritual studies; the doorway is called "enlightenment" or "illumination". Wouldn't it be great to find the steps to take to embark upon this interesting journey into new awareness, in which you could learn the different ways to perceive daily life, and in particular the notion of self, so that your journey became easier, more empowering, and much more joyful?

Wouldn't it be great to solve a riddle of the ages, keep advancing, and ultimately become the very creator of your universe?

ENTERING THE WISDOM GAME

Entering the Wisdom Game means stepping forward into something new. Even if you have simply stumbled across this book, happy wonderment lies ahead. Perhaps grace or good fortune has brought you to this point; perhaps it's been your own efforts to consciously evolve. In any case, you are at the entrance of a grand awakening, and can rightfully call yourself one of the enlightened. Insights, breakthroughs, and realizations will be milestones on your journey to wisdom, and on that journey you can see yourself as the entire universe evolving through you, becoming awake to itself via your perceptions.

The Key to move out of this Pre-Awakened state of ignorance or darkness and into the first worldview of new empowerment is to realize the role of choice – the *choice* to be you, and the choice in each moment to react in a fresh way.

HERE'S AN EXAMPLE OF A PRE-ENTRY LEVEL INDIVIDUAL, AT THE THRESHHOLD OF THE FIRST WORLDVIEW

Distraught and feeling completely victimized, when Client D first came to see me, she was stuck in a painful residential situation, feeling friendless, not making sufficient income, and endlessly sad. She had tried other avenues of counseling without results. What could I offer her? The first thing I suggested was to name the screenplay of her drama, her personal movie! What was on the marquee? She immediately came up with a title which (no surprise!) was rather gloomy. Next, I asked her to design the movie's lobby poster. I told her there was to be a looming monster, a damsel in distress, and a hero to her rescue. She fleshed these categories out by naming and describing them. Impressively, her heroic figure was quite spiritually conceived. Then I asked her by what device the hero would save her? She construed a light-bearing instrument that would awaken her own heart-powers that she might ultimately wield them independently. The watching crowds would cheer her on, I said, hoping that her success would be transmitted to them eventually too. Lastly, I charged her with playing this out in "real life" now. That's the soul's wisdom game!

~~~

THE FIRST WORLDVIEW

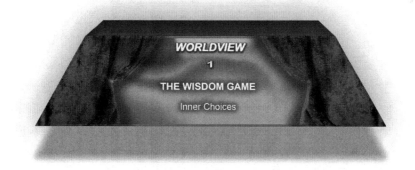

UNDERSTANDING THE FUNDAMENTALS OF THE SOUL'S WISDOM GAME

GATE/ WORLDVIEW	APPEARANCE	LANDSCAPE// REALM	KEY	ABILITY	METAL	TOOL	RESULT
AT THE ENTRANCE	Everyday Life	Fog	Karmic Predicament	To live	Lead	Passion	Suffering
1	Curtain	The Wisdom Game	Choice (The Quantum Shift)	To switch out of negativity	Iron	Emotional Mastery, Control of Thought	Wisdom
2	Door	The Law of Attraction	Power (The Art of Manifestation)	To co-create what you desire	Copper	Conscious Co-creation	Joy
3	Bridge	Continuum	Vision (Capping the Point of Awareness)	To realize who you are and overcome the fear of death	Silver	Intuition & ESP	Light
4	Portal	Mind of God	Service (Merit)	To know truth and be the Way	Gold	No-Ego, Surrender	Bliss

What are the components of wisdom, and why is it important to accrue? In this first worldview, we start to examine concepts including the nature and experience of wisdom; the idea that gaining and using wisdom is a Game – *The Game of the Soul* – and that Earth is a school to teach you to play this game well; that you have a Personal Energy Pattern (karmic pattern) which can be unblocked and shifted by recognizing your karmic dilemma (*the "hole in your soul"*) and overcoming it; that you have made choices, *including choosing your parents* – choices that are shown clearly in your horoscope – in order to evolve; that emotions play a key role in causing pain and suffering, thereby blocking energy, but that a new understanding gained through quantum physics regarding the way the mind creates reality offers fuller choice and unlimited possibilities in the creation of your reality henceforth; that scientific breakthroughs concerning the quantum theory of entanglement and in holography are revealing how to dynamically reframe your life in each moment (The Quantum Shift) by mastering emotion and holding a new vision; and that you are really playing a soul game of wisdom in which, by learning its rules and applying its clues and strategies, you can actually "win" by choosing joy and visualizing results. **The big secrets learned at this worldview are that you are actually both actor and director of your life, that your choice determines your reality, and that you live within a hologram wherein you can make instantaneous shifts in consciousness to improve your drama.**

One day, by the grace of your good karmic potential, you find yourself at the gate to The First Worldview. (That could even be through reading this book!) Your lucky stars have led you to what seems to be a large

GATE/WORLDVIEW: 1

APPEARANCE: **Curtain and Stage**. The theater of life. You see that you are an actor in a movie. Somebody writes the script; somebody directs the action.

LANDSCAPE/REALM: The Wisdom Game. Life is a gameboard or stage.

CURTAIN. Near that is a strong KEY. It is made of IRON, a durable and useful material. Harmonious sounds emanate. Pieces of knowledge are seen strewn about, as clues. Curiosity moves you; suffering spurs you on. You put down your leaden weight, pick up the key of usefulness, and lo, the Curtain rises.

> GATE/WORLDVIEW: 1
>
> **KEY: Choice (The *Quantum Shift*)**. The actor finds a device to alter the script moment-by-moment. The Director seems pleased.
>
> **ABILITY:** To switch out of negativity whenever you choose, by an act of will.
>
> **METAL: Iron**. A symbol of usefulness and strength with the means to cut through the fog. More light can penetrate.

You enter The First Worldview, and find yourself an actor on a stage. The lights go up, and here is what you find.

KEYS OF CONSCIOUSNESS FOR THE FIRST WORLDVIEW

What if life were really a game that you were playing and didn't realize it?

What if you had once known, but had since completely forgotten, the object of this game and the rules of engagement?

Your life is a spiritual game. It is all designed. However, you can change it. You are the designer of your game plan. You designed it to have some challenges and to follow your passions. You designed it so that you would be born at exactly the right moment when certain energy patterns would be in effect, which would allow a measure of potential to arise and a degree of challenge to be faced.

There's a way to play this soul's wisdom game and wake up within it. At The First Worldview, the whole point of existence is to figure out how life works, how to get needs and desires met, and how to get happier and more fulfilled as you go along. Some choices work well, and some do not. This is the soul's wisdom game you've always been playing.

The parts you need to grasp to play better are: Who You Are, Why You Are Here, and What Is The Soul's Wisdom Game That You Came to Play.

Welcome to your Wisdom Game! You have stepped on stage and can now look at yourself as both the actor and the director.

Your Personal Energy Pattern

What is your Personal Energy Pattern? It is a unique blueprint of mathematical (energetic) combinations that's revealed at the time of your birth. The pattern contains both harmonious and discordant patterns, some of which allow energy to flow easily and some of which cause energy blockages. It is a map of your core wisdom game plan.

Everyone plays The Wisdom Game to the same basic end - the goal of which is to gain wisdom by expressing energy as your unique pattern and to uncover what there is to discover about the value and the experience of the journey. But there are as many ways to play the soul's wisdom game as there are an infinite number of possibilities around which energy patterns can form. So the same game is played in order to express unique harmonic or mathematical patterns.

People choose patterns that may be more or less harmonious, more or less challenging, and with harder or easier parameters. We call this luck or bad luck. We see it as an accident or a random throw of the dice, but in fact it's self-designed to make use of existing threads that have already been sent forth and formed in order to put a life together based on returning actions. In other words, as karma and karmic possibilities. We also play the soul's wisdom game to accomplish a self-chosen task or reach a self-chosen agenda. These goals are given to us by no one other than ourselves in the formation of the soul's wisdom game plan, the life plan.

Everyone has different motivations or passions, which reside in the soul as *the dream*. Playing the soul's wisdom game well helps to alleviate the obstacles faster, get closer to the potential or realization sooner to bring about the creative possibilities that are inherent in the mathematical pattern. (Another word for which is your personality.) The personality is a blending of chosen talents and chosen challenges. In other words, a mixture of karmic threads from the past. Did you choose your parents? Why are you who you are? What brought you to Earth, and what are you wanting? Yes, of course, your parents conceived you and you were born - on a certain day, hour and place. But there's more to it. You know this because you remember or recognize certain things that are familiar to you even though you've never encountered them, and other things that are distasteful to you even though you have no reason for that. And so, if you stop and think about it, you have a familiarity with life that is self-apparent and need not be proven scientifically.

By waking up to this and not just being carried along "willy-nilly" and by seeing the plan and identifying its components, the individual awakens, sees what needs to be done, understands how best to operate within it and applies techniques whenever necessary to unblock energy, release passion and realign thoughts. There are general perceptions to understand and there are specific ideas to grasp.

Your Personal Energy Pattern not only reveals your basic makeup but also an overall agenda, or soul purpose, to pursue and accomplish. It's great to be in control of your P.E.P. because by figuring it out, you gain empowerment and reach your goals more easily, at the same time you find calm and joy sooner.

Your P.E.P. is vibrational in nature, and follows a path of flow as you create what you do from moment to moment. There are many games being played in life; you could be playing the game called Control Over Others, or The Rat Race, or Poor Me, or I Give Up Don't Bother Me, or the game called If I'm Really Nice Someone Will Love Me. You could be playing a Fame game, a Money game, or a Power game. Will these games bring you to what you want and where you truly want to be, which is a place of empowerment and joy?

The one game that is the most important game to understand and master – the one game that will put you in charge of your own life – is The Wisdom Game. Learning its four Worldviews will allow you to access your internal wisdom system.

The Wisdom Game is the mind's awakening. It is a fresh perspective on your life – a perspective previously hidden or masked – that shows what the meaning of your life really is, why you came here, what your soul purpose is, what role pain, suffering and struggling really play in your personal experience, and what game you are participating in day after day that you may know nothing about.

By figuring out what this soul's wisdom game is, what its rules are, what you need to do to play it better, to strategize more effectively to master the context, you can learn to view the world in a fresh new way, accept your struggles and pain, quickly transcend your issues, bring more humor and perspective into your days, and become stronger and wiser overnight.

Suppose there was a way to remember the rules of the soul's wisdom game and see how to apply them to your life to bring more joy, fulfillment and success much more quickly at the same time to reduce the pain and suffering that you might be encountering? Now suppose there was a way to really strategize so that you came to an understanding that you were the master of the soul's wisdom game, the creator of the circumstances, and not just a pawn?

This is the point when you realize that you're in The Wisdom Game.

What is Wisdom?

People tend to think of wisdom as something that takes a long time, requires discipline and meditation, and removes you from the world like the monk sitting in the forest. Well, yes, there is certainly great wisdom in serenity and detachment, but that type of wisdom seems a long way away, boring to do, and truthfully seems rather unobtainable in today's hectic, over-tasked world.

However, the truth is that wisdom can be something else too. Wisdom is available at every moment. Wisdom gives you knowledge about how life works, what in life feels good or hurts, and how to make better choices each time. It gives power, clarity, joy and, finally, compassion. It is what puts you into an awareness from which all things now become possible.

Wisdom is not only serenity, but is electric... an *ah-ha* thing! Often it's the bolt of insight, the exhilarating flash of understanding that clarifies and brightens the picture. Like an electric realization, a jolt of energy, a zap of awakening, an intuitive flash, or instant perception, wisdom can be the electrifying moment of knowing, the insight that charges up your system, gives you realization, and shows you who is really running the show in your own personal world.

It's not that we're asleep. It's just that we're unaware of this electric energized state that's available all the time, and as we comprehend and connect the synapses, our brains respond. There's this aware moment. A flashpoint! Wisdom comes in flashes of insight… it wakes you up! I've seen this happen with my students time and again as their minds expand and principles are grasped. One person, who was mentoring me on technology, began to see the outlines of the soul's wisdom game of life as I ran through my blog curriculum, then started asking question after question as flashes of insight arose and she "connected the dots". Her awareness level shot up exponentially just by being exposed to concepts nobody had ever presented to her, and the quickness of her mind made fast work of the new data.

Awakening is electric! It's not ohhhhmmm…it's *"hel-lo!"* To come alive, to wake up, and to see – we often need the bolt, the zap, the instantaneous electric flash. That's what awareness is. Awareness feels very **awake**.

However, that said, there's no shortcut to gaining wisdom. You can't learn it intellectually. Life must be experienced to do so. Even if your mind comes fully awake, the essence of life is trial and error.

Life can't avoid making mistakes, sometimes deadly ones. That's the "error" part. Life implies a degree of painful suffering from these mistakes. There's no way around that. It is the suffering that produces the wisdom. Once you gain it, you don't need to stay in the suffering any longer… at least for that round.

The Quantum Shift

The very first realization of Worldview One is that life is a soul game, a drama. The new paradigm, or realm, that you will step into is called The Stage, or Theater. When you see yourself as the actor on the stage, and your life as the script, you gain the awareness that before entering your body you've deliberately chosen to be this person within this set of circumstances. An entirely new perspective has arrived.

To play The Wisdom Game well, begin to see the world as inside you, not outside. This means that you examine your thoughts and emotions constantly; that whenever you encounter an event or a problem, instead of focusing on what it is that you see happening in terms of another person or of circumstances, look instead to your inner state. Pay attention to tension that you are holding in your muscles, in your gut, around your shoulders or temples, and track that to a thought that you have regarding the circumstance. Also, of course, track the emotional reaction that's taking place in you as you have this thought.

With a little understanding, you'll begin to see that whatever the event - whatever you are encountering - you are processing it somewhere within your mind and your body chemistry. There are plenty of wonderful methods available nowadays, such as yoga and stress management, to help you defuse the body's tension while you learn to go deeper.

Your primary tool in playing The Wisdom Game is the control of your thoughts. Here is where you will need an IRON will. As you see and understand yourself participating in karma, reaping the results of past behaviors, you realize that you can frame a thought about the experience. And you also realize that you have the choice and the ability to decide what the story's going to be. *"Let anger go, let aggravation go,"* says The Brotherhood. *"Watch the One Energy play with you. Laugh at the play. See the game. Adopt new strategy, and it should include a big dose of humor at others' wickedness and tricks."* In reframing experience, and acknowledging that you already made a personal choice and came here in order to do what it is you had designed, your view changes the pattern of energy. You get energy flowing, and thus energize creative potential. This is the beginning of learning that your conscious mind can start to manifest new possibilities.

Real-life possibilities can become available through new and deliberate thought-creation, because this is where your mind manipulates energy. And (as science is showing us), energy moving around us is *all there is.*

Subatomic physics – which is the scientific search for what's happening in the most infinitesimal stages of matter – has discovered that, in the deepest levels, there is no longer anything that can be described as solid. There is no "there", there. Rigorous scientific observation has found only energy (waves of probability...or potentiality).

In actuality, as science has found, everybody and everything are simply interminglings of energies. The nature of energy is that of being creative, always moving, and with no boundaries. There are differences in strengths or frequencies, but no differences insofar as distinguishing separate bits of matter. It's all just various forms of energy. This means that we, as material beings, are not separated things but are interconnected, or "entangled" with everything else. So the statement "We are all one" isn't just a lovely ideal but a scientific fact! Which means, of course, that each of us contains or embodies the whole world – chairs, tables, teapots, and other people – within the self. As Gary Zukav puts it in *The Dancing Wu Li Masters*, "At the subatomic level there is no longer a clear distinction between what is and what happens, between the actor and the action. At the subatomic level the dancer and the dance are one."

Whatever is done **here** affects what happens **there**. And whatever occurs **inside me** is not isolated from what's going on **outside me**. *As above, so below; as without, so within.* Not just metaphysical platitudes but cutting-edge science!

Seeing reality in terms of this new paradigm – not outside of self, but within, able to be controlled creatively through mental processes, i.e., mastered – is the single most important change that's happened to humanity since the caveman.

A fundamental change is in the works in our lifetimes. Its effects are profound. It is a complete shift of identity. We are realizing that we aren't material beings who are trapped in a limited reality, but are energy beings who can influence – indeed, control, create and design – the life experience through the mental process called **conscious creation.**

It is as though the creator of life is waking up and remembering everything.

This is the profound change that's been called The Shift. This alteration of standard thinking process is fundamental to realizing why life is now seen as a game... a wisdom game.

First, we have to understand that the concept of who you are and what the world is, is undergoing a rapid change as quantum physics reveals the truth about nature - that underneath the appearance of solid form is really nothing but frequency, waves, flows of energy, and potential, but not really solidity.

Next, we begin to see that what we identify as our self, as a person, a consciousness, is in fact the way the brain is structuring its input through the five senses. (More on this later.)

Finally, we see purpose behind this illusion that there is a "me in here" and "a world out there" - which is called duality. We see the purpose of duality as simply providing contrast. Providing the field or arena where one aspect of energy gets to play with a contrasting aspect. And if it's all just non-solid flows of vibration (energy) then we're seeing energy playing a game with itself, making something look solid or real when there's actually nothing there.

As energy continues to play within this illusion of separation, it seeks something that could be called a form of knowledge, but which we've given a more profound name, called Wisdom. Energy seeks to know itself, to know the results of activity undertaken within the illusion of duality (separation). It seeks to evolve its conscious knowing. What happens when one aspect of the "self" butts up against (runs into, encounters) another aspect ("the other")? What are the results?

The really cool thing is that, in playing the soul's wisdom game called "life", or called "self versus the world", energy has created a very powerful and advanced experience called "emotion". When there is no emotion, and no sentience (self-awareness), there is nature. Nature playing with itself results first in experiences within the mineral kingdom - that is to say, stars forming out of nebulae; worlds – fire, air, water, earth (i.e., elements) – forming from stars; rocks and stones forming out of molten planetary material; and finally plants and animals forming out of rocks. That's nature's result of playing its soul's wisdom game of contrast prior to the initiation of awareness. But as the evolution of nature progresses, nature develops reactions which we call emotions, which are comprised of chemicals at work within the physical structure. Again, all basically energy patterns, but nevertheless perceived by brains (that are also structures of energy patterns) to be pleasant or unpleasant.

The development, therefore, of emotion is a key stage in the universe's advancement of wisdom because life's game is to see how the self perceives the world, how nature impacts upon itself, and finally how sentient creatures deal with other selves and with nature. The game, then, of wisdom is to learn more and more powerfully, more and more quickly, more and more insightfully, what feels good versus what doesn't. What hurts and what doesn't. What is sweet and what is bitter. What action brings what result.

And so we participate in the universe's game - we are the universe's game - and the game is conquered by knowing that it is a game and reaching more and more satisfactorily the state felt and known as joy.

An understanding of holograms and virtual reality helps you to see your game plan.

We have five senses: hearing, seeing, smelling, touching, and tasting. The entire world is known through these five perceptions (which are really different vibrations). Our sense organs receive information and translate it in our bodies into chemical reactions. These perceptions are then layered in our brains to create that which is called experience. Other than this layering of information, the term "the world" carries no other meaning, for it can't otherwise exist.

Think of it: you stub your toe. A message of pain is felt through touch. Another message sees the door you banged into, or even the bruise or blood ensuing. Yet another message hears the "thwack" of the impact. Subliminally, you might smell the door or your own perspiration. All these vibratory encounters are handled by the brain, which stacks them up into a "form" and conveys to you that something real has happened.

But on the quantum level, the truth is merely that various vibrational energies have encountered each other (since solid matter doesn't even exist). Therefore, the brain, in stacking up the perceptions, is the generator of the illusion of reality. The brain is the device that accomplishes that feat. The human brain acts as a holographic device, using increments of moments to build an illusion of solid form (i.e., three-dimensional reality).

It is a holographic generator, like *Star Trek's* "holo-deck", or "The Matrix" in the film of that name – a virtual reality maker. All the layering of vibrational information into a general perception of reality is holographic. The brain is a holographic device to build the illusion of solid form.

You built much of your particular hologram before birth. You chose a brain that was designed to formulate the ensuing holographic experiences in a certain way. That was a big part of your soul's wisdom game plan. The particular crafting of this lens was part of your choice, causing you to always structure your world according to its design. At least, until you wake up and do something about it… in your mind.

> *"What the mystics had been saying for centuries was true, [that] reality was maya, an illusion, and [that] what*

was out there was really a vast, resonating symphony of wave forms, a 'frequency domain' that was transformed into the world as we know it only after it entered our senses." – Michael Talbot, *"The Holographic Universe"*

The Hole in Your Soul

Everyone has karma… **it's the soul's wisdom game**, and if played right, it leads to empowerment. Karma is the way we are entangled in the world, reacting to past drama and creating future drama without perspective or awareness, without detachment.

The dictionary definition of karma is as follows: "In Buddhism and Hinduism, the doctrine of responsibility for all one's acts and all incarnations that explains and justifies good and evil fortune. Loosely, fate or destiny."

Karma is Cause & Effect. It takes wisdom to understand the Law of Cause and Effect.

Karma is the thread of energy that we send out when we take an action or have a thought. And since energy is never destroyed, the thread of energy keeps going until it completes itself. In a closed universe (which is what any universe is*), this cascading energy returns full circle, insisting that we face that which we have sent out previously as an action. The universe is in perfect balance, and so karma never makes a value judgment other than the natural completion of its own behavior.

---

* Our entire universe, being just one of multiple universes, while possibly infinitely expandable is certainly not eternal. It has a built-in life span (in Hinduism: The Days & Nights of Brahma). Thus, the ripple effect of karma in the time-space continuum can exist, whereby the consequences of a thought or action, having been sent outward, shall be reencountered. Ripples return only in a closed system.

Karma is a given; every time energy moves, it's set on a path and its end result ripples back. Thus, your entire life design can be said to be a pattern of *karmic threads*, chosen to rebalance earlier actions while exploring new potential. You see original choice and then moment-by-moment choice. You can then understand the dance of life, which is based upon previous actions – Karmic Threads – that are spooling themselves out. These threads are encountered as consequences of past actions, and you can then see why there are certain challenges in life and how best to make new choices around them. Fate is then seen as a participatory soul game.

Realizing that you're in this wisdom game causes you step onto a threshold; it's a threshold of new awareness about your karmic entanglement. On the other side of this realization is a new perspective that allows you to see the soul's wisdom game from a broader viewpoint. Your perspective is lifted, and as it's raised you gain control of all the reactions and all the entanglement that you otherwise cannot see while you're participating in these karmic returns. Karmic threads can be "good" or "bad".

The karmic predicament ("K.P.") is the "hole in your soul", the big issue you signed on for (in fact, designed for yourself) that would prod you to grow... it's the problem in life that hurts, but which insists on being solved. It's your life's "dramatic tension". It's absolutely required to play the soul's wisdom game, and is built into the nature of reality.

Sickness? Money problems? Tough relatives? Sad love life?

All of these are part of the game – The Wisdom Game.

These situations, sometimes temporary, sometimes lifelong, are part of what's called your karmic predicament. Problems such as these cause the pain and suffering in life.

Did you know there was a way to overcome karma? A way to see your predicament differently, to put it into context differently so that you are not a helpless victim of your karma but are able suddenly to see clearly through the fog of misunderstanding into the sunshine of awakening? Awakening to the structure or framework of the soul's game – the game of life, The Wisdom Game – is the confirmation that you are now at Worldview One.

If you find yourself in pain and suffering, the new perspective can lift your self out of its clutches, can frame it as the challenge you have presented to yourself in order to grow. You can choose the avenue to move along, the fork in the road labeled, say, Getting Well or Remaining In Illness.

There are ways to make this choice. The choice is made intellectually (with understanding) and emotionally (with growth). But once that choice is made, the mind shifts, the thoughts form differently and the body responds joyfully to its own healing process. You accept your karma consciously, and work within it.

Let's say your K.P. is around finances, and you're struggling with money. You find yourself in troubling circumstances. Do you frame the thought around it that it's your lot in life, it's where you're stuck, you can't change it and must always strive... or do you take the other road choosing instead to align your consciousness with the belief that money is coming toward you, that as soon as you remove the boulders in its path it will pour in, and that you have the ability to be creative to allow its manifestation in your very near future? Even if you've been Madoff-ed or downsized, the point is not to magically and instantaneously sprout wealth, but to get out of fear and set energy in better motion.

Choices like this lift you quickly out of suffering. You begin to see life as creative play. First, you might begin to see simply that there is even choice. This is big. The concept of being able to choose your future is not readily apparent, and certainly not taught. However, being comprised mainly of energy, thought can zig or zag.

Do you zig or do you zag?

As energy, if you choose to zig toward creative manifestation, not only do you see yourself as having made choice, but you begin to see that by following energy along a positive new path you create more and more of it. Positive energy flows towards you; you flow towards it. (This is the Law of Attraction.) All of a sudden, life changes. If you choose wellness, life changes. If you choose prosperity, energy changes. More and more of that choice becomes available, and comes down the turnpike at you.

Well, this certainly begins to feel more enjoyable! More empowering! That which felt out of your hands, out of your control, or helpless, begins to feel alive and vibrant, electrifying, jazzy, and really desirable. You start to take control. Where? Not of others, not of things and stuff, but of your own head. You start to take control of your thoughts and emotions. When you are running the show, you feel very alive. You begin to see that the game of wisdom works, that the game of understanding brightens and illuminates you. You begin to see life from a larger perspective, to lift above yourself and see the broad scope. You begin to see the places where choice can be made, where there are forks in the road. You begin to see your role as not only participant but as creator. You begin to see life as your particular drama, and you as the maestro.

To put this another way, you are not a victim of your life. You are not a pawn.

You are not the helpless individual being buffeted by peoples' choices, being subject to accidental events, being lost in despair. You are a Wisdom Game player. You are a soul who has deliberately embarked upon a life experience. Pre-birth, you have chosen the exact time and place – the mathematical conditions – in which to enter life, and have the experiences contained therein. You have chosen those parameters that contain some measure of struggle and pain so that you no longer had to remain merely energy. You didn't want to be stuck in eternal energetic formlessness; you wanted to participate in the physical world. You wanted **experience**.

> *"A child is born on that day and at that hour when the celestial rays are in mathematical harmony with his individual karma."* – Paramahansa Yogananda quoting Sri Yukteswar, *Autobiography of a Yogi*

You have chosen to be who you are with all of its drama, and in fact you have decided just what the drama will be with the understanding that this will be a soul's wisdom game from which you will learn. *"You can't change the neural pathways that have been set down during the critical period of growth; you can't change the hard wiring,"* says physicist Fred Alan Wolf. *"All you can do is realize that you don't have to illuminate the hologram in the same way each time...[it] is just a program set down when you were a child.."** You will learn to be savvy. You will learn what is bitter and what is sweet. You will learn to see others with greater compassion. You will learn how to awaken and how to create your world, and thus how to help the greater world.

You're here quite deliberately to pursue something that you feel strongly about wanting, which can be called your passion. By identifying it, you name a key part of your Wisdom Game, your positive ability, your forte. You may not know what your passion is, but it's there deep-down because you come alive talking about it, you lose track of time doing it, and you feel really fulfilled upon completion of any part of it or any experience of it. At the same time, you're here because you have a challenge. You're using this challenge, perhaps to grow but certainly to make life real and give you something to gnaw on. Your challenge may be part of your history, or current in your relationships, or lifelong in your genetics. It's unique to you; it's nobody else's set-up, and it's a pretty continuous obstacle. There's a name for this challenge, as we've talked about: **your karmic predicament**. It's built into your life and designed to make your life more rewarding because without it there would be no chance to grow, and no joy in overcoming. So between your passion, which lives in your heart, and your karmic predicament which is part and parcel of your life's design, you've gotten two-thirds of the way to figuring out your game plan.

---

*   *The Dreaming Universe; Investigations into the Middle Realm of Consciousness and Matter* (Gnosis mag., Wint. '92)

It's suggested that you spell out your K.P. to yourself by listing your birth conditions (e.g., parents, gender, ethnicity, appearance, health – in fact, all the givens before age seven – plus your major adult relationships), and then naming your significant life dilemmas.

The last third is called the task you gave yourself to achieve and complete. This task is harder to discover in many cases than your passion or your predicament because this task can be hidden deep within you. It can be as simple as developing self-esteem; it can be as complicated as finding and rescuing another soul. Whatever it is, it's part of what brought you to Planet Earth once more. In my case, for instance, it took me half my life to figure out mine, which is to raise the planetary vibration by teaching, communicating and counseling.

For people who discover the three parts of their soul's wisdom game plan, a large-scale pattern is revealed that can then be utilized and deliberately worked with. That person can now step back from the daily grind, take a broader view, and begin deliberately to control the usage of energy in the life. Can, for instance, identify a passion and spend more time enjoying it. Can realize a soul task, and set about making efforts to achieve it. And, most wisely of all, recognize karmic predicament, and as though life were a symphony, soften those notes while emphasizing the more pleasant ones just by the process of self-awareness. In doing so, many things come together within the comprehension, and a step forward is accomplished in handling the journey to awakening.

Your Horoscope Shows Your Original Choice

A Personal Energy Pattern is also known as a horoscope. Keyed to your first breath and crystallizing the mathematical structure of various energies – harmonious and inharmonious – it sets the tone for your personality, reveals your karmic predicament, and is a blueprint of your life plan. We put the package together according to what we want to play out, pick the moment when energies are converging in mathematical resonance with what we want to experience in life, and we choose that time to be born. Then, under the veil of the personality, we enter into the illusion that we're solid, while in truth we are nothing but energy patterns.

Like any blueprint or map, it can be navigated. What's required is to understand the initial or original energy pattern – the karma – and, instead of remaining unconscious within it, begin to wake up to its demands and potential. Upon a birth as a soul, the personality doesn't remember anything; it has instant amnesia. That's called The Veil. Until you awaken, you can't pierce the Veil. But once you lift in consciousness, you see that which was Soul Choice.

As a child, nothing much can be done with what we are thrust into, but as an adult, we can lift our perspective above the karmic predicament of the everyday world's demands. Remembering that we chose our bargain, bargained for it, and created it, we can begin to understand what karmic patterns were selected (e.g., the genetic flaw, the skill set, etc.) that have molded us for a certain number of years but can now in adulthood be transformed. We can see it from a new angle, no longer completely overwhelmed and stuck within its patterns. We can instead wake up and start to harmonize with our own vibrational pattern.

Energy is vibration. This mathematical structuring is the interior relationships... *like notes in a piece of music.* We are vibrational energy. So we can wake up as we go along, and see how we're vibrating, then apply consciousness and change the vibratory pattern of our own musical score so that the harmonious aspects of our equation are emphasized, and the disharmonious are accepted and processed. We can use patience with them and reduce or diminish them so our personal symphony becomes smoother and more powerful and more attractive. It becomes more joyful.

We are *aware energy.* That is a definition of spirit. Can you call it Intelligent Energy? Same thing. When you sync and harmonize with your karmic patterns (the flow of your life, the vibratory energy of your world), and you have awareness of that, then things are going to manifest more easily and you're going to process differently.

There's an exact science to conscious creation, and there is unlimited creative potential.

The first thing is to *know thyself.* In other words, to identify the potential of your Personal Energy Pattern, or PEP. In order to achieve your life goals, you have to figure out first what your dreams are. You've chosen this pattern, which embodies an ultimate reachable potential.

A very strong part of the Brotherhood's message about The Wisdom Game is just this: Identify the PEP as best you can by figuring out what makes you feel most alive. What talents do you have and what is your dream about using them? If you don't have a dream and you're not in touch with it, the next thing would be to simply unblock the emotions and thoughts that are masking your passion. Everyone has some vital life force that stirs the senses and makes a person come alive, makes you sit up more in your seat, makes your face flush when you talk about it. Some people find that this has been very numbed and deadened, perhaps by medications, perhaps by other substances, cigarettes or alcohol or drugs. Some people have been given negative messages that they can't do it. These are all blockages to expressing your potential.

As soon as you were born, you contained a unique desire to be made manifest. It is your essence. Your Personal Energy Pattern - a constellation of set energies – wanted to explore its self-realization, bringing it into reality in this material world (i.e., in everyone's brains). Deep down, you can find it and feel it. It is your deepest truth. As layers of masking are removed through the process of gaining wisdom, your passion is brought to light. You remember your soul purpose. It's full of vitality and life force.

You may not be conscious of your life's passion, or your soul's dream, but you can find clues to it by observing yourself.

When, as great interest, you feel a strong vitality about a subject matter or a task, you're getting a clue that this is something that you hold dear. This is something that charges up your system. This is something that makes you feel alert and alive.

Another clue to having found your deep passion, otherwise masked or cloaked, is to notice which task so fully grabs your attention that you lose a sense of time and even a sense of self. If you zone out into a state in which nothing comes between effort and results, have no sense of yourself and no sense of the passing of time, then you can be sure that you have tapped into a passion.

It may not be your only passion, but it is one of your passions. It may be physical, in which your body becomes so engaged in sports or running or dancing or labor that you feel completely alive and at the same time not really there. Or maybe intellectual, in which you apply the faculties of mind, so focused away that, again, the room disappears and there is nothing left except the brain and its attempt at a solution.

These are all clear indicators that you are getting close to finding your core truth, or your soul's dream. Explore this, for it is a pathway to your light. And that is one of the first steps to reaching self-realization – the declaration to yourself of your passion or your dream.

So if you don't know what your dreams are and you can't figure out what your passion is, the first step would be to unblock it.

Unblocking your potential requires a new way to look at the role of pain and suffering.

Part of choice involves suffering. It seems to be the most powerful way people grow, change, and thus gain wisdom. So, pain happens. The suffering is, initially, always part of your original choice. It's part of your karmic dilemma. Many people at this stage voice something along these lines: "What, was I 'nuts' to choose this path?!"

Remaining in suffering is also part of your choice. Until you understand how to play The Wisdom Game, you don't know that you have the power to switch out of suffering, that you can shorten it, that you can take control of it, that you can, in fact, change your emotion on a dime.

When you're sick, pay attention to what thoughts have been draining or disempowering you because often sickness follows not just stress, but emotional weariness. Sickness is a reflection of the soul not in harmony with its own energy pattern, blocked from manifesting its dreams.

Just by understanding negative thought forms, it becomes possible to switch gears. There are techniques* to face these repetitive blocking thoughts, to look at the swamp of negative emotions that you may find yourself returning to time and again, and to switch by choice into a more positive framework, to frame your story differently, to tell yourself a different tale about what's happening. This will help you to better find your power. This will help you to realize that there is always choice, and this will put you on the path toward mastery. For instance, after Hurricane Katrina, I was speaking to a group and asked what if anything could be framed differently regarding people who were directly affected by this disaster. One woman suggested that it might be seen as a chance to make a fresh start away from the entrenchment of poverty. *What doesn't kill you makes you stronger.* Just about any experience can be seen to have a silver lining although that might not be obvious at first. Most people, when asked if they could re-live things, would choose not to forego their experiences. "It's what made me, me", most say.

> **GATE/WORLDVIEW: 1**
>
> **TOOL: Emotional mastery.** In a breakthrough realization, you learn to use your device to master your thoughts about a situation, and thus control your reactions.

So, just by knowing that you have a choice to reframe, switch gears, and move into a new emotion, in itself usually curtails pain. *"It's life itself that is your biggest risk,"* The Brotherhood advises, *"and which could be looked at as the game of woe that will bring you to the seat of wise (wisdom)."*

Some pain, of course, is physical, and needs to be healed. That entails a different type of transformation, but even physical pain can be reduced or lessened by mental effort and the application of methods that are within your control.

---

*   See The Second Worldview for some Techniques.

As you become more proficient in recognizing your ability to control a reaction, at first simply identifying it and eventually gaining some power over these processes, you'll begin to see that you can release muscular tension by breathing or by another calming regulating process such as exercise, running, napping, or simply modulating the thought. You'll also begin to see that you will have gained mastery over your emotional reaction, moving sometimes slowly but later as you get better at it, more directly from difficult thoughts to more tempered ones. Thus you will see more and more that the world - your world - is taking place on the interior, and in fact can be controlled from there.

As this occurs, another result will begin to show up: the more harmonized inner state will begin to produce more attractive results so that the very problem that set you off into this interior journey offers ways to resolve it. The outer world begins to provide opportunities that are more in keeping with a better harmonized inner state, and the dilemma begins to resolve.

A student, C, had been depressed about her life for awhile, especially feeling deadened by her job. After a few classes in a course I gave about Releasing Your Creative Potential, she saw herself in a new light as the creator of her fate. Her face brightened, but even more startlingly was her phone call to me right after class: driving home, she saw an injured animal on the side of the road and stopped to help it. This synchronistic event served to remind her of her love of veterinarian science. Within days, she reported quitting her boring job and getting one in the right field. Needless to say, the depression lifted quickly.

5 Rules of Wisdom – Why Is Wisdom a Game?

There are rules to The Wisdom Game, rules of engagement. Let's clarify the rules, and learn better strategy:
    The key concepts about the soul's wisdom game are:
    First of all, awakening, realizing that you're in it.

Second, finding techniques and doing the inner work to reach a more joyful, centered and whole place within yourself, having come to the realization that you're playing this soul's wisdom game.

Third, understanding that the whole exterior element of the world is really an aspect of yourself, a reflection of you.

This is where wisdom eventually takes you to. And then your interior work is not only to manifest your personal desires, but to continue into your journey that eventually allows you to help the whole world, and brings forth finally and ultimately a happier society. This is the logical place that The Wisdom Game will end up.

But for now, you're just realizing there is a soul's wisdom game in which you're engaged, though you don't know the rules. You are being introduced to the fact that you are a whole person, or energy pattern, that you are not fragmented, separate and disconnected components that are called "romance" or "career" or "health" or "offspring", but are a whole complete and contained energy system. When that energy system is blocked, and not able to manifest its full realization, then in fact that energy system is blocking everyone else. To not reach self realization is to not help the world.

We were given the rules of the soul's wisdom game, channeled from the Brotherhood of Light Workers, and here are their words:[*]

- Rule #1 is to remember your greater self *at all times* while in form.
- Rule #2 is to see all that is occurring to you as part of your bargain, and not as the trap or mess you have fallen into.
- Rule #3 is to remember that, on a soul level, you have devised the very traps, messes, and dilemmas that are causing you so much pain and discomfort; no one else has done so.
- Rule #4 is to remember the methods to change the very problem into its opposite.

---

[*] Wisdom's Game, Judi Thomases, Cypress House 2005.

༄༅ And Rule #5—for now—is to utilize your trump card, your ace in the hole, which is none other than the control of thought.

In order to win the soul's wisdom game, to play well, to not feel victimized by life, we must understand wisdom. Wisdom is the ability to surmount the negatives in life, the suffering, the unlucky hand dealt, and to recognize that as karma, and to eliminate wrong attitudes. *"The world's a game, a dance, a playground,"* says The Brotherhood. *"Learn better rules to shift your position to one of advantage. Face the tiger, and laugh."* Winning the soul's wisdom game means focusing on the target of joy, and on self-realization and peace. Wisdom becomes a trick to apply something that you've already got but have forgotten that you know and must find all over again. Again and again. The answer to the game of wisdom is already there. But we have amnesia, and are always in the process of remembering our truth. There's no way else to discover this except by playing with emotion and consequences, which is called karma. Only by facing who we are as human beings and what we have sent forth can we regain wisdom, recapture lost understanding, and return to our truth. The soul's wisdom game, in other words, is about awakening.

Awakening to wisdom allows a person to see the way through and return again and again into the right path – the path of joy, empowerment, and self-realization. Awakening to your own internal wisdom brings forth your latent potential, the potential of playing a game like a master: manifesting rapidly and fully that which has always been underlying. Being awake to your own internal wisdom gives you full and direct access to whatever creative potential you have designed in order to manifest it. It gives you access to "The M Field", allowing you to start consciously creating from the raw material that exists before space and time. In other words, to tap into Creative Power. (More on The M Field later.)

Awakening to your own internal wisdom is exciting and empowering. It's a process, a series of steps to surmount obstacles such as negative emotions, false beliefs and self sabotaging destructive attitudes. It's to work consciously with thoughts at all times, to change negative emotions to positive ones, time and again.

To be a person of awakened wisdom is to have the ability to utilize energy upon demand to align it and bring positive results.

The benefits are: less stress, more joy, fulfillment of your dream, and feeling as though your life has been meaningful.

Four Wisdom Exercises for The First Worldview

Here are some simple exercises to help you begin to see the game, to shift the storyline, to use a mental trick to remove yourself at will to a nicer thoughtform, and thus to gain empowerment.

> **FOUR WISDOM EXERCISES FOR WORLDVIEW 1**
>
> 1. Find space between any two thoughts
>
> 2. Reframe and rename
>
> 3. Create a Place of Joy
>
> 4. Use other methods to transcend emotion's thrall

1. Find the space between any two thoughts, thus learn how to get into the gap between the chatter in your mind. Paths such as breathing exercises, meditation and martial arts allow this. As a result, you will start to realize that you exist separate from the constant thoughts that are chattering in your mind. As soon as you are able to shift perspective from your daily thoughts into that of an observer of them, or simply that of an awareness of being, you grasp that you are not the same as the endless stream of your thoughts. Your self-perspective changes and broadens.
2. Reframe thoughts. See yourself structuring reality by the way that you build the story about it, and if this story causes

depression, fear or anger, decide to build it differently. If you can't do that, find a guiding expert who can help you to reframe your thoughts. (Examples: psychotherapy, Options Process, astrology, The Work, etc.) Above all, don't frame your story as that of victim.

3. During calm times, prepare an emotionally pleasant place – a Place of Joy – that can be an escape or sanctuary when needed. (Examples: an old memory of the best place you ever were, or a wonderful imaginative fantasy.) Practice returning to that positive moment or place, thereby using the pleasant memory, the Place of Joy, as an escape valve or a switching point when necessary. You don't want to live all of your life there because that's self-defeating escapism, but you can use this technique simply as a temporary release from negativity to shift the emotion that you're currently in, i.e., just as a mechanism to regain some internal power.

4. Explore other techniques, perhaps under the care of expert practitioners, that allow a similar freeing effect, such as Emotional Freedom Technique (EFT, the "tapping method"), biofeedback or even humor. The point is to become well-versed in the methods of getting out of the thrall of powerful negative emotion and into detachment or observation, the place in which you can reframe thoughts. The entire point is to find the way – on the inner plane – to see that you have the choice to create your reality. Continue to create, but just try not to generate extraneous thoughts because then all you're doing is creating extra energy with no pathway to utilize it (which, after all, is the "formula" for agitation!).

Step by step, a new understanding and different concepts are being built. The realization of the inner self – the designer at play in the field of life – is the connection to what is called the soul. The understanding of the amnesia that clouds your remembrance of the soul's wisdom game and of your original choices is called the Veil. The encounters with positive or negative patterns, luck, or its lack, are the recognition that there is something called karma that is simply the way energy behaves in a closed system. And finally, the understanding that you have designed the soul's wisdom game plan with a predicament – the "hole in your soul" or the karmic "pickle" you're in – existing for the very purpose of forcing you to surmount it by the accumulation of wisdom, is the light bulb that flashes.

These new insights and new perception put all of life into a different perspective. You see yourself forevermore as on a stage, or in a Theater of Action.

It's Really A *Game*, With Clues!

Here we are, then, completing The First Worldview, the understanding of The Wisdom Game. It's a game! There are clues all along the way. There are steps to playing it.

The major components that lead you to this understanding, and then through it, are pieces of a Wisdom route*. The Worldviews describe the discovery of the soul's wisdom game, its nature, and the steps required. The soul's wisdom game involves discovering the existence of "The M Field" – or the realm beyond the physical, a.k.a., *the Meta* – and then figuring out how to access it at will, even though it's veiled and can't be seen easily with the logical brain.

The discovery as part of the soul's wisdom game is also an understanding that life is like a perfect

> GATE/WORLDVIEW: 1
>
> **RESULT: Wisdom.** The fog begins to lift, and understanding dawns.
>
> **GETTING FROM HERE TO THERE:** You started out as life's victim – a pawn of others or of circumstances. You'll now learn how to control your emotions and thoughts (mastery), thus becoming savvy and amused.

---

*   This is what I call The Wisdom System.

hologram, with the five senses contributing to the sense of solid reality, when in fact, nothing like that exists and it's all just the mind conjuring an illusion.

So this Wisdom Game presents us with clues, with consequences, with the chance to awaken, with strategy and five rules, all of which can be applied. And then energy wakes up to itself, sees The Wisdom Game, tackles it, and wins! Wisdom applied is life-mastery.

~~~

Once life is seen as an experience that was deliberately chosen, an entirely new perspective arrives. Without effort, the mind enters a different reality. As soon as the individual realizes that he or she has chosen to participate in a drama of life with its challenges and blessings, and becomes fully appreciative of the richness of the experience and the self-chosen aspect of the game's design while remaining willing to work within its parameters, that person then automatically moves on to a second Worldview. The second Worldview has been called The Law of Attraction. It can also be called Creative Potential Energized or The Art of Manifestation.

As the mind grasps the fact that choice brings results and alters future outcome, then the individual **gains realization that fate is pliable**, and that the creative element exists within the self's awareness and not "out there". Many pieces of understanding contribute to this new perspective, a perspective that can also be called Overcoming Fear. You are in a hologram. You are the captain of your ship.

It is exciting and refreshing to grasp that your mind is creating what you will next encounter, and that rather than being magical or mystical, this concept is fully supported by science.

Dawning Awareness

My first book, *Wisdom's Game,* contained channelings that spoke of people being actors in a story of their choice, and directors of that story as well. But several years before *Wisdom's Game* was published, an entry in my journal spoke of this same thing:

You are our actor. You are a central figure in our drama. You are not alone/Judi/yourself. You are not just a single player, a little woman, a lone participant in a cosmic tale of woe. You are the lighted core of our work. You are the screen upon which we can mark the diagram of our intentions. Don't you see yet? You are stuck inside the role and can't see the audience. You are lost amongst the rest of the players and can't figure out that you also wrote the darn thing.

This guidance continued by advising me to step back, sit in the director's seat, especially during any crisis scene, to view it from the higher vantage point. It further suggested that I change the next act into what I now wish to create by residing in spirit within my role as actor, having the heart connection, understanding that I am the larger self rather than merely the small impotent human being named Judi—the very understanding at the heart of Worldview One.

THE SECOND WORLDVIEW

MASTERING CREATIVE POTENTIAL

GATE/ WORLDVIEW	APPEARANCE	LANDSCAPE/ REALM	KEY	ABILITY	METAL	TOOL	RESULT
AT THE ENTRANCE	Everyday Life	Fog	Karmic Predicament	To live	Lead	Passion	Suffering
1	Curtain	The Wisdom Game	Choice (The Quantum Shift)	To switch out of negativity	Iron	Emotional Mastery, Control of Thought	Wisdom
2	Door	The Law of Attraction	Power (The Art of Manifestation)	To co-create what you desire	Copper	Conscious Co-creation	Joy
3	Bridge	Continuum	Vision (Capping the Point of Awareness)	To realize who you are and overcome the fear of death	Silver	Intuition & ESP	Light
4	Portal	Mind of God	Service (Merit)	To know truth and be the Way	Gold	No-Ego, Surrender	Bliss

54

What are the components of emotional mastery, and where does it take you? In the second worldview, you will encounter the following concepts: beginning to see yourself as energy, not solid, and then working with your energy body and with the lower aspects of your PEP to switch your thoughts from the negative to the positive at will, thus unblocking from negative emotion at the same time your awareness begins to expand (The Quantum Shift), and you find yourself taking steps to reach personal empowerment via the control of thoughts and the conscious application of choice; you also begin to see yourself as a hologram – a holistic reality, or structure of light – that is mentally able to play with possibility and consciously create your life moment by moment by drawing to you that which is similar to the new you (i.e., that which you wish to attract, The Law of Attraction); furthermore, as you realize the new truth that you are not your thoughts, that your mind is the builder, that a secondary self has appeared who is neutral and detached (The Observer), and that you have unlimited creative potential to play with energy, several unusual things happen: you find your identity inhabiting a holographic universe, i.e., a vast field of energy (The M Field), in which you can connect effortlessly to your higher self, receive insights, and get spiritual guidance; you find yourself developing latent psychic and intuitive abilities in this "higher realm", and experiencing a surge of new-found energy as a result of greater self-realization, empowerment, calm, joy, a feeling of safety in the universe, and the skill to manifest your passion and soul purpose (The Art of Manifestation); and you learn to spot the link between your personal identity (small self) and greater being known as The Higher Self (or God) in the evidence of synchronistic events connecting your thoughts to episodes, thus validating your interior realization; the concept of "two are one" begins to take hold as you toy with playing "the god game", but you also learn that you must synchronize your individual frustration or dissatisfaction to the universe's pace – a technique called "surrendering to the flow"; each time you get it right (i.e., become the flow, find yourself in harmonic resonance, apply wisdom), the surge is unleashed; and you see that you are playing the soul's wisdom game successfully. An additional concept forms as a result: it's the recognition that long-prophesized changes to humanity are occurring via this fresh perspective, and that human invention, in keeping pace with spiritual evolution within the psyche, is now shaping a different world – one that is global, empowered, and aware; and that the seeds have been planted to raise the level of consciousness in both the individual and the planetary arena. **The big secrets at this worldview are that the inner thought-life creates the outer world; you are becoming a new type of person, empowered and globally-oriented, working inwardly through intuitive awareness of energy patterns and creative potential, to recreate life and the world in order to reflect their greatest potential.**

Now that you've realized that you have the power to choose your reactions to fate, and choose even how to describe and name it – that is, to design your reality – you've stepped into a new realm. Fog has steadily been lifting, and clarity has been increasing. The mind has started to realize its role in using choice to affect outcome. The world is now seen as fluid and malleable. And by redirecting all that great energy that heretofore went into emotional drama, it is as though a valve got turned open, or a train got rerouted, whereupon a cascade of fresh "juice" pours forth.

GATE/WORLDVIEW: 2

APPEARANCE: Door and Threshold. A hologram. You are at a gate or doorway, and hold a great key. Another way of life beckons – a way that goes past everyday reality and changes you forever.

LANDSCAPE / REALM: One of life's chief mysteries is unshrouded: *The Secret of the Ages*. A magical place. Things don't appear as solid as they once were, and the edges are vague. You get a glimpse of a strange and wonderful field beyond.

So as you look around, at the far end of the stage, you see a DOOR. In it is a great KEY made of the metal COPPER, associated with Venus, a symbol of fecund creativity. This is the door to conscious co-creation. Past its THRESHOLD is even greater illumination, and in fact an odd shimmering quality.

As an aware game-player, you realize that this new landscape will be a journey into new places in your own mind. You are drawn toward this compelling evanescence, and as you step over the threshold and into the new holographic realm, here is what you find.

> GATE/WORLDVIEW: 2
>
> **KEY: Power (The Art of Manifestation).** The tides of emotion pull less strongly while your thoughts are freer to dance in right rhythm. In fact, you see the energy dance. By directing energy, experience is yours to pull into being, or conversely, to avoid.
>
> **ABILITY:** To co-create what you desire.
>
> **METAL: Copper.** A symbol of creative pliability. It is shiny and attractive.

KEYS OF CONSCIOUSNESS FOR THE SECOND WORLDVIEW

We're all on a colorful game board, like a chessboard, as players, but also we are here while bi-located elsewhere on a higher plane watching ourselves act in our soul's wisdom drama (much like the movie, "The Matrix").

The more we can gain a new perspective and shift our awareness to the divine (higher self) playing the soul's wisdom game – the more we can participate consciously in the moves we make and choices we decide – the more the world will be improved or saved, and our personal lives made more joyful. We think we're individuals, but we're really the Divine playing this game called Life.

Here, then, are some key questions: How do I apply this new awareness? How do I use it in my daily dealings? How do I apply the flashpoints to get to the higher consciousness? How is practical wisdom applied to create that awakening, to make the viewpoint zoom out even to know I'm a player on a chessboard? Then what do I do with this new perspective when I get it? How do I apply wisdom flashes (the flashpoint) in my interactions with people? To leverage myself out of the hole I find myself in? To make life happier? (The more joy, the better the world.) How do I teach it to other people? As I become more aware, how can I use it to become more personally powerful?

All the answers to these important questions reside in mastering The Second Worldview.

The Second Worldview is the real "meat" of The Wisdom Game. It's where the greatest "pay-offs" are, and the strongest challenges. It is by far **the most important step for human development up to this point.** It's all about unblocking frozen energy and clarifying personal potential. But more than that, you have started to realize that you are not only the actor on a stage, but the director-designer too.

In short, once you realize that you're in a soul's wisdom game, The Second Worldview is when The Law of Attraction kicks in. The use of energy becomes tangible and the application of wisdom provides clarity. In this new paradigm, it's logical and rational to wield The Quantum Shift as a tool to help you overcome karma, conquer lethargy, fear, and resistance, and transcend emotional dilemmas. You see that there is methodology to leap out of the old paradigm into a new one.

The Second Worldview shows the need for the mind to begin to align with the universe and gain the cooperation of forces of energy.

The Second Worldview means that you recognize the role that intuition plays; you no longer act blindly, but check everything against an inner guidance system.

The Second Worldview is the point at which you become very aware of who the self is in relationship to playing the soul's wisdom game.

And The Second Worldview is when all experience begins to be chosen consciously so that the mind can reframe the point of view, can stop and unblock or use techniques to shift energy at will and master reality. Possibility-thinking ensues. A shiny surge of potential dances into your mind. You are half-way to realizing your true soul purpose.

Now we can look at specific practical ways to overcome barriers, and different ways to approach reality in order to shift the mind into a new paradigm…a paradigm that puts *you* into control.

The Self As Energy

Remember, in The First Worldview we encountered the idea that quantum physics shows that there's no such thing as solid material; that at basis, everything is just energy moving or vibrating. Well, the experience of the five senses certainly has to do with vibrational patterns. That's what emotions do to us: grab hold of our mind and our physical system, cause it to vibrate either with the intensity of anger, or with the disharmonious vibration of upset, or with the sluggish vibration of depression.

Whatever emotion you can name will translate into a brainwave activity, a chemical pattern and a mental story that contributes to and emphasizes that vibration. But since thoughts are what structure the reality, and since the mind can learn to work with thought and change the thought even while in any particular vibrational pattern (i.e., switch the thought from a negative to a positive, or at worst a neutral, with the use of reframing, which is to say, altering your story line), now you realize that the inner self can viscerally, as conscious awareness, alter reality by choice and with practice.

Just knowing that the self is not a solid block weighted down, stuck in matter, and at the mercy of its own vibrational patterns, is the liberation. The liberation of understanding is the entrance into The Second Worldview

The Second Worldview says: This is a new piece of wisdom. What do I do with this? Now that I get it, now that I have lifted my perspective above my karmic dilemma and am watching myself in my karmic dilemma reacting, feeling that I'm stuck in emotion, what do I do? How do I change things? How do I begin to behave?

The answer is: As the master, not the victim.

There is a process at work in which the mind is becoming attuned to the current, and recognizing that emotions are obstacles to the smooth unfoldment. The process is one of **realization of energy patterns being made more visible** by the very fact that you're no longer propelled forward in thrall to overpowering emotions, nor are you stuck and glued down in thrall to stagnating or numbing depression.

By stopping to detach yourself from your emotions and the thoughts around them, you're recalibrating. You're also listening on a level that has nothing to do with sound, but has to do with feeling.

The goal is to get your energies moving, to hook up with the universal flow or pace of available energy, and to **get yourself out of the way**. The desire to have more, to have results faster, whatever it is, is where you are not in alignment with the pace of the universe. The goal is to align yourself with *vectors of available energy**, slowing down your pace or speeding it up as required, in order **to flow.**

Energy, as we've seen from physics and through mathematics, such as the Mandelbrot Set, reveals itself as in constant motion, ever creative, following natural patterns of formation, and always new, always discovering a fresh avenue. How wonderful, then, if you can get onboard deliberately and knowingly; if you can eliminate frustration by first realizing, and then listening to or discovering, and then aligning yourself with this natural flow. This is exactly what happens when you overcome blocked energy with **a new approach to emotions, a new mastery of thinking patterns**, and **an elevated connection to your own intuition**.

The Brotherhood says, *"Just keep that energy moving, even if you don't know what you're doing, even if you're afraid of failure."* Because to move forward is the key, to get unblocked and even to attempt alignment, is the doorway that opens you to all your creative potential.

By saying that we're energy in formation, we can overcome our blockages by applying The Wisdom Game to our own processes. Accessing our own internal wisdom means inquiring, discovering, and opening to guidance and to inner answers. Aligning means getting past the lower ego, getting into sync, and harmonizing with the flow. This results naturally in greater calmness as well as in **a huge sense of joy.**

The joy is particularly strong when we see that this inner work results in a boon, or in good fortune. This is often shown to us through synchronicity, and results in a sense of power when we see that something that we have done inwardly has brought to us just that which we desire outwardly. This is the experience of **greater connectedness and of harmonic resonance.**

---

* From the Michael material (Chelsea Quinn Yarbro)

The Gateway to the Higher Self

The thing that occurs when you calm yourself down, remove emotional blockages, and reach a place of greater interior peace, is that a gateway starts to open up.

Whenever there is less turmoil, less storm, and greater peace, then quieter, subtler and less obvious aspects within you become more apparent. These are seen as another aspect of self standing to the side of, or next to, the obvious part of self – an aspect of the self that can be called elevated, **or the observer, the witness**; an aspect of self that seems to have greater wisdom, that can be conversing with or guiding the more immediate inner being.

Now, this aspect of self, known as the higher self, is still you, and has always been in there but has been masked or covered up by the lower mind's constant dialogue with itself, and by the emotional maelstroms in which most people spend their waking moments. Thus, wisdom means reconnection with this interior part. Once the reconnection has been established and the doorway opened, a path is formed allowing guidance and insights to make their way from the higher self to the lower mind. This is often called **intuition**, but is sometimes also received in a more direct form as **channeling**.

Depending on the individual's makeup (the way their brain works and their natural abilities), insights can be received in different forms, such as through dreams, through intuitive guidance such as precognition, through psychic hunches, or sometimes through channeling. So long as this is a true path to the higher self and not dark imagination to the lower, fearful *Id*, the messages will be helpful and pull the individual towards his or her own light.

An interesting thing occurs as the doorway opens and the messages come through: just like on any road or avenue, a return route is at the same time established, and the individual self now has the means of expanding so that the lower mind can start to search into this area or realm from which this higher source seems to emanate. And here we have the road taking you into the Meta, the place beyond, the place where extrasensory perception originates. Here we have the route into *the field of mind* that we will call **"The M Field".**

The M Field is a name for a source of limitless light and unbounded energy. It is a name I've chosen for the place or realm beyond space and time, beyond the three-dimensional known universe. This is a place from whence the expanded mind receives guidance. This is the place to which the questing soul searches to connect with something beyond its known parameters.

Some scientists have called this higher realm *the implicate order*, an invisible matrix from which all patterns emerge, from which all energy emanates, and which is the creative fountain underlying the world. Kabalists call this realm Ain Soph, meaning "no thing" or "without end". It's also called, in Kabala, limitless light. It is an ocean of energy, undifferentiated as yet. Information that comes to us (human beings) from this place can come through dreams or visions, and seem wiser and more divine. And that's why it's called "higher" or "elevated."

Some dreams can therefore offer answers.

Let's get acquainted with this relatively new concept I'm calling The M Field, but which is also being dubbed The Source Field[*] by some researchers (for science is without doubt moving inexorably toward the same understanding held by mystical masters of ancient wisdom).

What is **The M Field?** M Field is just a shortcut name to define and encompass many concepts.

The M Field is not really a place, but a realm. For instance, M can stand for **metaphysical realm** beyond the physical because "meta" simply means "beyond".

The M Field can stand for **the mind, the higher mind**, that which is beyond the everyday thoughts and the holographic illusion constructed by our brain.

---

[*] The Source Field Investigations, David Wilcock (Plume)

The M Field is also a good name for **the morphic resonance field** (also known as The Morphogenetic Field) discovered and named by biologist Rupert Sheldrake, the scientist who studied the "hundredth monkey" phenomenon, so named after observing behavior in monkey communities who, although separated by oceans, were able to transmit a newly discovered way of utilizing tools from one isolated community to the other once a certain mass number of individuals understood the concept. Thus he explored a field that showed proof of existing, but which seemed to lie outside of the brain's interior experience.

The M Field can also stand for **the matrix**. The matrix is a name for a grid or pattern of energy holding all that is. In Hermetic Mystery School teachings, this matrix or grid is called the Akashic Records – it contains the energy pattern of everything that ever was, including every thought ever created. Energy cannot be destroyed, it can only continue to move and explore. So the matrix, or Akasha, holds the record of the patterns it has previously explored.

The M Field can also stand for that which is beyond **Maya**, i.e., the illusion of the holographic experience of life. In other words, accessing that which is beyond the illusion.

The M Field can also be defined as **manifestation, the Art of Manifestation,** which is the ability of an individual mind to travel outwards, or upwards, or beyond, into the realm of pure creative energy, and begin to magnetize, or draw to itself, those desirable patterns that want to be lived out, experienced, made manifest.

The M Field, of course, can also represent **the iMplicate order**, the invisible realm behind matter in which all potential resides, as we'll explore further later on. This has also been called the Frequency Domain.

The M Field can also stand for **the Mandelbrot Set**, a mathematical formula discovered in the late '70s by Benoît Mandelbrot, the father of fractal geometry, showing the very basis by which energy comes into being, or plays with form…the very patterns being expressed as infinite potentiality, the dancing energies of endless possibilities and eternal expansions.

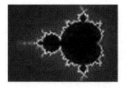 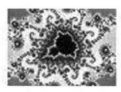 

And finally, The M Field can represent **the Mind of God**. Because once the human brain travels outward, gets beyond the illusion of time and space, and gets into the very stuff from which matter emanates, those coordinates can be none other than the divine realm.

Once consciousness has managed to expand sufficiently so that it sees itself as all others and no longer sees division between the inner and the outer, it has succeeded in raising its vibratory frequency enough to align with frequencies existing beyond the illusion of embodiment, of captured and isolated self-ness or physicality.

Consciousness experiences epiphany and can no longer think in terms of separation of you and I, or self and other. Consciousness instead discovers itself in a different field, a new paradigm, an ascended and expanded level. At this point, consciousness recognizes itself *as* the frequency domain.

There have been many names for this awakening. The *music of the spheres* is an ancient one meaning the perception of a greater frequency. Also, it has been called in Kabala *Ain Soph*, which can be translated as "nothing but awareness" or "only wisdom" and is also translated as "limitless light", a fountain of ever-creative energy bursting forth from before and beyond creation. In mathematics, this place or realm is called the implicate order, because all that can be implied as possible – all potentiality, in other words – exists prior to its formation. These names are simply ways to use human language to describe an ineffable experience of which consciousness is capable, and in fact within which it always exists, but of which in human form is rarely cognizant.

Once consciousness finds itself able to wake up and remember its presence in this sphere – of one self limitlessly dancing to a high frequency, choosing and playing at the soul's wisdom game of knowing what it is capable of – then it can be said in truth that the self is reborn as its divine nature. But an interesting thing happens at this juncture because you recognize your very nature as the divine creator and at the same time, you understand that this aspect of Being is that which is described as *the Now,* or *Presence,* by Eckhardt Tolle. The self wakes up and realizes its greater reality in the eternal present.

The Second Worldview opens the doorway to "The M Field".

The Hologram that is Your Energy Body

Everybody has an energy body beyond the physical body. Everybody is energy. Everybody exists in a sort of a dream of being physical, whereas the truth is, everybody is really just vibration, or energy moving, vibrating, constantly reflecting or experiencing life as energetic movement. *"The dream is dreaming itself."* say the Kalahari Bushmen.

> *"The idea of a constant 'self' undergoing successive experiences is an illusion."* — Fritjof Capra, *"The Tao of Physics"*

Part of The Second Worldview is to understand that energy must keep moving' that there are flows of energy greater than are perceived by the individual brain or lens; and that, as the brain shifts focus and understands this truth about life – that the individual consciousness can direct the flow of energy and can also align itself or jump onboard the direction that energy is already moving – harmony results, as well as more creative potential. So reaching The Second Worldview, reaching the understanding of a greater field of energy beyond the brain's illusion of individual selfhood, means beginning to access **almost magical power.**

In Tarot, the Magician represents this understanding: the basic truth that the consciousness can pull or draw from the greater field of energy, and through will or intention, focus that energy into **manifesting**, into forming a thing or an experience of life; in other words, into creating the world. The Magician is the self. It functions unconsciously most of the time, just in being...just in being a person who is experiencing the world.

But how powerful, how magical do things occur when the individual self realizes this power and specifically uses it as if there were a giant lens called "Awareness"! And when that lens is plugged into or taps the great field of energy, and focuses in a narrow beam, so to speak, to achieve or create or produce a result – in fact, when the lens uses its focus *to name the result* it's shooting for – then that is magical power. And that person becomes **a magician, or wizard,** in life.

All things then become possible when the self identifies its being in terms of focused energy patterns. Quantum physics calls this *collapsing the wave function.*

How can we activate our inborn creative potential?

Shifting focus to a quieter, more aligned interior state allows energy to flow in a simpler and more direct path.

The flow of energy from your thoughts and through your emotions to others, interconnectedly, begins to provide pathways in which two things occur: first, your own creative potential – that is, your own resources of energy in the form of ideas, imagination and effort – starts to flow outward as though you are clearing boulders off a path. Thus, the avenue opens up; it smoothes; it's paved; even its bumps are evened out, and your own interior flow seems to pick up speed, become more productive, follow openings, branches, roads you always wanted to go down but felt unable to.

At the same time, this open avenue provides potential for wonderful opportunities to travel towards you because, of course, there are no more walls or boulders. **The interior calming relaxation, quietude and peace** is not a dull monotonous state but rather an ongoing energetic construction site, only this time the construction is providing materials, time frame, structure, so that your inner work is actually the builder of an exciting future. Look at creative potential as a two-way street; energy that flows out from you in a free and smooth way, and opportunity that flows towards you, untrammeled. How much can be accomplished when all the mess is cleared out and you've gotten out of your own way?

Looking at the experience of life through the lens of quantum reality, we begin to understand that no experience can be outside of the idea of energy moving, recombining, and reforming itself into patterns. If the world exists within, and consciousness is the world, then all of its experiences are within the realm of choice. And here again, choice is everything because consciousness can begin to direct these patterns, take control of choice, and arrange the life experience to be more pleasant, more harmonious, and sweeter even under dire circumstances.

The concept of energy is one of unlimited creative potential.

This opportunity to make awake (conscious) choice, and then utilize a pool or reservoir of unlimited creative energy to do so, is the second large concept against which to apply the idea that everything is chosen. Not only have we engaged in original choice regarding our life's parameters, but within its structure we are able to choose what direction we want to take our lives, and what things we want to create with it. The structure itself has vast potentiality. So we find that, having made original choice, we engage with life based on an inner approach, and then we can create things or experiences while we're alive... the more consciously, the better.

We are talking about The Art of Conscious Creation. (More on this later.)

Reframing the Karmic Predicament

Our lives are spent caught up in our karmic dilemmas.

Within our K.P. (karmic predicament), or "hole in the soul", are the challenges of any particular lifetime: relationships, health, money, children, careers. And some or all of these items are what bug us, where we keep tripping up, from which negative emotions are generated. It's like we're in loops going around and around the same stuff, re-encountering it, never able to rise above it.

The Brotherhood says, *"The birth is at the end."* Most people have to wait until they die to look back and have *any* perspective or panoramic view of the lessons learned during your journey in earth school. But what happens when, in the middle of things, at age 20 or 30 or 40, you wake up and you realize, "I'm in this game, these are the challenges I agreed to, the lower aspects of my PEP, the b-s I keep encountering. But now I see it and I have answers. I have techniques, I have perspective. I've been taught and can now integrate what happens when I remove myself emotionally, and tune my thoughts to a different perspective and begin choosing how to create, and deciding whether I want to get trapped and caught up in the same-ol' same-ol', or whether I want to switch gears. And if I want to switch gears, what are the rules for doing it, what are the tools to help me? What do I have to do in my mind, my heart, and my intuition, to make this change real, and turn a lemon into lemonade?"

So, we're not saying that you have a bed of roses or you can ignore your karmic dilemma. We're not saying that at all. We're saying that wisdom, The Wisdom Game, is the next level of evolution, for everyone. The power to be the creator of our future from now on, has to do with seeing our original patterns in all their messed-up glory, and deciding to shift gears, deciding and knowing how to apply a process.

Once we understand truly that within our consciousness resides duality, that we are both the observer and the experiencer, that we are humans and creators at once, that we are the witness and actor simultaneously, then we recognize duality in ourselves as well as in the world, allowing us to become more flexible, to see the two aspects and to figure out how to switch between both dual realms whenever we want. This is great power and it is something new for the human race.

How can you realize that you are greater than your thoughts?

As the self begins to shift identity patterns, seeing its small identity as more often and regularly being replaced by the understanding and awareness of its expanded nature, you begin to understand the personal power in choosing to go this way or that way, to feel this or that, or to move down one avenue or another. The identity feels less small and more expanded.

The identity sees itself as being formed of choices, of directions, of willingness to "let go and let God". In other words, of a willingness to become more aligned with the patterns and vectors of flow.

In order to do this, the inner being is realizing it has **power to shift from one thought to another.** From one chosen outcome to another. This power lies in the ability to form a thought towards an intention and away from powerlessness. Thoughts are examined by the self. Thoughts are weighed and measured. Thoughts are understood as preliminary to the creation and the formation of potential. You begin to learn that you have power over your own formation of thoughts, and thus over the outcome.

Simultaneously, in order to create thoughts as freely as possible, the self begins to work with emotion, realizing that emotions can propel the self onwards toward the desired goal if they are positive, and can also, if they are negative, resist the flow and botch up the works.

Client M, an excellent yoga teacher, needed a certification in order to move on to the next level with her students. She told me she was having problems with presenting forms (*asanas*) whenever she was in front of the certifiers but had no such hang-ups during normal routines with her students. So time and again she was failing these tests but knew she had the right stuff. When she came to me for choosing the best date and place to take her next test, we approached it from a completely different angle: we talked about The Wisdom Game, specifically The Second Worldview. The time or place of her next test wouldn't matter as much as her mental state. She had to get out of her own way! Understanding this gave her empowerment; as a result, she sailed through the next challenge because she stayed in the state of *flow*.

So, the self begins to learn the power to switch from one thought to another at will. This underlies the magic. Behind such an ability is the growing awakening that the self is something apart from its thought and its emotions. In other words, the self is not simply the thought, or the belief, or even the feeling about what is happening, but is some process that's deeper or more removed that a person can observe, can witness, and can stand apart from, and direct the show. This thought is simply part of the process, the tool to produce the outcome. But the thought is not the self.

And this is an even greater secret.

If people understand that they're in a soul's wisdom game, that they're playing with this stuff that sets them off, that gets them depressed, or kicks them into their the weird states that they don't like being in – sadness, anger, upset, anxiety, whatever – yet then realize that they have conscious control over such, here we have what "overcoming" is about: knowing how to leverage ourselves out of our typical life predicaments.

It's a very large perspective though. It's not just self help, breathe deeply etc. It's about **reframing reality.** Other components (e.g., psychological expertise) might eventually be needed to help people work more deeply with their emotional malaise – but now we have the overall perspective on what's happening, kind of like a zoom-out. The camera is close in on the action (the soap opera in the room), then it suddenly zooms out – what you see isn't simply the building, it's the lifetime; and then the context of the soul. So you're zooming out into the metaphysics, into the cosmic Worldview of what you're undertaking.

You know that sometimes you catch yourself having very dark, habitually negative thoughts. Some are repetitious loops that you've been basically recreating for years.

But it's really helpful to begin the process of awareness: to catch yourself in the middle of one of these thoughts...to stop and see it as just a thought, not as reality, just a creation that you've made. If you can catch yourself seeing that... in other words, if you can split into two... (well, as long as you're here, you're dual anyhow...*duel*!), one part of you can observe the other part thinking. The observer can realize that the thought is just that, a thought. The observer, without putting too much blood, sweat and tears into it, can dismantle the thought and let it go. This is what this book is all about.

When you manage to become more conscious during the thought process, to monitor and edit your thoughts just as you would as a writer scratching out sentences and replacing them with better ones, what you're virtually doing is changing your life, your reality, giving energy to something better, and removing your energy from something negative. This in itself is the power to change something that's blighted, or seems depressing or full of anxiety, and to change it in the moment. That's untold power.

Your viewpoint becomes a little bit more amused, a little more detached; you have more power over it. You see yourself as a piece on the gameboard; you see yourself as the director of that board game. It's nobody else pushing you around that board.

Above all, see the immense value in unblocking from negative emotion.

One of the key tools or tricks when you're in negative emotion, when your health and your body are being affected by it and your subsequent thoughts are being formed out of that emotion... is just to recognize it and decide by an act of will to get yourself out of it. Negative emotion is based upon faulty thinking. Thinking that leads you into imaginative scenarios in which danger or heartache, distress of many sorts, can be imagined and then given weight or substance.

Negative emotion is like a huge boulder that's placed upon our shoulders and weighs us down and stops us from forward motion and really impedes creative potential.

Who gives us this negative emotion? Is it something that appears in our lives from outside of ourselves, created from a place outside of our minds? Well, sort of. It's chemical reactions in our physical body, and sometimes is even based upon our genetic make-up.

But negative emotion is not something that intrudes upon us and is punishment *from outside*; instead it is simply our perception of an experience and projection forward as to the outcome that we expect. If we are in an experience that in and of itself generates fear or distress, such as natural disaster and similar situations, we are right to react strongly, and as the event unfolds and resolves itself, we may find that our fear has saved our lives or that our anger has motivated us into action. All of this is part of the experience of life, of being human.

But when negative emotion is just free floating, based upon "ancient" history or bad future expectation – when negative emotion, in other words, does not have its basis in an immediate event – then we have a choice, which is to wallow in it endlessly, or to recognize the habitual pattern of placing oneself into that feeling, and then going around and around, creating thoughts about it and basically placing its burden upon our own shoulders.

It is this type of negative emotion that we realize we have the freedom to control.

Client V came to me with a long history of difficulty in relationships. New awareness of her karmic predicament had been growing over a series of sessions. Her newest relationship presented similar patterns: an insensitive guy who hung with his buddies and took her for granted. What had changed significantly was her awareness, her understanding of where and how she sabotaged herself or became over-emotional and disempowered. Emotional mastery was like throwing a switch. The light dawned. The same set of actions was being played out, but quite differently. The boyfriend continued his old patterns but her emotional reactions changed. It was she who was learning to be in the driver's seat. The other party was perplexed, thrown off balance. Now he couldn't take her for granted, and sought to please her. She became very upbeat about the new situation.

Techniques for The Quantum Shift Into Empowerment

By now we know about being in our karmic predicament, and being thrown into a negative emotion.

How do you get to a place of wisdom?

The first technique is to acknowledge and explain to yourself what you're undergoing. This technique can be called **observing**. It's a technique of detaching from the emotion long enough to explain to yourself its parameters, and just by doing so, the mind (which is always dual in nature) can see its elevated awareness observing its small self undergoing its "pickle". A good example occurred very powerfully for me when I was in consultation with two lawyers and both were badgering me, and I was able to still my mind momentarily just by closing my eyes and detaching myself from their drama. That moment of recentering calm was all that was needed to regain not just composure but empowerment as to whose agenda was to be honored.

Clarify this observation, perhaps by **journaling.** Writing down the nature of your predicament can emphasize it, but can also give you some space from your emotion.

Identify your emotion. Is it an emotion of fear, of anger, of upset, of anxiety? Now look at the thoughts that surround that emotion. Clarify the story you're telling yourself about the emotion you're feeling. Why are you feeling it? What has happened? What is the definition of the predicament that's generating the emotion?

Practice a method such as one of the following that not only gives you detachment, but can actually change the emotion. For example, breathing. The technique of **breathing** – specifically called The Box – is a yoga technique that's very useful and easy. It requires you to keep an inner count of four or five beats, visualizing a vertical line as you inhale, then holding the breath to another four or five beats while visualizing a horizontal line attached to the vertical one, then exhaling to yet another four or five beats while visualizing a second vertical parallel to the first and extending from the corner of the horizontal, and finally keeping exhalation out for still another four or five beats while visualizing closing The Box with a second horizontal. In other words, your breathing creates an invisible box; by maintaining this measured deep breathing, you will slow your heartbeat, slow your brain, and naturally fall into better alignment, which shifts the emotion. The technique of the box for breathing can be used in tight quarters when there's tension and stress. A good example is when you're in the dentist chair getting your teeth drilled.

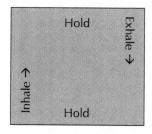

Breathing exercises are one of the gateways into **meditation,** which is the process by which you center yourself, learn to access the essential you (the conscious awareness that lies between any two thoughts), and remain there until you realize that you are not your thoughts, your emotions, or even your body. Repeating a mantra is another gateway thereto. When you meditate very quietly, calming all chattering thoughts, sometime an intense blue light appears in the third eye field of vision (middle of the forehead). This blue light, just like the pilot light on a stove, can be seen as pure light or can be formed (by visualization) into the shape of a tiny Buddha. And as you are drawn towards this, the world changes instantaneously. (This meditation device can even be used as a powerful aid during sex, an aid that will further the exploration of sex as a path to God, also known as *tantra*.)

Another technique is to **apply humor**; that is to say, to see the humor in the human drama. To lighten it by laughing about it or seeing it as ridiculous, trivial, or not as big a deal as first thought. Humor is a long-recognized remedy to negativity and in metaphysical studies is recognized as the antidote to evil.

Yet another technique, as mentioned earlier, is to **establish a Place of Peace (or Joy)** in your mind and in your emotions. This is done by visualizing a time, a memory, or even an imagined fantasy, in which you place yourself into a framework of great enjoyment, pleasure and peace. And by having that inner sanctuary created and built up during pleasant or calm times in your life, you can always return there during crisis. And once again it will be a method that changes the vibration of emotion while you're in it.

Another approach can be the **use of patience,** the understanding that life unfolds at a tempo. The inner self, when in fear or anxiety or upset, often wants to speed that up to get out of it much faster, or conversely to push it away indefinitely, whereas the Zen master simply allows the process to unfold, and detaches the emotions from the engagement of the tempo, and thus achieves patience, calm or non-attachment even while the story plays itself out. This is a form of mind training.

There are further techniques that are offered by experts in fields such as **Emotional Freedom Technique, or The Work, The Option Process, or other such internal methods** that promote a shift in emotional energy or a rearrangement in thought formation.

Also for those so disposed, there's even the technique of using modern computer terminology to tell the mind to pause, **to hit the pause button** in the on-going reaction, and just stop it. Or, similarly, to envision a "control+alt+delete" of the reactiveness – a reboot returning the inner self to its neutral default position.

Similarly, you can change an outcome by quickly saying (and meaning) **"Cancel, cancel"** after the unconscious creation of a negative conception. It works!

Reframing is another technique. This simply means telling yourself a different story about what has happened to you, putting a more positive spin on what you believe has just occurred. For instance, (not to be flippant or uncompassionate) even those who suffered through nature's worst might choose to reframe the experience as the forced push that has catapulted one into a new start. Large-scale natural disasters also serve as the device to make the entire human species more compassionate with one another, more globally aware.

Working with **true, not blind, faith** is excellent. This requires a true understanding of what karma means, and a clear realization that "What goes around, comes around." Such a philosophy allows you to "let go and let God" – in other words, to allow the universe to return that which you are (positively) sending forth. Then all you need to do is make sure you're sending forth the good stuff, and wait for its return!

The shift **into love and away from fear** is yet another excellent way to move quickly towards wisdom. Situations that might provoke anxiety or separation are changed and softened by the deliberate shift from the feelings of hurt and isolation, into that of connectedness and union. As you do this, the outer world conforms to the new vibration and approaches you with its better energy.

The Brotherhood Of Light Workers recommends **the control of thought** – the understanding that a certain train of thinking is being brought to bear upon the situation, generated either as a reaction to the emotion of fear or anxiety, or as a precursor to the emotion, such as habitual negative programming. Either way, if the mind understands that it is the originator of thought, but not the thought itself, then the mind sees its power to shift, even as it's in the middle of a chain of thought, to a different story line. The Brotherhood says, *"This is our most powerful tool."* So that, while you're in great fear, and experiencing chemical reactions to the fear as well as a new stream of negative thoughts emanating from that emotion, you can, at will, realize the process and determine the conscious choice to shift from that series of thoughts into an entirely different one in which you present yourself with better options... in which you rewrite your movie.

When the mind understands itself as the creator of reality and the master of thought, the self begins to see its true power. Now you have the potent tool and method needed to leverage yourself out of your karmic hole, to apply the internal wisdom to the external situation, monitoring thoughts, guiding them towards a more harmonious flow, and to begin to notice results appearing.

Until you find this internal power, your karmic predicament will continue to execute, but once you become aware and start consciously working with your karma, this is when emotional blockages are removed and a surge of power is unleashed.

The value of wisdom is to remove these blockages and get energy flowing, connected to its vitality, its passion. When energy is reconnected and is seen as controllable, or able to be mastered, something else happens. A doorway to a larger realm becomes available because the mind has expanded beyond the limitations of the karmic self, beyond the limitations of its emotional rootedness, and has seen itself as larger and expanded from the restricted individual identity.

Consciously Creating your Reality

When we look at mathematical formulas, such as the amazing patterns of the Mandelbrot Set in which we can see fractals of energy forever zigging off in constant renewal, we have a clear visible image of life's eternal choices.

Since we are comprised of nothing but energy and consciousness, we begin to realize that the only thing that stops us from going this way instead of that way, or

> **GATE/WORLDVIEW: 2**
>
> **TOOL: Conscious Co-Creation.** In each moment you learn to equate your inner thoughts with the universal flow of energy. You learn to become aligned. You feel as though life has become play!

remaining in ruts of stagnating loops of habitual patterns, is what our minds choose. It is emotional choice that keeps us in our ruts. But we also see that at the quantum level, energy has choice at every instant. Everything is probability and potential. We can go down that old emotional road, or we can switch right in the midst of it, right in that moment.

"The point of power is in the present." (Seth) Jane Roberts

All human beings are flawed and have feet of clay. All human beings stand in the muck. But after making conscious choices in the midst of our emotional storms again and again, and after doing that sufficiently, we begin to feel the flow. We realize we can start drawing from an entire field of potential and not just remain stuck in our own small limitations. When we access this larger field of potential – The M Field – even miracles can happen. Unbelievably good things can happen to us.

You've got to activate your higher consciousness to see which moves you should be making.

As you begin to reach the higher development stages of The Second Worldview, you realize that your next moves will not only fit into better planning for your future, but they are the creators – these thoughts – of the future itself.

And so, you begin to tailor and structure your thoughts in order not just to move yourself to the next rung on your ladder toward success, but to actually create the next several rungs themselves. You begin building possibility. In order to do this, you must work actively and consciously with energy patterns, seeing which avenue you are being guided toward and aligning your dreams and desires with available energy.

This is an inner process. It begins as you learn how to think differently, and then practice the release of negativity. It continues as you experience more opportunities to feel and use your innate energies, and it reaches success as you apply this additional energy and diminish negativity toward the realization of your goals.

So, wisdom allows you to create your reality deliberately, and brings you to the place of more empowerment, more calmness, greater joy, less stress, and the further attainment of self-realization and manifestation of your dreams. Wisdom pulls you out of suffering.

One more thing that this conscious creation allows is a feeling of greater safety in life. Just as The First Worldview took you to an understanding that life itself is a soul's wisdom game that the universe is playing with its embodied self, so The Second Worldview takes you to an understanding that no one or nothing else is creating the soul's wisdom game that you are playing. **You only need to encounter that which you choose.**

Mind is the Builder

"For mind is the builder," the seer Edgar Cayce taught, "and…thoughts are things."

Cayce's quote describes the truth that the creation of thoughtforms is the initiator of reality.

How you think about something is what story you tell yourself. The story you tell yourself on the inside manifests the reality you encounter in the world. Every thought counts.

We've been talking about the concept of the **reframing of experience**. This means that you decide in one moment, in one second, to change the story you're telling yourself about an event. For example, you've just been treated poorly by another person who has insulted you or rejected you. You can tell yourself that it feels hurtful, that you are the victim of unjust behavior, and that you'll get even with their poor actions…or you can switch the story in your mind, telling yourself instead that the insulter is your teacher regarding detachment, wisdom, and self respect. Or you can tell yourself any other story that you'd like. Using infinite possibility in this direct and conscious way is what is called The Quantum Shift.

The more positive the new thought is, the better the outcome will be for you. It's not a question of getting even; it's a question of personal empowerment. Only you are responsible for your thoughts. Only you design your reality. Regardless of how we were taught when we were brought up, the truth is that we, in our minds, build our world.

And if we think we are going into a recession, then we will create it, and if we think we are in economic recovery, that is also what we will create, first on a personal level, and then on a societal level. The thoughts are the structurer or builder of the world.

Encountering The Surge

When you walk through a threshold, and stretch yourself in this fashion, you experience a delightful situation known as The Surge. You become a possibility-thinker. By removing emotional blockages, there is an acceleration of creative potential. Each time you go within, raise your awareness, increase your energy, and keep expanding in a positive way, utilizing Quantum Shifting, you are seeing visible results indicating that you're getting the highest pay-off in the shortest amount of time with the least amount of effort. Eventually, you realize that this will also be for the good of the world! Alignment with universal flow means that the universe begins supporting your interior efforts. Fortunate "coincidences" occur more frequently in life, and things happen more easily. Then a cascade of opportunity is unleashed. Possibilities unfold as fast as can be dreamt.

So just do something, even if you fail at first, because you want to keep energy moving in a directed way, to become self-realized and co-creative. It's important not to get stuck or stagnate because then the energy isn't doing what it always wants to do: flowing. (People get ill when this happens.) Once flowing, all of nature will then comply, revealing this collaboration via meaningful coincidences (i.e., synchronicity). Amazing help will appear. Even more doors will open.

As the mind realizes that it is the director of the show and no one else can force that individual to continue and propagate a situation of discomfort or suffering, then the mind has taken a giant leap from powerlessness to great empowerment. The surge is the reflection of that.

The surge occurs when the mind itself, at will and instantaneously, realizes it can choose what state of emotion it wants to be in and what thoughts it would prefer creating rather than helplessness or habitual stagnation. That mind has then prepared the way for a propulsion of creativity. That mind has cleaned things up. Done the yard sale. Gotten rid of baggage. Straightened everything out, and tidied up.

Within that mind is an open road. No bottleneck. A complete and solid conduit for possibility. Energy can rush forward, for there is no negative emotion blocking, and no discouraging thoughtforms impeding.

When energy rushes forth, it creates. It creates in a way that might seem miraculous, might seem disconnected one from another event, might seem amazing, and will always feel enjoyable. The awake and flowing mind is a path of rapid realization. It is a dynamo of possibility and all things rush forward toward it as it clears and opens. This is what as known as the surge or cascade of opportunity.

Seeing the Hologram as Life's Illusion

Remember how the notion of a holographic reality was touched upon in The First Worldview? Let's revisit holography and light at this juncture.

From the scientific point of view, the dictionary definition of light is "the form of radiant energy that stimulates the organs of sight." From a spiritual point of view, light is awareness, light is the opposite of darkness or ignorance. Light illuminates. Light is energy that shows itself, reveals something that is unenlightened, brightens what has been revealed or awakened and then shone to itself and brought into awareness.

So, light is **energy that is awake.** To be enlightened is to shine a revealing glow upon that which is unexamined, dark or unknown.

Lightness is the opposite of heaviness. Lightness is free. Lightness is happy and playful. To access and apply wisdom is to increase light inside the self and therefore in the entire world, to shine a beam of understanding into dark places and to work with energy in an aware fashion. To apply wisdom is to see yourself as awake or aware energy, the wielder of conscious power.

A hologram is constructed of light – laser light. It is coherent light.

Holography can be seen in a plate of glass.

A hologram is made when a laser is used to imprint an image into a plate, giving a three dimensional representation of the item. In other words, you can walk around the plate of glass and see it from different angles. If you make a hologram of a person, as you walk around it, you see their side and their back and then their front again. If you make a hologram of a glass of water, you can actually use a microscope and see the microorganisms in that water.

Not only is the hologram capable of capturing an exact duplicate of the three dimensional world, but it offers another similarity to real life, which is that if the holographic plate is smashed to pieces, the complete image remains in every sliver of that glass, no matter how small. The whole is contained in the minute. (In metaphysics, *"As above, so below"*.)

Holography is seen on a credit card when the image shifts shape as you twist it back and forth. A hologram is seen in the movie *Star Wars* when Princess Leia accesses her message stored in R2D2. A hologram is understood as able to be entered in *Star Trek's* spaceship Enterprise, when the crew needs to live through an experience, or take a vacation in, the "holodeck". And certain gamers experience holography as virtual reality when they become immersed in a video game by wearing a helmet and other sensory devices.

In real life, we see these items as images, as futuristic technology, and as virtual reality. But what science has begun to discover is that all of real life is virtual. We are living in a holograph that is presented to us through our brains. We see the world as solid. We see ourselves in time and space. But this is where the virtuality is, because all that we can ever know of the physical world is shown to us through our five senses: smelling, hearing, tasting, touching, and seeing. And these perceptions occur when one frequency of energy encounters and crashes into or parallels another energy frequency and produces the first stages of physical illusion. Thereupon, differing vibrations are "translated" into body chemicals and processes (still just energy patterns) that feed information to our brain about an event that seems to be occurring outside of us but is actually all taking place within ourselves in the hologram-creating device called the brain. These energy patterns emanating from the five senses are then stacked up to present us with the sense or illusion of a whole event (i.e., a moment in time and space). And so we have the first glimmering of existing in a place and at a time in which something has occurred.

Next, we have a series of moments in which our senses, as information from them is stacked up or layered, present our brains with a concept that another event, slightly different than the first, has now also occurred in time and space. And so on and so forth, so that our perception (that we have lived through and encountered something) is born of energy which forms sensory input, which in turn creates the Now, and then does so again and again.

And from this process of the five-senses-layered hologram comes the sense of an "I am." *I am* having a sequence of events occurring and these events are occurring in a linear fashion, giving me the sense of existing here, and furthermore, existing right now. And since this sense of continually-occurring momentary events shifts ever so slightly each time, not only *am I* existing and moving forward in time, but *I am* also moving or doing something in this sequence through space.

Here we have the root of the illusion of life. We have broken it apart in order to see that it is all anchored in sensory input from the five human senses and stacked up in the brain to form the illusion of solidity moving through time and through space. In fact, it is virtual reality.

How do we know that? How do we know – while we're *here* and appear to be *real*...and if we pinch ourselves, or if we stick ourselves and bleed – how do we know that we are in a hologram? Well, if we bleed, we see blood, we can taste it, we may hear something occurring from the bleeding, we feel pain, we have kinetic sense, and we might smell something. That's the only way we know we are bleeding, and all of that is part of the five-senses-holographic-reality, thanks to our wonderful human brain.

> *"Our brains mathematically construct objective reality by interpreting frequencies that are ultimately projections from another dimensions, a deeper order or existence that is beyond both space and time: The brain is a hologram enfolded in a holographic universe....we even construct space and time."*— Michael Talbot, *The Holographic Universe*

If you couldn't see, hear, feel, smell or taste something, would you know it had occurred? (In Zen, *would it have?!*)

Something unusual happens when this is fully understood. The mind expands sufficiently to be able even to perceive this illusion. The mind asks questions and takes a broader point of view, and begins to see that reality is occurring nowhere else than in the brain. And at that point, the brain becomes aware of **one more source** of sensory input. Only, it's not the five senses, it's the extra sense – the sixth sense – which is the intuition.

This becomes the point at which the brain allows intuition to enter the mix and become part of the virtual reality illusion, or a part of the hologram. An expanded field beyond the body must be acknowledged. Information or input is being received; it lands in the interior of the illusion but comes from a different source, a source that is both outside of the known boundaries of the brain and deeper within, from some subterranean level that is only beginning to come to the light.

This marks the stage known as the Piercing of the Veil. It is the boundary where the self realizes that it has constructed an illusion and willingly entered it and yet has left itself a bridge to its source, a source elsewhere and beyond, or very deep. At this point, the hologram begins to lose its rigid structure and reveal its magic secrets.

To understand the world realistically is to understand that you're living in a hologram.

What you see as yourself, as a separate individual, disconnected from other individuals, or from physical objects, is part of the illusion. Holistic understanding means realizing that all people are fragments of one energy, completely interconnected, only existing in a brain that is designed to separate energy into **the illusion of matter and objects**. Whereas the truth is: no such thing actually exists.

To wake up to the idea of the holographic nature of the universe is to realize, also, that not only are all people one but the rest of the world – things, and stuff – are also a part of you. And that there is no differentiation in a field of energy, i.e., that there can only be different degrees of vibration, but not true separateness. That in fact the hologram requires the understanding of the principle of vibrational rates or frequencies, and the ability of any particular consciousness to decide to get into greater harmony with another aspect of itself and thus form a bond, or a union. The entire world, this so-called outer nature of it and the more obvious inner nature of it, are all entangled, all one field of energy. Joined, unionized, and experienced as separate things only because of one particular part of life, the part called the human brain.

The human brain is the only aspect of all of the experience of life in which a sense of separation occurs.

In truth, two are one. *"You are I are not 'we', but 'one',"* said the silent guru Meher Baba. In this changing paradigm, duality is an illusion. The outer and the inner are its play. It's all taking place in the field of mind (consciousness) where duality is constructed, where the lower self (human) talks to its higher self (God) in a soul's wisdom game of contrast. Therefore, you are me. And I am the world. And there's no one else except the One anyhow.

I need *you* in order to discover being-ness. I need contrast to learn. You teach me the wisdom gained from interacting with the illusion of the other. *"Without contrarieties, no progression,"* teases the mystic-poet William Blake. If I want to win, then I have no alternative but to help you (because you're me). If I want to brighten the world with wisdom, joy and peace, there's no where else to start but within the illusion, changing myself as fast and as well as I can, and wanting with all my heart to leap beyond the illusion into a construction of oneness.

I have to bring you along to there because I can't get there any other way.

Continuum of Awareness

It's at this stage that a new perception of identity takes hold. If you are both the creator of reality and its experiencer, you find yourself located in a new role. Its location is no longer simply in your physical body (feelings and sensations, your brain), or even outside it in the physical world (events, occurrences, other people, objects). Your new location is in an identity that resides beyond the limits of these places. Sometimes you know yourself as the experiencer "on the stage", sometimes as the creator "in the wings". So where are you?

That becomes a deep question that you ask yourself. And it has only one answer: you are on a continuum of selves, a sliding spectrum of identity that is not fully in space or in time. You are Awareness that can inhabit its vehicle or can "float" above it as it pulls things into manifestation. You have gotten, as Kurt Vonnegut wrote, "unstuck from time"*.

---

*   Slaughterhouse Five

Furthermore, your heightened awareness can choose to locate itself in various "stops" along this continuum – here as your personal identity (with all its karmic baggage), there as your Higher Self who guides you always... and even midway as a witness who simply sees the larger perspective of your life at this or that moment. I have decided to call this effect *The Capping of Awareness* because, as in any dam of a river or endcap to a pipeline, the infinitude of possibility regarding your chosen identity at any particular moment requires a delineation to provide it with form. In quantum physics, this could be called *collapsing the wave function*.

Four Wisdom Exercises for The Second Worldview

Here are some simple exercises to help you refocus, lift upwards, connect thoughts with external occurrences, bring about that which you desire, and let your energetic potential rush forward.

> **FOUR WISDOM EXERCISES FOR WORLDVIEW 2**
>
> 1. Pull back the camera
> 2. Practice listening to your intuition
> 3. Keep a dream journal
> 4. Attract and manifest

1. Pull back the camera! Take a larger viewpoint of whatever is going on, and tell yourself that you created it to play with your innate potential. Instead of suffering, laugh at your tragicomedy (as best you can) and look ahead to your soon-to-be-changing scenes.
2. Practice listening to your intuition. In daily life, have you just gotten a hunch that someone will call? Did you just "hear" yourself telling you to pick up an item at the store? What about that parking spot at the Mall? The smallest, most trivial feelings might be your inner guidance system aiding you... or it might just be your over-imagination! Only daily practice will help you

develop true intuition, from baby steps onward, until you can really hear your "small, still voice within".
3. Keep a dream journal. And make note of any paranormal event you might encounter, including "signs and omens" from the universe. Put limiting beliefs aside, and open up to cause-and-effect. After all, if you want to "swim" in The M Field, you must "suspend disbelief" and pave the mental way.
4. Attract and manifest. Pull to you that which is similar to your new desire by seeking out people and mindsets that reflect the new you, then ask for a need to be met (yes, prayer is one way). Wait quietly for its response. If it doesn't happen, repeat the previous three exercises.

Results may at first seem almost magical. But soon you'll feel gleeful as you witness your own forgotten powers being resurrected.

Recap: Playing The Wisdom Game

In short, everybody is playing the soul's wisdom game, basically to the same end: to experience life, gain wisdom from placing value on certain experiences and seeing other experiences as distasteful or leading to suffering

At the same time that everyone is playing the same soul's wisdom game, there are different versions of it. Everyone is expressing a unique mathematical (harmonic) pattern. People are choosing patterns that are more or less harmonious, more or less challenging, and with harder or easier parameters. People also challenge themselves to fill an agenda, to discover the nature of the chosen pattern, to accomplish a self-chosen goal, to complete a task, and to be differently motivated by inner passion (what we call our dream).

There are infinite ways to play The Wisdom Game, but generally, the key concepts are: to awaken to the fact that we are in this soul's wisdom game; to understand it; and then to learn methods to reach a more joyful centered and whole place within. Once we learn how to do that, we eliminate our obstacles faster, get closer to our possibilities sooner, and begin to manifest the creative potential that is inherent in the mathematical pattern in the first place. This is the pattern which we call our personality, a pattern that combines the karmic threads from past actions into combinations that reflect our current talents and challenges.

Once we wake up to the fact that we are playing the soul's wisdom game and we see what needs to be done, how best to operate within it and what techniques to apply, we are no longer carried along haplessly, but are motivated to see our actions and identify everything from this new point of view. We begin to grasp the individual and the overall general concepts that need to be understood. We see the rules of The Wisdom Game that apply to everyone, regardless of what individual or particular game we have chosen to play within a certain unique pattern or personality.

We see that there are general rules that can be applied, we see that there's nothing magical about this, but that it's in fact scientific and fits completely into a new paradigm of reality. We understand that the outer world is completely entangled with the inner self. We understand that the other person is really an aspect of the self. We grasp that this is the very place that wisdom carries us.

We have named this The Quantum Shift because we see that our interior process is entangled with our exterior experience. The shift is really a shift of beliefs about what is possible within three dimensional reality and about how that reality truly works. We see that we can manifest or co-create with the universe, and that what's going on in our minds (our thoughts and our emotions) has direct bearing on what life offers us.

We understand that this is the true secret. We see that we each choose skill sets to acquire and internalize this new understanding, and in turn become able to reframe all experience using the rules of The

Wisdom Game to unlock the key to our own soul's wisdom game, to make life work for us, to make it easier. We understand that there are no separations between people, between aspects of our lives, such as business, health, or love life; we see that our goals are entangled with everyone else's; we see that we are whole persons; and we see that by identifying that which gets us off-center and impedes growth also identifies what blocks manifestation. Finally we see that these obstacles along our pathway are absolutely necessary in playing The Wisdom Game.

A client, whom I will call "S", came to me with a story of strife on the job. A new boss had come along months before and was creating pressure, stress, and turmoil. Client S was in a pickle. Should she leave and suffer the loss of livelihood or should she continue with aggravating circumstance? Her Personal Energy Pattern revealed that she was indeed going through a very stressful period, but that she was built to endure it. She was made to withstand the pressure, not only to exist within it, but to thrive and prosper. If she maintained right attitude and kept going, not succumbing to the manipulation, threats, and difficulty, but constantly shifting perspective, this very troublesome boss would become the instrument of her growth. She would become a much more powerful individual herself, and eventually in due time, be released from the circumstances. S made her decision to stick with it because she now has the tools to do some maneuvering herself.

Such mastery of your inner life underlies the turning point of your awakening.

The Quantum Shift is the understanding that what happens on the inner level has a direct bearing on what happens to you on "the outside". It is the shift in perceptions.

Now the connection between the self (the inner world) and the outer reality is seen as an illusion, and the shift is in the realization that what goes on in the inner world in our thoughts and feelings can change reality. It's the interior work that actually dissolves the barrier that is stopping the flow. You must not only work on what's in your mind or your thoughts, but you must also engage your heart and emotional self, too. All must be brought together.

This is a process, and does not occur instantaneously. Techniques must be deliberately and consciously applied in order to win The Wisdom Game. The ground rules include seeing each emotional issue as it's occurring, bringing the understanding of it to the surface of your mind, identifying it, and also identifying discouraging thoughts that lead to negative emotion as well as positive thoughts that re-energize. The ground rules include trying to work within this understanding – not just repressing an emotion, but accepting it. At the same time, you are asking your higher self, or the Observer, to integrate it.

As you're going through the emotional issue, meantime you continue to practice your techniques (whatever you find is working for you), such as going to a place of joy or reframing a current experience into a thought about it that changes it into something more thrilling or useful.

After doing this type of process several times, something new begins to occur, the confirmation that this inner change or quantum shift is working. How do you know that? Often, the confirmation is given by synchronicity. Synchronicity is defined as the wild and "coincidental" occurrence that shows you that what's going on inside you is bringing outer results. Synchronicity is that which reveals the entanglement. Psychiatrist-metaphysician Carl Jung saw synchronicity as the manifestation of a higher principle, while others feel it illustrates a larger intelligence at work in the universe which some might call God or Source.

Eventually, you begin to do this process so swiftly and so well, and you begin to dissolve your boulders so quickly, that there's no blockage anymore. Creative potential, which is always in you, starts to flow, at first gradually, and then in a torrent.

Each individual has a dream, a passion to fulfill. That is what is flowing. That is where creative potential wants to go. The faster your obstacles are dissolved, the smoother the flow becomes and the torrent moves forward as a river, unstoppable.

The confirmation is not simply psychological; it becomes visible. This is **The Surge**.

You can see that creative potential is now flowing, and other people can see it as well. The Wisdom Game hands you your own power. It gives you awareness and validation regarding the deep inner work that you are doing…in other words, the choices that you are making.

Where you've stumbled before is exactly where you now have choice, and you see that making wise choice smoothes and increases the flow. This of course makes you joyful and shows you your own power as the creator of reality. You see that you're no longer a helpless individual against large forces, which you can name as society, as the world, or even as God. Instead, you see that you're now in charge, running the show, and that you can keep doing that at every turn.

Once you've done this often enough, sufficiently enough, and powerfully enough, you realize that you have **become the flow**. You're no longer an individual against the world, but you are the energy of the universe itself. By accumulating enough validation about how the process of The Wisdom Game works, you are able to hit a threshold, or the next Worldview.

By fully manifesting creative potential, and by feeling fully empowered in the world, your goal changes. Your purpose in life shifts from fulfilling individual need to serving the greater good.

If The Second Worldview teaches the usage of creative potential and the access to The M Field, the next Worldview, The Third Worldview, brings you to Global Identity. And so, by mobilizing the interior journey, The Wisdom Game's ground rules can't help but reveal that your further goal is to help the whole world to become a happier interaction of individual selves, a happier society. This is the logical next step on the continuum of Worldviews.

The Law of Attraction – "Like Attracts Like"

The phenomenon known in recent times as **"The Law of Attraction"** is about the power of focusing intention, aligning your emotions and will clearly with it, and drawing results into existence.

It is a secret not only because it has deliberately been hidden for ages (cloaked), but because what's going on is not obvious or apparent. It hasn't been for mankind throughout the ages, as the brain evolved and as societal structures developed and as knowledge accumulated. The Law of Attraction has waited all this time, until man entered the Age of Aquarius, the current epoch, in order to be revealed to many.

And the revelation is not because some ancient hidden tablet was discovered, but because **science has revealed** the phenomenon of the entanglement of everything in life, in the world, in the universe, in one constantly fluctuating energy field (Quantum Physics). Science has shown that our brains are devices that form the illusion of matter or reality out of this fluid mind stuff (the holographic universe).

The Law of Attraction is being revealed to us not in spite of science but because of it.

One way to work with the Law of Attraction is to understand and align with frequency, or vibrational patterns. In other words, to flow... **to go with the flow.** When you align your PEP (Personal Energy Pattern) with that of the universe, you bring yourself into vibrational harmony. By offering less resistance via negative emotionality, you clear away the interference (static).

If you encounter resistance, you use inner understanding to soften emotions and develop patience. In other words, you slow down as calmly and as centeredly as possible, and continue to move but at a slower rate or lower frequency.

Conversely, if you find that a fear or anxiety is holding you back when the energy seems to be increasing and the flow is speeding up, you soften the resistance (fear) within your inner awareness, and trust or learn to have faith in this flow of energy, thereby jumping on board and working harmoniously, or stretching with what is being asked.

This alignment of inner placement with larger forces is called **harmonic resonance.**

By consciously reducing the self-created and self-sustained obstacles, thus removing your opposition to the world at large, the sense of ego diminishes while **the sense of oneness moving within itself** increases. You are no longer separate from the universe, but are in fact the embodiment of its unfolding. That's what is meant by *becoming the flow.*

A good way to work with this is to use sentences that replace the word "I" or "me" with the phrase "Creative Potential", and to practice doing this frequently. This will result in amusing and simple everyday situations in which one says to oneself, instead of "I have to pick up the dry cleaning" that "Creative Potential has to pick up the dry cleaning." Or instead of "I can't manage to finish my work," change it to "Creative potential can't manage to finish its work." And so on, all day long, until one realizes that it is not just the self that is at play, but the entire field of energy, attempting to manifest its potential in as creative and flowing a way as possible.

This shift in personal identity broadens the awareness so that The Law of Attraction, or the Art of Manifestation, is not happening only to people on TV or in a book, but to the very self as the self begins to see its individuality as the field of energy at play.

"Earth is a school, no matter what you think," says The Brotherhood, *"and here's another lesson to be learned and mastered. The lesson of flowing."*

Seven Cosmic Laws

An even better way to utilize your new skill, The Art of Manifestation, is to understand hidden laws of existence that are more explicit than merely The Law of Attraction.

We have spoken extensively regarding the **Law of Karma** (the law of cause and effect) as a primary basis for the blueprint in your Personal Energy Pattern. In addition to the law of karma, there are six other cosmic laws, and these have bearing on this material.

The first law is the **Law of Mentality**, or mind, and it says, in essence, that all is spirit or consciousness. And of course that is the gist of this entire concept of the Continuum of Awareness.

There are other cosmic laws given to us in the secret teachings down through the ages. **The Law of Correspondence**, or analogy, the second Law, tells us that *as above, so below; as within, so without.* And this very much speaks of likeness, and attracting that which is analogous to your interior constructs. It explains the macro, the very large, and even the divine, as corresponding to the micro, or the very small, or ourselves.

Third is the **Law of Gender** which states that everything has masculine or feminine qualities. That is to say, everything in the Cosmos is comprised of the Yin and the Yang of essence, together, making the whole.

Fourth, as mentioned above, is the Law of Karma.

A fifth law is the **Law of Vibration**, which fits perfectly with the concept of a frequency domain: all energy having different qualities based upon the frequency at which something vibrates, and that everything is in constant vibratory motion. (String theory is called to mind.)

The sixth cosmic law is that of the **Law of Polarity**, or duality: everything in this universe has an equal and opposite reflection; the Universe is comprised of this duality and can't be other. When you think of it, this is quite awesome; it's as though the nature of life offers not oneness but two-ness, and it is only through consciousness that this basic dual essence can be transcended and reunited.

Finally, the last of the seven cosmic laws or principles is the **Law of Rhythm** or cycles, often called the Wheel of Existence: everything has its ascendancy or descendancy, and is in constant exchange in that regard.

The funny thing is that, in naming these seven principles as the basis for all that is, and seeing how they correlate to the description of the Continuum of Awareness and the truths that are found in pursuing its understanding, it becomes obvious that there's no specific Law of Attraction, the very thing that *The Secret* was based upon, and which has gotten so much buzz and so much interest in recent years! The Law of Attraction is in fact, a combination of many of these principles. When you are aligned in your vibrational expression, when you realize that the interior and the exterior are analogous or correlated, when you understand and harmonize with your karma, when you grasp that everything is mind and not solid form, then you are able to resonate in a fashion that draws to you that which is desirable, and can attract that to which you are harmonious and what your passion and heart's desire seeks to realize.

Therefore the basis of much of this era's striving is to understand and manipulate cosmic principles in order to improve the current sojourn of each life. The Law of Attraction is secretly the translation of basic cosmic principles available to the person who raises vibration and expands awareness, and who can begin utilizing creativity *by design.*

Having accrued new wisdom, what are some ways to utilize it? Well, one of the things you want to do with wisdom is capture it in a fashion that makes it real, accessible, and structured. As we go along in life, there are many, many experiences that are giving us a piece of wisdom on an almost continuous basis. But it's rare that anyone will sit down and actually outline it or detail it…although it is very valuable, like a treasure! So, perhaps keeping a journal of your insights would be a very good thing to do in the journey.

Another thing, of course, once you get a piece of wisdom, is to apply it to the specific thing that is your particular karmic dilemma. In other words, to get yourself out of the hole

THREE WISDOM USES

1. Keep a journal

2. Leverage out of your "hole"

3. Increase joy for self and others

that you always find yourself in, the "hole in your soul". Whatever it is that you have realized as a piece of valuable treasured wisdom, once applied to your particular unique dilemma, begins to chug along, pick up steam and bring results. The results are always seen as a reduction of the problem and a concomitant increase in joy. You know when you are getting yourself out of your karmic predicament because you feel more in control of your life. That will make you feel calmer, less stressed out, less victimized. You will find yourself feeling happier, of course, because you have less problems. You'll begin to realize that your inner self can get to its goals and can discover its purpose faster because there will be less obstacles in the way. The world won't seem as dangerous. By mastering something deep down, the accumulation of wisdom and the application of it brings a sense of greater security into life, even a protection against the threats that the world continually throws up. These threats are seen as within the individual, subject to the application of smart wisdom techniques. And so, the world begins to seem safer and less threatening.

Finally, the accumulation of wisdom, and the deliberate application of it into techniques, brings you into greater joy that also radiates outward onto others. So, you seem like a person who is managing life better, who is more in control, and perhaps even someone who reflects a certain amount of luck or the ability to manifest positive results more quickly. People become drawn to you.

This is what you can do with wisdom once you get it.

The Art of Manifestation

There is a science to conscious creation. An artful science. It's what The Law of Attraction is teaching.

Matching your personal vibration to that of the present moment (universal flow) is the beginning of a kind of magical ability that is often called The Art of Manifestation.

First, you need to learn the ability to switch out of negativity by the control and production of your thoughts. This has to become routine or second nature.

Second, you need to identify what your true desire is, your passion, something you can feel very strongly about to use imagination to develop, and to use positive energy in the form of intention and expectation to strive for.

Third, all that happens to you on the way to this desired end is reframed as self-created challenges within your soul's wisdom game strategy.

Fourth, is simply to take action, to take some kind of action that will get the energy moving and will get you out of your rut. So we have statements such as, "Just do it!" or as the Brotherhood says, *"Take action!"* Even if it will result in failure. Because in order for conscious creation to undertake and achieve success, the prerequisite is to get energy moving forward under conscious control.

Fifth is to intuitively align your energy – in other words, your vibratory frequency – with the universe's intention, otherwise known as Greater Will, and to feel when you are in the flow and when you are meeting resistance. If the latter, apply game strategy and switch from negativity to positivity. Spend time appreciating, spend time visualizing.

Put will and action together with desire and creativity, and you will get results faster. You will begin to see the desired results manifesting.

The secret to manifestation resides in the emotional power and the focused intention that are placed upon the projected desire. This is what The Law of Attraction is all about. It teaches how to draw to you that to which you are resonating. *"Like attracts like."*

Here is a Quick Check List to utilize your tools, including visualizing your desired results, to be emphasized with the power of repetition:

A QUICK CHECK LIST TO IMPLEMENT THE LAW OF ATTRACTION
- Have a clear intention
- Make sure it's designed as something positive, in line with your overall life plan and core beliefs, harming no one, and serving a larger need.
- Charge it with emotion ~ intensify it with visualization & emotionality ~ e.g., create a Vision Board
- Realize there's a scientific reason that your inner world and the outer universe are completely connected
- Send your intention outward as a ripple
- Declare it with confidence
- Repeat it frequently
- Don't dismantle it with negative thoughts or emotions (examine & identify these)
- Adjust thinking patterns, start attracting "like" to yourself
- Figure out what's your To-Do list, or where something higher must help
- Do what can be done by you, then release your intention ("let go and let God"), and ask the universe to fulfill the rest of it
- Stay in the moment, feel gratitude for your creative opportunity, choose joy and peace
- Act and feel as though it's already coming
- Affirm that it is
- Enjoy abundance & realization of desires!

Applying The Rules Of The Soul's Wisdom Game

You're not a set of individual needs all disconnected from each other. You're a whole person with an inner goal striving to express something in life. You have a set of skills and abilities. Certain obstacles will present themselves. As a whole person, you can't separate your business and your personal life. You need to recognize that obstacles in one area will block you in another area. You need to recognize that your outer obstacles are not separate from your inner self.

> **GATE/WORLDVIEW: 2**
>
> **RESULT: Joy.** Boy, does this feel good!
>
> **GETTING FROM HERE TO THERE:** You were just the actor or game-player but now you are the creative do-er, the creator. You've embarked on the journey of manifesting your intentions. The little actor is becoming the Designer. Soon you'll become the manifested experience itself. Fear will be removed; possibility will be all that remains. Then, your separate identity will begin to dissolve at the same time that your higher powers increase.

Learning to apply the rules of the soul's wisdom game is primarily learning to identify what is getting you off-center or what is blocking you.

To be successful in your soul's wisdom game, you realize that what is engaging your emotional self in negativity can be overcome by a process of seeing these issues, bringing them up, and learning to break up the blockage. The brain will open as it pays attention to positive results. The heart will respond to the shift toward joy as creative potential is released and the path is smoothed out. You become whole as you practice doing the hard work of conscious creation. You eventually become unconsciously competent at doing this.

All power becomes available. Everything flows easily. The universe supports the person doing the conscious creating. The person feels complete, healthy and joyful. Other people are seen as aspects of self, and embraced by the opened heart. The opened heart starts loving all others as itself. There is nothing but unity. It's humanity, elevated to its perfection. It's a great place to be!

~~~

Now you are inside the soul's wisdom game, playing it consciously, switching back and forth between actor and designer. As long as you hold mastery over your emotional drama, and apply the device of shifting thoughts at will into positive directions (reframing), you embody a new type of human living in a changed type of reality. From this fresh perspective it becomes obvious that it's easy to design new and better possibilities from a limitless well of potential; at this new paradigm you not only see yourself as willingly participating in an ingenious game, but as the co-creator of the general design, and as the moment-by-moment author of its particulars.

As this back and forth process continues, like a camera zooming in and out, or a novelist changing voice, your point of view keeps switching from participant to designer. Soon, realms merge – the gameboard and the hologram become one... and suddenly you are standing outside of both, no longer thoroughly in one or another. You are in a field of no limitation – a boundless energy realm, an ocean of limitless light.

Upon this natural and comfortable realization, you instantaneously overcome the illusion of duality – interior versus exterior, or self versus other – as a new Worldview makes itself apparent. The Third Worldview can be called The World. Its Key is comprised of the metal *SILVER* which, like that of the Moon, has the quality of reflected light. By understanding your relationship with so-called "exterior" events, you see the entire dance of life, from planets to starbodies, and from insects to humans, as the creation of mind...*your* mind.

This is the restless, never-ending outlet for energy in its innate quest to explore avenues of potential and discover all there is to be learned about the drama – a drama that's named Wisdom's Game. The metal of silver is appropriate because you are seeing everything else beyond your personal framework as a reflection of yourself, and as none other. You have swallowed up the world, so to speak; at the same time, the world has gulped down you!

Growing Awareness

My husband, Carl, and I were watching an action-adventure movie in the local multiplex, with the usual high-volume soundtrack and all kinds of destructive violence on the screen. Midway through, my perspective automatically shifted. I found myself watching not just the movie being projected onto the movie screen in front of us, but the entire theater. All of it—its walls, stadium seats, exits, all the people sitting there—began to recede in linear perspective in front of my eyes and gave me the distinct feeling of being inside a hologram, inside a holographic illusion made up of projected thought.

The movie continued toward its finale, and I kept shifting back and forth from being in the natural world to being inside the hologram. But the holographic point of view was so strong that as we got up from our seats, walked out through the lobby, crossed the parking lot and got into our car, then headed home driving down darkened country roads, everything remained a hologram. In fact, the headlight beams reinforced the impression as they projected forward along the road.

I don't remember the precise moment when it ended; I think that the hologram just dissipated, and the strong sense of its illusory nature changed, and I was back into normal everyday life. But what I retained forever after was the sturdy sense that how I saw myself in the real world could be changed and shifted instantaneously to the perspective of consciousness participating in a holographic experience (like the *Star Trek* crew entering the Holodeck to participate in a story that was indistinguishable from the real). And I saw, from then on, the world as illusion—very detailed, a very good illusion, but a projection nonetheless—just like the breakthrough in Worldview Two when the barriers between the dream of reality and the true nature of existence begin to dissolve.

THE THIRD WORLDVIEW

YOUR TRUE RELATIONSHIP WITH THE WORLD

GATE/ WORLDVIEW	APPEARANCE	LANDSCAPE/ REALM	KEY	ABILITY	METAL	TOOL	RESULT
AT THE ENTRANCE	Everyday Life	Fog	Karmic Predicament	To live	Lead	Passion	Suffering
1	Curtain	The Wisdom Game	Choice (The Quantum Shift)	To switch out of negativity	Iron	Emotional Mastery, Control of Thought	Wisdom
2	Door	The Law of Attraction	Power (The Art of Manifestation)	To co-create what you desire	Copper	Conscious Co-creation	Joy
3	Bridge	Continuum	Vision (Capping the Point of Awareness)	To realize who you are and overcome the fear of death	Silver	Intuition & ESP	Light
4	Portal	Mind of God	Service (Merit)	To know truth and be the Way	Gold	No-Ego, Surrender	Bliss

What are the components of piercing the Veil, and how does that transform your identity and purpose? Many fresh and amazing concepts become evident upon transitioning into the Third Worldview as the distinction between the world and oneself blurs, the connection with your higher self increases, and profound insights abound. Age-old questions arise and are answered: what is soul? What is spirit? Who is the observer or witness? What are angels, spirit guides, and teachers (known as The Counsel of Elders)? Who in fact are the Brotherhood? You start to see your identity as sliding back and forth along a continuous bridge ("the continuum") between the everyday egoic self and the advanced mystical consciousness, temporarily and continuously relocating itself at various points (i.e., "capping the point of awareness"). The intuition is activated as never before in order to probe the mysteries of oneness, duality, and multiplicity, and to flow through the incorporeal realm called The M Field (a.k.a. The Akasha, The Implicate Order, The Frequency Domain, Ain Soph) via out-of-body experiences or through hidden knowledge (the occult) in the passage known as piercing the veil; paranormal awareness becomes the norm as past lives, soul ages, soul ties, soul agreements, soul missions, and your larger purpose are made obvious through life reviews, while a large-scale design (the cosmic plan) is simultaneously revealed that fits with ancient prophecies, scientific discoveries, astrological patterns, and even the metaphysical symbolism incorporated into the Great Seal of the United States that calls forth "a new order of the ages".* You realize you are becoming a foretold New Human for which inner guidance is the norm, the validity of the supernatural is comfortable, the traits of sensitivity and receptivity are increasingly evident ("yin rising"), the resistance of orthodox science is outmoded, and the heart is opening itself to all souls who, after all, reflect the oneness of life; inspiration and wisdom begin to alter your values and goals, and give new meaning to worldly events; and you are ready to flow with the wisdom of psychic tools (oracles), and to grasp

---

*   See Appendix B.

and align yourself with cosmic laws. **The big secrets at this worldview are that the awareness known as You is participating in a continuous spectrum (continuum, rainbow bridge, Jacob's ladder) within a holographic illusion of three-dimensionality; and so therefore, within a hierarchy of expanded awareness in an oceanic oneness of waves of energy, you are also your spiritual guides and even God.**

Now you are flowing, surging... both I and Thou, moving from Here to There, back and forth. When Here, you are in pure personal creativity, happily manifesting; when There, you see a moment-to-moment temporary identity that is simultaneously self, other, and world. This is a place of great illumination. It is a vast field stretching to infinity. There is realization that you can be You-Here, or You-in-the-Past, or –in-the-Future. Death isn't an ending, merely a passageway. That other person? An aspect of You! The world? Still an aspect of You!

> GATE/WORLDVIEW: 3
>
> APPEARANCE: Bridge. A passageway that knits a divide, or overcomes an abyss.
>
> LANDSCAPE / REALM: Continuum. A limitless path whose way-stations are infinite, temporary, and continual.

Now something amazing happens as you come to the gateway to the next Worldview. Your heart opens wide, and love fills you to capacity. That's because across the immeasurable and illuminated new landscape, all you see is a reflection of yourself, designing the game and entangled in it. It's all you, and you want to help your beloved self.

But wait! In this revealed infinitude, it's also seen that you are the reflection of God as well. And now God (the universe) wants to help you, its beloved. In the reflected view, you realize yourself as the world, and realize how to gain the universe's assistance. You realize how to create miracles!

A BRIDGE to infinity stands open before you. Carrying the SILVER KEY OF TREASURED MIRRORING, you are about to be given your miraculous powers and discover all that is and ever was. You are about to recognize your role in the entire planetary drama.

GATE/WORLDVIEW: 3

KEY: Vision (Capping the Point of Awareness). The ability to *see* (be a seer). An epiphany that shows the true nature of consciousness, and gives a remarkable answer to the mystery of our spiritual guides.

ABILITY: To realize who you are and overcome the fear of death.

METAL: Silver. A beautiful, malleable material of intrinsic worth that can capture an image and reflect it back to you.

KEYS OF CONSCIOUSNESS FOR THE THIRD WORLDVIEW

Heretofore, most popularized teachings about the Second Worldview, known by names such as The Law of Attraction or "The Secret", have been narrowed to a destination that is self-centered since they speak primarily about learning to manifest one's own desires, to focus on self-realization, and to reach creative potential. That's all well and good, and a necessary earlier step, but it's quite self-directed. Whereas, the truth is that total realization of The Second Worldview – that is to say, the complete mastery of the physical world's emotions and the Wisdom Game – automatically brings you to The Third Worldview.

The Third Worldview is ushered in when you understand and know your very being – the self's very essence – as the same as all other selves...the same as the world. And of course, then The Third Worldview becomes all about the opening of your heart center.

> **GATE/WORLDVIEW: 3**
>
> **TOOL: Intuition and ESP.** The connection to your divine self. Guidance from higher sources. Inner knowing. A foolproof way of negotiating experience.

Once you understand yourself as not separate from all others, and see a reflection of yourself mirrored in every other person, the development of the particular type of wisdom called compassion begins. This is the highest level of wisdom.

"If there must be compassion for the 'sins' of others," say the Guides, *"it must also be weighed by their inner ability to separate right action from foolish (i.e., harmful or worse) action. In other words, by their level of awareness as they wend their way through the thicket of lifetimes and its various lessons in earth-school. Wisdom would seek to reject [choices made unwisely] as wrong, or wasteful, or ultimately foolish*

(and even worse, if it creates karmic ribbons such as through mortal harm to another), whereas compassion would see in such behavior the entire human predicament that lays hidden in the game of life."

Furthermore, this understanding of oneness or complete entanglement (complete merging of self and other selves) goes hand in glove with the recognition of, and facility within, the M Field. It stands to reason that by lifting your awareness up and beyond the boundaries of the personal self, you instantly and automatically find yourself swimming, as it were, in the field of consciousness, in a realm beyond the body, beyond the personality, and beyond the individual brain but in an expanded awareness in which it's easy to maneuver from individual (personal) consciousness into other individual consciousnesses; in other words, psychic or paranormal development. Within this new realm, you also automatically gain entry into the impersonal or ultra-consciousness... what metaphysics has always called super-consciousness, and what Jung called the collective unconscious.

Once you get comfortable swimming in the field of expanded awareness, delving into nooks and crannies, feeling liberated from the boundaries of the Personal Energy Pattern, you begin to understand that this is the resource from which to tap into truly unlimited creativity.

This domain is known by many names. It has been called by some mathematicians the Implicate Order, for it is an energy domain full of potentiality not yet realized, or manifested into physical expression. In Kabala it is also called *Ain Soph*, which means both limitless light – the same as a frequency domain – or no-thing, which means pretty much the same thing: the realm of potentiality before it is made manifest. In Hinduism, it is called Brahman, the Divine Ground where all partial realities have their existence. In Perennial Philosophy, it is called the Akasha—and also the Akashic Records, to define the eternal residue of energy that cannot be destroyed. It can only transmute, reform itself, bounce against itself, or take on different principles or expressions. And since energy can never be destroyed, it stands to reason that it must leave a trail, it must leave a footprint, or some sort of eternal pattern (matrix, record) of its perambulations. If energy can only spin and move and transform and journey, but never be destroyed and never disappear, then every single wave and particle of its expression must be retained or stored in some fashion. And if so, then there is some way of "reading" that record. And, if in that M Field we have surpassed the realm of time/space (i.e., of form), then that Great Record will contain energy patterns of "the future" as well as of "the past". Out in the M Field, everything that has been, or will be, is already imprinted!

Client R was concerned about her studies and asked with anxiety if she would fail. We examined her Personal Energy Pattern (her horoscope). It showed a terrific combination of aspects at a certain date in the future, a combination that was conducive to writing, studies and communication. I asked her, "What is the significance of such-and-such period of time?" She answered: "That's when the course will end and the test will be given". The answer was then obvious: she would pass her course of studies with flying colors. Her successful conclusion of exams was already patterned in the M Field and simply had to be lived out! The "future" was already spelled out. When she ultimately caught up with this date and this pattern, it "came to pass" and so she passed her exam.

This goes to the issue of free will. Does free will exist or are we simply going through the motions? The answer is yes to both. If there weren't free will, there would be no point in the soul reincarnating, making choices and learning lessons primarily from the consequences of those often painful choices, lessons that lead to wisdom. On the other hand, outside of three-dimensional reality, time and space do not exist. All energy patterns that ever were or ever will be are already contained in the ocean of oneness as though the system is both fluid and static at the same time, depending on the perspective. From God's perspective, it's all one; it's eternity. From our perspective, there is past, present and future; only the present being real or interactive, and wise choices are the whole point of the soul's wisdom game.

> *"When the understanding is great enough, one sees all events as inevitable."* – Builders of the Adytum

Thus, once we are freed to circumambulate around the M Field, we can, through ability and practice, learn to retrieve stored information, we can access past lives, and we can tap into long-ago personalities or information of those who once lived but no longer do. That which is called paranormal is in fact perfectly normal, but beyond the limitations of most personal physical experience. The expanded mind, however, is not limited and can, through thought, enter this realm, the M Field. That's what Edgar Cayce, "the sleeping prophet", was all about.

As awakening humans, our faith that has heretofore proclaimed that we are all one is being supported by science that says there is nothing out there but entangled energies, and that even in the observation of this dance of nothing-ness, our consciousness affects the outcome and indeed creates the observed reality.

We must look at reality in a new light and from a different angle. You and I are two aspects of a single no-thing. Put a different way, we are two poles of a single dance of energy, which is constantly fluctuating, changing, creatively renewing and at the same time, not even really happening.

What goes on in the "I am" consciousness is reflected, then, as an aspect of the other, or the "you are." It's always just the surface of a mirror.

Our new understanding will take time to accommodate; it will take a broadening of perspective. We will learn to see the other as not so different or so separate, but as ourselves…or even better, as the "I am." Similarly, we won't see the natural world as separate or different from the inner self. And finally, probably most difficult of all, but most powerful, we won't see the small self as differentiated from the divine within us. The theory of entanglement promises union between people, between humanity and nature, and between the self and God.

This beautiful, fascinating, complex and deeply rewarding journey into the M Field becomes immediately available for anyone who rises above The Second Worldview.

Piercing the Veil

The scientific approach can never reach the ultimate mystical truth of the secrets of consciousness… because the logical brain-mind has to be surpassed to get there.

"I Am" awareness in its pure state is *beyond* 3-D form. The mind must learn to expand out/in/upwards to reach it. Mind *can* go there, beyond form, but only when form (ego-structure, 3-D identity) is allowed to give way and be transcended. Meditation is one conveyance; psychism is another. In metaphysics, it's called *piercing the Veil*.

Thus, the mystic's journey is the only path to show the logical brain the way to pure self-realization, the knowing of self as God. It can be mapped out. But disbelief must be suspended, and the supernatural (sup*r*anatural?), a.k.a. the paranormal, must not be resisted. It's the only gateway… and you'll see why as the pathway is mapped out.

The scientific mind has been very resistant to the metaphysical path, but in today's theories of quantum physics, dark matter, implicate order, and multiverses, the two poles (of reason and mysticism) are converging into one simplified concept anyhow. As soon as even one scientific brain allows itself to overcome its prejudices (self-imposed limitations, i.e., false illusion) and accept a mystical experience, the deed is done! The connection is made. Someone – whoever that will be – will stand with a "foot" in both camps, that is to say, a fully expanded mind. That someone will be a pioneer. That someone will be God analyzing itself.

Consciousness sees itself dialoguing, observing, and creating the splitting that is called *you* and *me*, or me and it (the world). And at the same time, consciousness creates the magical amnesia to protect and sustain the illusion (game) of life. As soon as *we* wake up and see this core dynamic, we see the puppeteer, the masked devices, the manipulated actors, and all the rest of the game's parts.

In "Wisdom's Game", the Brotherhood of Light Workers tells us that there are three "easy" steps to attain spiritual connection: stilling the mind, releasing skepticism while integrating the teachings, and then letting go of the illusion of the small self.

The first step is the same as meditation – a way to find the spot between any two thoughts. This immediately allows the universe to reach you as you simultaneously open the door to a greater presence. Such opening of the mind overcomes limitation and expands consciousness at the same time it allows greater *permeability*.

The next step is to willingly suspend disbelief, allow the connection to occur, listen to the spiritual (inner) guidance that ensues, and align your vibration to it. This is the process of becoming a metaphysician... in other words, of developing a mind that is ready to go *beyond*, and of a heart that is prepared to feel a presence approaching. At this stage, there is intuitive knowing and clear cognizance.

Finally, only when ready and not before, you recognize your larger identity, realize that it is the very stuff of your own inner connection, and realign your characteristics with that of your greater nature. The small self and the large self are seen as one. The individual as creator of experience and mirror of the expanded awareness grows ever more powerful.

Here is the gateway. In Tarot, it's the Star card. This process takes you to your true destination at warp speed.

Once, I had a nightmare in which I was in a cave filling with water and was about to drown. And in my distress in the dream, a voice spoke to me through the fear. It said, "Then who is doing the observing?" Of course, I woke up at that point, a little shook up, but also profoundly altered. The dream was a metaphor: no matter what the lower self is experiencing, however overwhelming, there is always the higher self present, witnessing it, but not participating.

It is here when we truly encounter the aspect of self called The Observer, or Witness.

There is a part of your soul which is engaged in the inner dialogue. Usually without awareness, you participate in dialogue or conversation with this other aspect of yourself.

For example, when you ask yourself a question deep within, or weigh a decision, there is an aspect of yourself that you turn to and from which you expect, if not an answer, then at least a judgment or an alternative. This aspect of the self is often called the higher self, but it can be named more neutrally as the observer or the witness. It is the same part of yourself that sits to the side, even during crisis or emergency, but also during everyday mundane life, and just watches. This part of you is unemotional and detached. It is that which answers the question: "While I'm going through the event, who is naming it? Who is realizing that it is happening?"

In recognizing and acknowledging your higher self, or observer or witness, you are thus immediately establishing a connection. You are building the bridge that enables you to move from typical daily life, or the lower mind, right out of it, upwards or away into a detached perspective – the perspective of the observer of the life. This is a wise thing to achieve.

As you become acquainted with the wiser, more expansive, deeper, and more ancient part of yourself – also known as your Higher Self – you immediately overcome a limitation of perception that is a function of being trapped in the 3-D illusion. The reunion of your lower and higher selves pushes you into a brand new view of reality.

The Veil is the name given to the amnesia that separates your daily consciousness from all of your past lives, all of your alternative selves, your higher consciousness, and finally, The M Field.

In learning to connect with Source, and to build a bridge to your observer or higher mind, you will automatically pierce this veil of separation. You will find yourself in another realm.

You will, as it were, look behind the curtain. You will see from that vantage point how your life is constructed. You will see the game that your soul is playing in entering your life and accepting its illusion. You will see multiple times that you have done this, and you will feel as though a veil or fog has been removed from your vision.

Piercing the Veil is another way of saying that, as a soul, you have lifted your head and awakened. There is a story about the Buddha, looking out over *the Buddha-fields* and watching to see who lifts his or her head. When a soul lifts his or her head and starts to look around and truly see, the Buddha smiles. It is another way of describing the moment when the consciousness, known as your soul, wakes up and sees itself as eternal spirit. It is a moment of great clarity, and once achieved, cannot be forgotten. It is a threshold, and forever more, you will not be able to remain fully clouded in life's illusion, but you will be straddling two realms.

It is the definition of metaphysics, for you will have gone beyond (*meta*) the illusion of the physical world.

The Veil is shown in the Tarot as behind the High Priestess. It is not the conscious mind that will take you through this passage, but the subconscious which will be able to do this work, for that is what she symbolizes. When the conscious mind understands this purpose and allows this process to continue, then the subconscious mind can do the work and bring you to the gateway faster.

Once through, and reconnected, the "small, still voice within" becomes more pronounced. It is your intuition. Intuition... it means the same as *the inner teacher.*

Within each person is a guidance system, a navigation system that speaks telepathically to you at certain times. Often, when least expected, this inner aspect of you gives information from a higher knowing. And since it is not as clear or as loud as emotions or as the logic, it is often ignored.

It is called the teacher because it has the capacity to give insight or awareness of what is not consciously known. People experience intuition sometimes as a gut feeling, or "a vibe". The logical mind does not necessarily know why a person or situation is setting off this feeling, and only learns or finds out about its wisdom later on, after the fact.

Another name for intuition is the hunch. Often, people with leadership abilities will act on their "hunches" (gut feeling), even after they have exhausted a logical analysis of the situation. Because the intuition presents us with information beyond our experience and not tied to reasoning, it is proof that an inner connection reaches to a higher Worldview, and that there is a Worldview that can provide flashes of insight or clear knowing that would otherwise be unavailable or inexplicable. The intuition is therefore being presented at The Third Worldview because it is a human faculty that starts being consciously developed somewhere in our human experience as though there is a radio station to which one can be better and better attuned. And when accurately focused, can provide a continual bridge between the lower reasoning centers and the M Field, or expanded energy realm.

The intuition is not the same as superstition; it is not the same as instinct. It is full knowing, instantaneously, or a direct link to truth.

Once, many years ago I was invited to share in an event in which a female guru was presiding over a large gathering in an old and large church in Manhattan, the Cathedral of Saint John the Divine. At one point, the guru suggested that someone in the audience wanted to sing a Hebrew song! Startled by this request, the audience stayed mute. The guru was insistent; yes, someone here wants to sing a Hebrew song! The guru was firmly rooted in her intuition and wouldn't give up. Finally, a lovely voice arose – it was very tentative, but it continued. As the singer sang, her creative inspiration came clearer and her voice strengthened. A little-known song lilted through the cavernous church, and began soaring with every new instant. A chill went through us all, and we surrendered to the melody, allowing it to lift us upward. Our energies met at the cathedral's peak, and we were all hushed and exhilarated. The guru's intuition, joined with the singer's creative potential, was merged to the benefit of all. It was an unforgettable moment of oneness.

Past Lives

One of the most immediate things to be found when one pierces the Veil is the encounter with one's own previous lives.

This is so because it is seen that life is a soul's wisdom game entered into willingly by the consciousness deciding to partake of a pattern of existence which includes personality, heredity, karmic predicament, and other unique typical characteristics and qualities. Furthermore, it's seen that each entrance into a unique pattern is an occurrence that is repeated many times in order to gain the wisdom available from each experience.

Once this viewpoint is gained, the consciousness then separates from the current lifetime's perspective and gets what could be called a panoramic view of the existence – the particular existence as well as the multiple varieties of existences. We call such passages into the between-lives state "crossing over" or *devachan*. Devachan has been described as "the state of consciousness which the Ego eventually reaches after the death of the physical body and when the desires of the personality have been discarded. It is often referred to by Theosophists as the second death."*

We also call it *life after life.*

Once you have made your way through the Great Divide, and found yourself in a new realm peeking "behind the curtain", so to speak, looking at where you just came from, you understand that you have moved into a place (really not a location of time and space, but a new perception or awareness) from which you can see that you have stepped through this veil many times and entered into a variety of experiences, called lives.

As in Kurt Vonnegut's book, *Slaughterhouse 5*, where the protagonist becomes unstuck from time and space, we begin to see that each life is its own bubble or sphere in the time-space continuum, but the eternal

---

*   www.tscardifflodge.12freeukisp.co.uk

consciousness takes many journeys in and out of different bubbles or spheres, in other words, many lives. Books have been written to explain this, such as *Many Mansions* by Gina Cerminara, or *Journey of Souls* by Michael Newton.

From this new vantage point, you can see that it's neither weird, nor specifically religious, nor even "paranormal" to accept the fact of past lives or reincarnation. Reincarnation is simply a way of explaining how the self steps in and out of various bubbles in the time-space continuum. Reincarnation is a necessary part of the wisdom journey. It is by having physical lives full of challenge, growth and learning, that wisdom is accumulated. Without doing so, there would be no way to participate in contrast and follow the threads of past actions. Karma and reincarnation are inextricably linked. Karma propels you into further experiences that reflect the consequences of previous choices in other lifetimes.

It's essential that the unencumbered consciousness willingly chooses to engage in new lifetimes over and over. The name of this process is called The Wheel or cycle of existence, and has also been named "the only dance there is."

A client, L, revealed an astounding karmic journey through early abuse, poverty, rejection, chaos, and non-existent self-esteem. A turning point had already been reached; the turning point away from drugs and alcohol and towards spirituality. The soul task would be all on the interior from now on, studying, growing, awakening, putting the parameters of her soul's wisdom game into realization. The astonishing thing about her path was to be the amazing amount of growth from where in life she began to where in life she was reaching: summits of wisdom, clarity of soul purpose, inner peace, recognition of drama, and stability and strength to return to all the earliest memories and re-examine them with an open heart, a clear mind, and courage, putting everything into a new perspective, seeing the resolution of much negative karma in the service of huge personal growth. The victory is immense and continues to increase to this day.

WHEEL of FORTUNE.

Let's revisit the channeled message first discussed in the Second Worldview when discussing Reframing the Karmic Predicament. The message was quite brief but spoke of a profound concept, namely, the Life Review.

Once when I was on a radio show, talking about Wisdom's Game and The Brotherhood of Light Workers, an odd thing happened: the interviewer (rather than myself) received a channeled message from the spirit guides while on the mike. *"The birth is at the end"*, she blurted out... meaning the awakening (overview or wisdom gained from each life experience) is usually revealed upon death. Death is then seen as the passage of the consciousness from inside the time-space bubble of existence to that of being outside of it; in other words, into the M Field.

Not everyone who has an out-of-body or near-death experience will immediately see previous lives, for that takes some gain of perception. But it is a given that upon piercing the Veil, past lives become available and are no longer seen as hokum, because the vantage point of awareness has profoundly shifted.

The phrase "the birth is at the end" is then understood as a profound shift in perspective, a paradigm shift in which you grasp the meaning of the experience of that particular life, of that particular soul's wisdom game or movie script, a meaning which cannot be seen while one is on the stage. It is as though the actor – you – needs to develop some distance, achieved through crossing over, in order to begin to perceive the lessons learned from that occurrence, the new values to be applied from then on, and the significance of various relationships during that life.

For the rare soul, awakening and wise perception can take place before the end; that is to say, while one is still alive. In fact, the new human being that is developing on Planet Earth is just such a person, just such a creature who will be able to see past the illusion of time-space, perceive the other side of the Veil while still physical, and enjoy the expansion of mind that is occurring as the human species evolves. This new human will wake up sooner, will learn wisdom faster, will apply insights previously available mostly after death, and utilize these insights consciously and deliberately to create more beauty, joy, and personal empowerment in the daily life.

So, an eon's-old paradigm is shifting, and now the birth can be before the end.

It stands to reason that, from a greater perspective, while considering available lifetimes and deciding how to put together your next life's parameters, you'd decide to hook up in the new go-round with others who are in similar between-lives design mode. You'd co-create the patterns with them.

In constructing the framework of the next life, karmic threads previously set in motion will be taken into consideration. Relationships that are "unfinished" must be addressed. Goals to be met must be arranged. Tasks to be undertaken in the hopes of completion must be assigned. The conscious self must put it all together and call upon other aspects of itself – in other words, related fragments of spiritual energy – to participate in that life.

And so, there will be fated relationships. Some relationships will be casual, fleeting, and insignificant except for the variety of experiences, while other relationships will be profound, deeply impactful, and sometimes enduring. The nature of relationships will go by various names. Some will be soul ties...that is, those with whom agreements have been entered to come together for periods within time to fulfill needs, meet tasks, and further goals. In some cases, these soul ties will occur just so that you can move from point A to point B, and then the job is done. A friend, J, living in New York City, met and fell in love with someone living in California. It was mutually decided that J would relocate to Los Angeles in order to live together. She did so. However, the relationship quickly fell apart after the move. It served its purpose though as the catalyst for J's relocation.

In other cases, the soul tie may occur even though people are physically separated, perhaps in different parts of the globe – for example, two politicians in different countries accomplishing entwined leadership goals for their respective nations. A client, D, formed a close business and personal relationship with an individual originally from a far-distant birthplace. Their collaboration – a transcendence of age gap and geographic complexity – demonstrates the hidden purpose of soul ties.

There are other types of soul ties in which the heart's center is to be deeply affected. These types of ties can be called "soul mates" where the bond is deep and true and the relationship itself is most or very important as the life experience.

Not every life will include a soul mate, but most lives will include soul ties. Agreements made between lives can be honored or not (because free will is operative within the life), but karmic relationships must always be honored and cannot be skirted because, once set in motion, the balance of the universe must be maintained via the completion of the ripples.

Karma often includes deep lessons; at its heart is the attainment of compassion as the end goal. By experiencing the receiving end of what one had previously sent forth in an earlier passage, the two sides of a single karmic relationship are exchanged and rebalanced, and the universe maintains its perfection.

Entering The M Field

To be in The M Field is to grasp immediately what is being described in Kabala by the phrase "limitless light."

In The M Field, there are just no boundaries. Form or solidity (resistance, material substance) simply doesn't exist. The M Field is beyond the notion of life, beyond three-dimensionality. The soul is comfortable in The M Field, as it is during dreaming. The soul can also experience The M Field in bliss and in meditation, in complete unity with nature, and in the phenomenon of the paranormal.

To move beyond the physical body, or escape limitation, is possible during life by the process of reconnecting with pure conscious awareness and "locating" one's self in spaciousness, in peacefulness, in the place of no resistance, the place of no thoughts, and in the place of no ego-identity. Entering here, you begin to realize the vastness of your being and the fullness of your potential.

In this frequency domain, there is nothing but expansive creativity: every conceivable pathway to explore, every possible combination to attempt. Nothing to limit or stop this process. The realization of the utter truth of full creative potential is at the basis of Kabala's phrase for The M Field, "a fountain of limitless light." It's been called an ocean of oneness in the sense that all consciousness reunites, finds itself beyond duality, beyond separation, beyond *you* and *I*, beyond small identifiers, seeing the esoteric truth that there is really nothing else than the one consciousness, or the *I Am* realization.

And so, the individual self immediately flows between previous versions of itself — itself in the guise of other people, in the identities of those who have passed on, and even in the identity of those who have not yet but will take birth in the "future". There is no time or space, no limitation at all in The M Field. This is the realm from whence gurus can *bi-locate* (be seen as solid in two or more physical places simultaneously), and from whence Jesus created his miracles.

In the soup of The M Field, all is known, all is possible, nothing is prevented, all is blissful, all is love, and there is only one, one of us and nothing else, no worlds, no people, no things, simply energy. Heaven! This is exactly what John Lennon is describing in his lyrics for the much-loved song "Imagine".

In the M Field, in the moment, in the Now, all sensory input coming through your ears, eyes, nose, etc, and all sense of time and space or separate identity blend into one interior awareness. It would be great – blissful! – to be able to remain in such a state always, as some advanced sages can, but barring that state, there are ways to get there purposefully.

I like to use moments such as airplane landings to shift into "Presence". It's a valuable instance for focused and expanded awareness. Here's what I do:

As the plane readies for its landing, I meditate until all thoughts halt. In other words, the story of what's happening subsides. No longer am I telling myself about how I feel or what I think; all of that ceases. Instead, all cabin noises – including other passengers' conversations or physical clatter – become part of the moment. The moment is one long suspended "event"... or even better, one long Now. There's no longer any Me there. There's only the breath. Inhalation and exhalation. *Prana*. Prana – a Hindu word for life-force – is the marker of existence. When consciousness wants to live, it begins breathing; when it wants to exit life back into non-being, breathing stops.

But the Witness – the "Self" – remains ever-present. That from which Siddhartha* sought to escape can never be removed, for it is the eternal observer and creator of all experience. The higher self becomes present in the Now. It's always there, but moves to the forefront of awareness when the lower self – Me – and all its drama gets out of the way. And since the higher self is the same as the expanded consciousness, from this new perspective a permeation of others' minds becomes easy and

---

*   Siddhartha, by Hermann Hesse, 1922

natural. All others aboard the descending airplane become myself, each with personal storylines, hopes and fears. The heart follows the mind's expansion instantaneously; all are embraced in love, no matter their personalities. In the Now, all are Me. The plane's descent and landing is actually the momentary illusion... and despite the moment's power, nothing's actually occurring!

Yet something does occur. It is this: in the expanded state, perception can shift from personal to elsewise. The "Me" can become the "Other Person". I'm suddenly in another's eyes and brain and even heart. I can see the experience, not from my own (the passenger's) point of view but from the pilot's. He lives for the challenge of setting the aircraft down just right. Each new opportunity is a chance to top his personal best. So what might frighten Small Me thrills him. In this second, I'm reborn! I'm "here" but I'm also experiencing life as someone else. I am all types. *Tat Twam Asi.* "I am that, too."

Being in the Now is to attain peace... but also to *become* the M Field! It is the point of no-limitations. That's our reachable goal in this era.

As previously said, the M Field is another way of regarding the "ocean of energy" known as The Akasha.

The Akasha is the holographic imprint into the fiber of being, into the ocean of oneness, the trail or track of every electron, every particle, every quantum, in all its multiplicity of expansion. The Akashic Records hold all that ever was, and can be accessed through the paranormal (metaphysical) experience of entering The M Field. In a closed system (i.e., the universe), the Akashic Records, also called the Matrix, is what remains eternally from the universe's attempts to continually expand and discover.

The Akasha is very similar to the title "The M Field," the only difference being that the Akasha refers to the recording or capturing of all that ever was created, attempted, experienced, and even all that was ever thought. The Akashic Records is the storehouse of all previous energy patterns. And of all "future" ones too!

Here's an example: It was not easy to write this book. It was difficult to organize into a whole the many concepts, years of studies, history with clients, and received teachings. It was daunting and especially in the early stages, when it was most disorganized, I felt despair. But I took a look at my Personal Energy Pattern and could see completion. Psychic colleagues in my field whom I consulted could also see a published work. It was as though I was given confirmation that the task would be completed even as I was experiencing the most difficult portions of the work. It existed already in the Matrix, and therefore, somehow or another, I knew I would get it done. I would travel *from here to there*. And here it is!

> "The holographic theory suggests that...our own past instead of fading into oblivion...remains recorded in the cosmic hologram and can always be accessed once again....In addition to images and sounds, emotions being felt during an event are also recorded." — Michael Talbot, *The Holographic Universe*

A mediumistic personality such as Edgar Cayce can swim easily through this record of all being and pinpoint your "past" lives, or your "future" patterns. The mediumistic personality is merely the type of individual who is so constructed as to be able to permeate the Akashic Records and then bridge them to their 3-D selves.

There is a surprise to be found when swimming through the ocean of oneness, and that is that there is intelligent design underlying it. Not just Nature has designed all creatures and all things, but a Great Consciousness, whatever you prefer to call it. There is a predisposition to test out potential, to force awareness upon otherwise unconscious natural outcomes, and to move toward the reconnection of matter with its spiritual source.

What can be called a Greater Plan is afoot, and is eternally so.

When a quality is desiring to be expressed in the universe, a template is formed for such. Jung called this an "archetype". It can be described as a role that is calling out for fulfillment or embodiment.

All such information is stored eternally in the matrix of energy called the Akashic Records or Collective (Cosmic) Consciousness. When new, unique conditions require heretofore unrealized embodiments, the matrix reforms itself to express a certain type of individual. These invisible organizing patterns act like energy blueprints.

For instance, with Yin (or female power) now on the rise, it became inevitable that there would be females who expressed not only the bright aspects of feminine power, such as holding government office or corporate power, but the shadowed aspects of feminine power, such as emboldened strippers or prostitutes who, rather than being helpless and abused, have utilized (in fact, gloried in) the role of embodied female empowerment through the lower nature (vulgarly, "pussy power"). A spectrum in which every expression of female power will come to the forefront, from the most base to the most elevated, will thus be manifested. And someone will be born here and there whose soul purpose is none other than to fulfill that invisible template so that the universe can discover everything that there is to know about that role and that life experience, simply by calling it forth.

Similarly, invisible templates exist that offer minorities a more empowered role in society than heretofore. From sports to show business to the highest posts of office, an individual will be born who will step to the plate, and who is almost mandated to do so in order to represent an archetype being fulfilled. In that regard, empowered male and female minority figures, such as President Barack Obama, Governor Bobby Jindal, celebrities P. Diddy, Denzel Washington, Will Smith, and Oprah Winfrey, and a host of others step forth (are born) to play the part. (President Obama has said that he had always felt destined for his groundbreaking role.)

It is as Paul Simon says in his song, "Every generation throws a hero up the pop chart."

For instance, in my opinion a template exists right now that calls for a sexy and dynamic female within radical Islam's halls of power! That life may be a short one, but it would be influential beyond measure. Has someone already chosen a birth into it*?!

If the Akasha, with all its hidden potential, is now accessible, let's consider the methods of entering a field of oneness with deliberate intent.

There are several ways to get into the M Field. One of these ways is the Out-Of-Body. The Out-Of-Body Experience (OOBE), sometimes also called a Near-Death Experience (NDE) – not necessarily the same thing – is an entrance into expanded consciousness. The experience is that of transcending life… *knowing* – not thinking or believing or imagining – but knowing that you have gone beyond the illusion of time and space and beyond the daily story of mundane details, and have awakened to a place of being that is not inside the physical body, but beyond it.

Now, this can happen during crisis, such as surgery, or drowning, or other extremis, in which the awareness finds itself outside of, and looking down upon, or looking from a distance at, the physical self, observing everything, witnessing the body's ordeal, but not from an interior place. Scientists try to explain the near-death experience as the moment when the brain dies or the breath has stopped or the heartbeat flattens*, but have rarely tackled the conundrum from the viewpoint that the expanded awareness simply returns to its non-physical, non-local basis. This is in fact what happens. During an OOBE, there is a reconnection with light or spiritual awareness. There is a disconnection

---

* Yes! *"2 Nice for Tunis: Topless woman's protest spurs calls for death"* – New York Post, 3/26/13

* Some research has been undertaken to weigh the average person post-mortem or during OOBEs. *The Source Field Investigations*, Wilcock (Plume)

from the illusion of separation and physicality – a stepping outside, as it were, of the virtual reality hologram.

Interestingly, whereas some need crisis to offer the catalyst to propel oneself outside the body in this way, other people get to the M Field through a different route. In my case, before my metaphysical journey began, I had a moment of pure detachment from the interior physical experience wherein regular awareness was replaced with a sudden new perspective in which I was apart from and looking at my body in my vanity mirror (at that moment, just an empty shell), while I remained conscious of an alter-aspect of myself that was separate, intangible, and far more knowing. At that split second, my real self was standing invisibly to the left and behind the empty physical body. A shocking moment!

In fact, it was this greater self that presented the opportunity for such an alternative reality to occur… thankfully *without* the emphasis of crisis. From then on, for me it was a question of gaining understanding of what had happened, and of comprehending a far different reality than I had cared to explore or been led to believe was all that could be.

Entrance into the M Field and out of the body can also occur through bliss. The individual who raises his or her vibration to the point of total expansion and transcendent joy comes to a place where only beauty, truth, and love exist. Where separation, fear, confusion and illusion no longer do. This occurrence can happen through prolonged and deep meditation, through mind training, through sexual union, through great compassion and love, or through immersion into a passionate pursuit. Or simply, through grace. Once known, it can never be forgotten. Books have been written about this state, such as Eckhardt Tolle's "Power of Now."

Many true gurus exist in this advanced state continuously, a state that is called *Samadhi*.

> *"Presence: consciousness without thought."* – Eckhart Tolle, *A New Earth*

Entrance into the M Field ushers in a new perspective. The world can no longer be seen in the usual fashion. One can no longer just trudge through life, but becomes able to appreciate its every nuance, its every flavor. There is an old woodcutting in which a pilgrim, on his knees, peeks through the curtain of heaven and sees beyond the sun and trees, beyond nature, and even beyond the celestial field, into a new reality. It is as though this kneeling pilgrim has pulled aside a curtain and discovered truth. This famous woodcutting is symbolic of the self – the pilgrim or journeyer – discovering the expanded mind, or the M Field.

Last, but certainly not least, the way into the M Field is through death. The death is simply a return home, a reunion with one's source. As the spirit guide, Emanuel, channeled through Pat Rodegast, says (in the greatest one-liner ever), *"Death is perfectly safe."* The M Field is a place of return, a place of origin, a realm from which we continually re-emerge into physicality. The Out-Of-Body Experience is but one door into it. And death is another.

A strange thing happens once you've moved beyond 3-D reality and found your identity sliding along a continuum, and your current self encountering your past selves – you begin to redefine your essence and that of all life and the world. And you meet and greet your teachers! These are your Spiritual Teachers, and sometimes your Council of Elders.

We have already discussed that, from a quantum perspective, there is really no differentiation between the lower and the higher realms but that they co-exist at all times, and are interwoven in the same way that invisible radio waves permeate our physical world constantly, merely waiting for the appropriate device or antenna to receive them and make them apparent. In the same fashion, our spiritual guides are getting more involved with the process of the hastened accumulation of wisdom among the sentient creatures of the physical plane.

These spirit guides are actually ourselves, of course - the discarnated, non-physical aspects of ourselves who have already accumulated a very large measure of wisdom regarding life on earth. These elder statesmen, so to speak, form a union dedicated to service! Their job is to advance the human race.

In truth, spirit does not work physically, but serves the greater purpose of the universe: to throw forth material, see that it develops life-forms, and shepherd these life-forms into awareness. Once self-aware life-forms exist in the physical, then spirit's plan, in service of universal self discovery, is to advance self-awareness towards its own perfection. So, those known as spirit guides, angels, the Council of Elders, or your wise ancestors, are tasked with helping humanity reach forward and progress.

In order that the new human society be ushered in and guided toward its larger purpose, wisdom must be invoked.

Not only must people strive while in physical form to accumulate greater and more useful wisdom as they live out their lives (aspiration), but in order to hasten this process and to develop stronger spiritual muscle in us the higher realm must become very much more engaged in the process (inspiration).

"Spirit" means the same as energy but with one other defining quality: it is energy that is aware, energy that is conscious. It is consciousness disembodied, without form. Pure energy that knows that it is.

One of the definitions of God is *"I am that I am."* This means that pure being, knowing itself as such, is the same as what is called "God."

Spirit has no form. It is awareness disembodied, playing, and seeking breakthrough. Spirit wants one thing: that is to express its beingness while discovering what there is to know in doing it. So spirit plays a soul's wisdom game with itself, an eternal game. Spirit squeezes itself, reduces itself, limits itself into that which is understood as matter, or three dimensionality. (Four dimensionality, if you count time.) Spirit chooses to express itself eternally in this way so that it can play the soul's wisdom game of discovery.

In darker ages, spirit guides have the main task of helping each soul create its life design and make its best choices; they appear in people's lives only rarely, in circumstances that require a messenger or a protective guardian angel. However, in today's world, with humanity standing at an abyss and with crucial options facing us regarding choice of direction towards the light or towards annihilation – in other words, in End Times – humanity is in dire need of guidance. And so, part of the larger plan – a prominent part of it – requires that such guidance be provided more than ever, and that light stream forth abundantly wherever possible.

How does that work? Well, the universe collaborates with individual fragments, known as souls, to create some people who will have the innate ability or skill-set in their very nature to be receivers of guidance. The name for such people is "channeler" or "medium". And sometimes simply, "psychic". These individuals do not necessarily have a great amount of wisdom, but do have an ability to be a link or conduit for advanced information. It is as though the entire M Field wishes to create a bridge with three-dimensional reality, and does so through specific linkages. In fact, psychics can be receptive to all manner of input coming from all levels. And so, the psychic must learn to discriminate or shield from negative input and block that in favor of more enlightened information.

There is a special quality to enlightened information. It is being received in service of humanity and not for one's personal ego gratification. This is the broadcasting (transmission) from the higher levels of spirit, or the Council of Elders, attempting to reach into the darkness in people's minds, and to bring them a more rapid development of wisdom.

The happy news is that more and more people are accepting the validity and truths of this process and are actually opening linkages within themselves to become receivers. This, too, is part of the advancement of the human species. It is called *permeability*. It is prophesized that the next *root race* of humanity, the fifth, will be more permeable to the higher realm. ESP will become the norm in the next stage of humanity.

One of the chief qualities of form is duality. Whereas spirit – disembodied, eternal and unbounded – has no form and therefore is always one, the world of matter and form necessitates twoness. Its very quality, inherent in its makeup, is to see contrast and boundaries or limitations between one thing over another. Whether it's a rock or a cloud, a creature or a person, all of these material forms are necessarily described by limiting features. And so, as soon as spirit chooses to play the soul's wisdom game of contrast, of materiality, it instantly enters the world, which is that of duality. The world is instantly created.

"The Tao begot one; One begot two; Two begot three; and three begot the ten thousand things." - Lao Tse

Once worlds have been created, and matter has come into being, then nature takes over and begins the process of evolution of form, guided always by spiritual purpose. Nature creates ever-evolving form that grows in substance, and can become sentient (aware of itself). Eons are needed to develop this quality in the material world (in nature). Once it has been developed, however, and a self-aware creature enters the planet, then the process of evolution continues until the self-awareness – the understanding that I AM – grows further and develops a more profound connection with spiritual purpose; in other words, realizes the universe's game plan from the beginning.

It is this sentience that is called soul. It is a merging of aware spirit with natural form. A synthesis, it has been represented symbolically throughout the ages. A beast with the head of a human is a common symbol of it, such as the Sphinx. Or vice versa, such as Anubis, the Egyptian jackal-headed god who protects the deceased*. Also, symbolically, a six-pointed star comprised of two overlapping

---

*   Both figures are seen on the Tarot's *Wheel* card.

triangles - in other words, the Star of David - with one triangle pointing downwards (infusing) and another pointing upwards (aspiring), merged into one, is another symbolic representation of spiritual consciousness merged into natural form. Ditto the Trinity, merging Father (Godhead), Son (Soul, Person) and Holy Spirit (Infusing Consciousness). The soul is the *"I AM"* quality within the creature who has become aware of its own being. The spirit is the admixture of aware energy into that being.

Now, and only now, do you begin to see how there is no separation, no boundary, no time, and no limited identity. The questions *Who am I?* and *Who is speaking?* are answered by the realization that there is a spectrum across which you are spread, and that your identity rests at the position you temporarily place it. *You* are smeared across a continuum of possibilities, here being the persona you know as yourself in the current life, and there being the observer/guide who has an elevated perspective. And thus, you are no longer Little You and Higher You, but are simultaneously the journey-er whose mind is traveling along the bridge, back and forth again and again, capping the point of awareness along the continuum. You see how each thought is fluidly capped at whatever end it temporarily rests (that is, at *me* or *you*, or at guide or even God), and how this process forms the illusion of separation (duality) under which you have so long labored.

When I found myself at this bridge, my definition of lower and higher selves changed forever. No longer were my wise and wonderful spiritual guides, The Brotherhood of Light Workers, different and apart from myself; but both poles were united, sliding one to the other and back again. The end caps of each identity were just convenient fabrications. These "identities" were just ephemeral way-stations. The truth was that there weren't two opposite poles but one fluid connection. Suddenly, I was my own wisdom teacher. Suddenly, I was both human and elder at the same moment... and that moment existed eternally.

Yet another revelation is born at this stage: a larger purpose is stirring.

It becomes clear that the universe has an overall game plan, and that we are but fragments of it that need to be brought together to work synergistically, to understand the parts that we, as components, are playing. Such interplay can be called Intelligent Design.

The universe's game plan is one of self-discovery and awakening.

The soul's wisdom game plan can be called Energy Finding Out About Its Creative Potential. But since this is an eternal game, after millennia energy has discovered self-awareness, and self-awareness has discovered wisdom. Wisdom then seeks the most powerful and enlightened form it can embody.

After millennia, the name for this eternal self-discovery is the Divine, or God. It's the ultimate, highest reflection of the soul's wisdom game of self-discovery. Therefore, the universe isn't just energy potentializing, as the quantum physicists would have it, but is consciousness *being the best it can be*. And so, there is an awareness steering the entire effort of self-discovery.

Each individual piece of that consciousness or fragment is there as part of a larger plan that needs to be brought together and to work holistically in some fashion for the plan to be manifested. Sometimes, the fragments must clash with each other. Sometimes, whole cultures must rise and thrive and then fail. Sometimes nature must be dealt with and accommodated, and sometimes one individual here or there must stand out in greatness to shine the beacon for the next stage. But always, there is an overarching pattern that is being explored. That's why we all feel as though there is a larger guiding force, or Greater Being to whom we answer, or who runs the show. Man at his most primitive feels this, as does Man at his most evolved.

In fact, whether that's called the universe, or Source, or divine energy, or God, that is correct. It is also correct to call it Intelligent Design. The intelligence is the ultimate recognition of the Wisdom

Game derived from the exploration of life by aware energy in physical form (the soul).

From this perspective, life can also be viewed as a puzzle consisting of a framework of energy patterns.

For instance, in today's world, the worldwide web is such a pattern. It's like a geodesic dome of energy covering the planet. Within this central framework, all the pieces fit together; where the spokes meet are the nexus points that are critical in order that each individual and groups of individuals can play their roles in the great puzzle. By scooping up individual talents, joining any two various nexus points, and then connecting these to any larger nexus points, the worldwide web is creating global mind – another stage of human experience. This stage is occurring in cyberspace through digitized information (a binary world), and also as a spiritual web which some call the *noosphere*.

Your clues to understanding your part reside in your PEP, your Personal Energy Pattern. You can now see how the little pieces of your story can and must be woven together into a big picture. As a race, at this stage we are waking up to this insight and can begin to focus and work toward it to align our own efforts with the large pattern of the puzzle. The universe then assists as your individual efforts become harmonized with it; it speaks to you of their realization, with the result that you reach your potential more quickly and therefore feel more joyful. There is a synergy between receiving guidance or intuition, using your will or intention to participate, and getting rid of unconscious blockage. Winning the Wisdom Game means evaluating your goals, aligning with your deepest (highest) ones, and not letting anyone or anything else uncenter you. Because, at The Third Worldview, everybody wins. Inspiration that moves you at this Worldview is the win-win kind. Your individual success and delight will simultaneously benefit the greatest amount of other people because, at The Third Worldview, you and they are seen as the same. You and the world are seen as one. *"The quantum view implies that what I think affects the world."* says author Dean

Radin.* Each person's soul's wisdom game is his or her own personal puzzle to identify and solve. And in so doing, the universe is solving the riddle of life, or of the world.

In reaching this point, wisdom questions the "why" of all actions. You look at your value system in order to understand what your personal goals are in contrast to the world's goals. Or, said in another way, as against the universal game plan.

People, being as they are, naturally ask the key question of anything that they do, "What's in it for me?" Everyone wants a better life. At The Third Worldview, it becomes clear that the deepest satisfaction is gained by pursuing an improved world and choosing goals that not only fulfill the self but also the entire planet. At this Worldview, it becomes apparent that such higher values are actually in your self interest because your expanded self now sees the complete unity and entanglement of all. Remember, now you *are* the world!

New pathways of energy are arising on Planet Earth that are specifically designed to help you universalize yourself by offering an abundance of creative possibilities that can become the blessing of many. Each of us can pluck our share of a cornucopia of life experience that is now available.

As at The Second Worldview you unblocked your energy, and latched onto your passions and inspirations, you began to feel a surge of energy and an abundance of creative possibility. Now, at The Third Worldview, saying yes to creative possibility means shifting from thinking just about the lower nature and instead getting onboard with the amazing new possibilities. At the same time your intuition is being honed, and you are becoming a receiving station or antenna for the signals or patterns from the larger realm. The dance then is simply to wait, watch, and see what shows up; this will allow yourself to become

---

* *"Quantum Mechanics and the Global Consciousness Project"* (Light of Consciousness magazine, Spring 2007)

more realized. You can partake of your own buffet at the cornucopia. As alignment succeeds, flowing begins.

When you get yourself out of the way, put your ego to the side, and switch from negative emotion to different thoughts that allow more positive emotion to come to the surface, you begin to flow.

Flowing can be as simple as catching a bunch of green lights in traffic or a parking spot near an entrance. Merely thinking about unity does not make it so. But when you are committed to it, believe in it, take a leap of faith, move forward with what you now know as the truth, hold good values in terms of your goal, and maintain intention and the will to do it, the flow begins. It becomes real. You are in the soul's wisdom game, consciously participating in it. You have grounded it, and synchronicity will show up; that is to say, the meaningful coincidence to validate what you're doing. At which point it's no longer a sacrifice that you are making for the larger good. It becomes a thrilling ride where your personal goals are so aligned with the universe's that all effort made in that direction can only bear sweet fruit.

To be in the flow means to be part of the grand design of the universe and to **let the universe manage the job**. The soul's wisdom game becomes very Zen-like. Wonderful and incredible results will begin to occur. Life becomes less about you, more about universal Will. Wisdom reveals the cure for suffering (peace, love, patience, detachment). Alignment increases your intuitive connection, and then *knowing* begins. You allow yourself to be guided, steered by deeper awareness and subtle signals. There is less reason to resist since there is less ego-need to be satisfied. A deep union is formed between Self and Greater Will.

You Become a New Version of Human Being

A new type of person is coming onto the planet, certainly being helped by a lot of fresh insight, information, and experiences that people are having so as to convey the very idea of evolutionary change. If you've read this far, then you are one of those who are becoming this new type of human. You are contributing to the raising of the whole planetary vibration. When a critical mass of understanding is reached, when enough people realize **the flashpoint of awareness** – the awakening of wisdom and understanding – the planet will be changed.

We have to get past the mess of so many different races and languages, cultures and all this separateness of the human race. We have to get into a mind-to-mind communication whereby we connect the planet together. The new generation of cell phone and internet users represents the human mind being receptive, through technology and through instantaneous communication around the globe, to this awakening, the nature of which is electric.

The human mind, sped up and interconnected in this way, really represents the development of Intuition…a new level of reality. Minds working together toward the same realizations, even if they're approaching that through different concepts, become harmonious and synergistic.

The concept of who is playing the soul's wisdom game/ what the soul's wisdom game is about is being redefined. It's being redefined – by science – so that we can understand that our fragmented, small, egotistical self is *one* with the Master Creator, and is completely intertwined and joined with what we have previously always considered above and beyond us… that is, God. So, the new human is beginning to see him/herself as godlike, or playing "the God game".

This term – "The God Game" – is a concept used in virtual gaming. Some video games offer a player the chance to create a particular universe. In these, there's a term that refers to the use of virtual selves. These are called "avatars", a word that gamers have co-opted from actual religion. In Hinduism, for example, an avatar is a master being or highly advanced soul who takes on a physical vehicle (a body and personality) only to serve a cosmic purpose of elevating humans and/ or alleviating their suffering. An avatar is free to act in accordance with this great purpose, and is no longer constrained by the limitations of karma or physics. (Avatars are cool – they never age, can blink in and out of existence, can manifest in the same form century after century, can bi-locate, and can perform "miraculous" acts as needed for their task, and can then simply disappear, neither dying nor corrupting.) In virtual gaming, however, your cyber-self is cleverly called your avatar. You, the human player, use this representative cyber-self to act in ways that are compatible with each game's rules. And in fact, you are, by working through your avatar, co-creating each new development within the game's parameters, each new alternate universe.

Applied to The Wisdom Game, though, another important concept – a whole new viewpoint – is revealed. You're not just put here on Earth as a puny game player. Part of you is the human actor immersed in the drama of life, but another part of you is the designer of the show, the puppeteer or co-creator, the Lord of Life, the Realizer, the Master. Part of you, in other words, is a godlike designer of the actions that the actor finds him/herself doing. And the new perspective lets you – the Self – switch at will between the two.

In this context, there is still pain and suffering and challenge, but it's seen from a new perspective. It's seen as an essential component of this God game, and immediately gives humanity the opportunity to create better strategy. We see how to maneuver within the frustrations, disappointments or predicaments of life. We see the purpose of life as bringing us ever more to an expanded awareness and to the fulfillment of the self-chosen inner passion. And in this process, our choices become clarified and the moves that we make get clearer. We see the role of conscious intention and conscious choice, and we understand that we are not victims but game-players improving the quality of life for the individual, and therefore for the race. We begin to understand that emotions can be mastered, and can be trimmed down in the equation of life. And therefore a new kind of liberation is available

In changing our point of view in this manner, we become more aligned with the flow of energy, with the flow of the universal patterns of energy, and we begin to see our hopes and dreams as ever more realizable. This is a very powerful type of human being: not seeing oneself as small and puny or a victim of circumstances, but seeing oneself as the master of reality.

Up to now, we have seen ourselves as individuals, as separate fragmented and disconnected people, but upon entering The Third Worldview there is no other perspective than to see all others as ourselves, to become deeply connected to the whole world and to each other (the definition of brotherhood, and keyword for The Age of Aquarius), and to see others' pain as our own.

We are speaking of the transformation of humanity. This profound shift has even been reflected in the stars!* Deep and profound, humanity's mysteries, reason for existence, nature of soul, and mission toward which it is aimed are slowly being revealed. The new human is coming forward, and is being birthed in pangs of difficulty and challenge (as all are), but nevertheless beginning to breathe the light of day. The new humanity will eventually take hold on Planet Earth and

---

* In the year 2007, from the point of view of humanity's home base, planet Earth, we looked out in the sky and saw a celestial event that had never been observed. Not because it hadn't happened before, but because humanity had no way to be aware of its occurrence until now.

The occurrence was the passage of planet Pluto across the degrees of 26° to 27° Sagittarius of the Zodiac. That particular point happens to be the center of our galaxy, or the black hole that is surmised as being the center point of the Milky Way around which the entire spiral galaxy spins and towards which it is receding.

The Galactic Center is symbolically significant as the pull towards which humanity and all the rest of its immediate neighborhood and far-reaching environs are embraced by and drawn to.

The symbolism of planet Pluto is one of deep transformation; of the probing of mysteries that lie under the surface – as deeply embedded as is possible, and as dark and hidden as is able. And whenever a significant passage occurs in its journey, some profound transformation of the psyche takes place.

be a much more masterful race, able to fathom the Grand Design and to work consciously in performing the Great Work...the perfection of form, the spiritualization of nature.

Well, this huge shift has been predicted all over the globe for centuries. It goes by different names.

The End Times have long been prophesized as a period somewhere around this era, often thought to be around the year 2012, in which we will either encounter Armageddon or be reborn... a phoenix rising from its ashes.

Many patterns are coming together. These times have been prophesized by many throughout history, from Nostradamus to the Hopi Indians, and from the Mayans to Edgar Cayce.

The general tone of the End Times presupposes gloom and doom. Something ends. Something is changed or destroyed. As Bob Dylan says, "the times, they are a-changing".

Yes, it feels like something huge is afoot. However, it is just now, during these challenging times, when humanity is being stressed and forced to change and awaken, that great advances are occurring in consciousness, such as the dissemination of spirituality, vision, and new awareness, and also in science by the very notion that all of three-dimensional physicality truly is a pure energetic ocean of oneness, as reflected in the total entanglement of quantum mechanics.

Perhaps as part of that wonderful synchronicity, there is irony. We've spent eons untangling the mysteries of the mind and the age-old questions about God, only to find, finally, that everything is entangled; that there is no "there" there, that all of life is an illusion, and all being is simply oneness. So the End Times seems more about ending the illusion of separation than of ending humanity.

Is it really here now, this era of profound evolutionary change? Are we really on a threshold?

Signs, Omens, and the Age of Aquarius

This is the era that has long been prophesized. All the signs and omens are appearing.

Native Americans for ages have prophesized the appearance of *the white buffalo* during the era of mankind's awakening. Recently (1994), a white buffalo was born in the Midwest on a farm. The buffalo was white, not albino, and when the first buffalo born failed to thrive, another white buffalo was also born in the Midwest.

Lakota white buffalo prophecy: the birth of a white buffalo calf would signal the nearness of the time when White Buffalo Woman would return again to purify the world and bring back its harmony.

In Africa, shamans have long considered *the white lion* as the spiritual symbol for Africa, a symbol of humanity's oneness, and in fact, there is today a sanctuary holding a small but thriving group of white (not albino) lions being funded in part by American philanthropy. National Geographic magazine has done a "special" on The White Lion Trust.

African white lion prophecy: the reappearance of the white lions – the "star lions coming down from the heavens", representing pure sunlight beyond all color, creed, gender or race, and purity and enlightenment in spiritual terms – marks the fulfillment of an ancient prophecy. The mysterious white color of the lions identifies these majestic creatures as messengers from God.

In South America, it was long prophesized that the true dawn of humanity would occur *when the eagle flew together with the condor* – the eagle being the symbol of North America and the condor of South America. And, in fact, there is a confluencing of Peruvian shamans with Native American medicine people and African shamans. The eagle and condor have met... and are offering workshops together!

Ecuadorian/ Peruvian eagle & condor prophecy =The period when the Eagle and Condor reunite is written in the stars as the beginning of a new time, a new light, when the two peoples can

take the Spirit into their own hands, move the spiritual energy, and reunite mankind.

And in Buddhism, the prophecy that *the Dharma would move to the land of the red man when the iron bird flies in the sky* came true when Vivekananda and Yogananda Paramahansa brought the tradition of yoga to the West and found fertile soil here in 1920. Many Eastern masters have followed. Hollywood celebs brag about their gurus!

Still more prophecies, including those of Nostradamus, Edgar Cayce, many psychics and the Hopi Indians, have all targeted this era as the wake-up call for humanity. The Mayan calendar pinpoints the year 2012 as the date of a so-called "End Times". We have not yet seen the *Blue Star Kachina* appear in the sky, as the Hopis have prophesized, but that might come as well (perhaps in the form of an asteroid plunging towards us).

Hopi, Blue Star Kachina = "When the Blue Star Kachina makes its appearance in the heavens, the Fifth World will emerge". The Hopi name for the star <u>Sirius</u> is Blue Star (Saquasohuh Kachina). This will be the Day of Purification "when the (Blue Star) Kachina dances in the plaza and removes his mask."

And let's not forget the Harmonic Convergence in August 1987, an astrological pattern presaged by the Mayan, Western and Asian calendars, in which a new era of brotherhood was initiated via ceremonies around the globe.

There is no doubt that we stand on the precipice and have the choice to fly or crash, but the signs are good. Meanwhile, any search of the internet will reveal massive numbers of communities of global spiritual intention that are striving to bring forth the positive turnaround – certainly a Third Worldview feat!

A very important part of the turnaround from Second to Third Worldview taking place within each of us as well as on the world stage is the shift from the masculine theme to a greater role for the feminine. Equality of the genders is necessary. In your psyche, the creative coppery fertility gradually morphs into a silvery luminescence.

Yin, the opposite quality from Yang, is expanding in the world in this era. An ancient beheaded goddess statue has had her head and torso reunited – a metaphor for the shifting tide of dominance through the ages. Whereas Yang is the creative thrusting principle of life, Yin is the feminine receptive principle. In history, there are cycles in which each quality of manifestation is emphasized and comes to the forefront.

We have just gone through a long period in which Yang has dominated, as seen by patriarchal governments, religions and family structures, and an emphasis on technology, materialism and wars. Prior to this Yang expansion, culture was more matriarchal and based upon the Earth, the Goddess, nature and fertility. A swing back toward this focus is taking place across the globe. It will be seen by women rising in power, and by women's concerns, such as family, nurturance, conservation and preservation of the environment, sensitivity, and other feminine qualities taking precedent over male power structures. Of course, Women's Lib is part of it (as is Civil Lib and Gay Rights), but was not the only example of this force, because in third world countries where women have been very repressed, this movement is taking place as well, albeit as yet mostly underground. Eventually, the male power structures will be threatened and some will dig in deeper, attempting even more entrenchment.

In fact, it is part of the Age of Aquarius to rebalance these energies, to be more egalitarian, to have a community or brotherhood of mankind rather than an imbalanced power structure where one sex or the other dominates. Equality of the sexes will become the new rule.

We have spoken of prophecies but we have not yet spoken of oracles.

An oracle, by definition, is a prophecy. In the "past", it had a ponderous implication but in today's world the term is used more casually. It means the answer given by any tool of divination.

Thus, the tools that provide non-rational, intuitive and psychic answers – Tarot cards, rune stones, I-Ching coin tosses, pendulums, tea leaves, shells and bones, horary astrology, and all their like – are each and every one considered oracles. Once a query is asked of it, the device casts a "reading". The reader's skill then determines the accuracy and insight of the forecast. Primitive tribes use such, and modern computers have also been programmed to produce random "throws" of digital bytes.

The reason an oracle works is that in quantum physics there is only the Now (the singular moment of time-space), and the All exists in that moment. Much like a hologram, everything is contained in the Now, and the oracle allows a read-out of a portion of it – the portion you have queried about. Depending on the interpretive skill of the reader, it's otherwise assumed that the read-out contains the truth of the moment. The human lens through which it is divined is the weak spot, and can make mistakes or not see clearly. However in skilled hands much help can be had in divining the prognostication of the oracle.

However, receiving the read-out isn't enough; you have to be willing to follow it!

As is understood on the spiritual path, *surrender* does not mean giving up, or being weak. Spiritual surrender requires wisdom and guts. It's the stage of allowing the small will to accept and follow the guidance of the Greater. In Tarot, it is represented by The Hanged Man. He has a strong light around his head because he is consciously accepting the surrendered position. His hair is gray because one must be quite an old soul to comprehend this wisdom.

Surrender means trusting in universal flow. Surrender means accepting the decision of the oracle. Surrender implies true, not blind, faith.

If you've gotten to the spot in life where you seek guidance of an oracle, then the wise route next is to bend to the prophecy and with free will let the forecast be your guide. Otherwise, what's the point?

True faith, rather than blind faith, indicates that you grasp the notion of a higher plan at work in your life, and that you have become willing to let wiser navigation tools (always in conjunction with common sense) be your directional finders, your inner G.P.S. True faith reveals that you have progressed in wisdom, acknowledged factors beyond your ego and brainpower, and are enthusiastic about integrating other awareness into your life choices.

Surrendering to the oracle means you prefer locating yourself in the M Field rather than in the everyday.

All of this understanding about the M Field, about expanded consciousness, about the evolution of the human mind towards self awareness (an awareness of the nature of the illusion of life, even from a scientific point of view) comprises the larger design created so that sentient life can proceed towards clarity, and towards the perfection of being.

And we are on that threshold now, and the name of that threshold is the Age of Aquarius. This is an era where the expansion of the individual mind into a larger framework is the beginning of a global community and a global mind.

The creation of the internet, or the worldwide web, has provided the wherewithal for all minds to interrelate and mesh into a global community, as a network of minds, each mind (in each personality) wanting to contribute its own gifts of talent, insight, knowledge and love, so that what is shifting is the authority of the few, and what is burgeoning is the growth of the multiple (global) mind. Built as a matrix of communications around the planet, through cell phones and computers, text messaging, and instantaneous transfer of knowledge accessing all parts of the planet, a grid has been created. This is a grid in cyberspace, and has its presence in electronics and technology, and in that sense, it is grounded in, and connected to, physicality.

Global Mind is not just people writing blogs and reading them (threads of conversation). It's not just the database of all the facts that ever were (Google, etc.). Global Mind is that which recognizes that each infinitesimal aspect of that mind – in other words, each person's contribution to life – furthers the entire race. It furthers all of creation. It furthers the universe. It is the sum of reports about what the universe is, what spirit discovers regarding taking form and being a person. It is the whole interactivity of individualized selves finding ways to testify to, and converse about, other individualized selves, other aspects of spirit. And there's nothing that's going to stop this because the whole thrust is to understand how *we are the world*.

But it also has a presence via cyberspace from mind to mind; many minds are creating not just a gridwork of connectivity but a gridwork of intention. Global mind is allowing the creation of *an intentional community*.

Which intention is followed will be multiple – as multiple as there are different personalities, different needs and different passions. Creative potential is the most important thing that structures the framework and determines the intention. A global wisdom community is being organized and structured; it has key nexus points. It covers the globe like a geodesic dome. It's built partially through organizations and groups, partly by key individuals who are the nexus points on the dome-like structure, and partly by the internet itself ("Web-2"), which links humanity on a mental and emotional level..

Eventually, however, another development is taking place as wisdom permeates and allows humanity to see beyond the physical. It is then that the heart's center is pulled into the global structure, bringing in knowledge and expertise and building the framework for something other than just electronics. As the framework begins to be built from the heart's center, where compassion and caring play a key role in the intentions, humanity sees itself rise above base desires and destructive appetites, developing instead a spiritual consciousness.

In the current era, this process was enhanced by an astrological configuration called *a mutual reception* between technology and spirituality* in the year 2011, then further enhanced as greater access to the M Field is opened. Understanding and heart-based energy will pour across the planet, allowing another level of the grid to be built, a level in which the entire planet is seen to be connected to spirit, and in which the entire world is understood as one energy or one interwoven and entangled, very complex system.

The spokes of the grid then begin to permeate the M Field and seem to shimmer, not just with electronic radiation, but with spirit. As they pierce and seek connection to the higher realm, humanity will then, in the course of the Age of Aquarius, begin to see itself as one body, one entity. As the Age of Aquarius proceeds, planet, human, self, and God, will ultimately become merged in conscious awareness.

In fact, the Age of Aquarius is related to The Precession Of The Equinoxes. As with all Great Ages, its duration is about 2100 years. It begins as we leave the darkest point on the cosmic cycle, otherwise known as the Kali Yuga, and tilts upwards on the return journey into more enlightened Ages. As a known and planned event, this bodes well for the future of Earth, of mankind, and of the awakening and spiritualizing of the entire Universe.

It cannot be otherwise, then, that as we apply our new wisdom to worldly matters, we bring into being conscious commerce. We bring conscious capitalism into reality. As consciousness awakens, a triple win will be created, whereby humanity is able to realize benefits for the people, for the planet, and for the bottom line (profit). This global community will be based partly on idealism, partly on science, partly on spirituality, and partly on the laws of the physical universe, including materialistic truths. Not just a growing spiritual wholeness, but the good life for all people (and creatures) – a world of abundance. This is precisely why *the dharma* (virtuous path of the universe) has moved to

---

*　This process has been enhanced by the recent "mutual reception" of Uranus (technology) in Neptune's (spirituality) sign, and vice versa, and is now further aided by Neptune's entry into Pisces (The M Field) in 2011.

the West: to realize the right use of the material plane (i.e., Conscious Capitalism) so long as no harm ensues for any. That means, of course, a rejection of war.

To be gathered together by our intentions is to create a community of intention: groups of people working together, forward thinking, on the cutting edge, who can see that this is the only way to go. The Third Worldview is the mind-meld. It is *the Firing of the Grid**. The Third Worldview is the Intentional Community, or Self as World.

Experts will be pulled into this global structure (Global Wisdom Community) who are able to help humanity rise above base emotions and destructive appetites, developing instead their spiritual consciousness. It will become the manifestation of the truth that "all is one".

Four Wisdom Exercises for The Third Worldview

These four exercises can help root you firmly in a greatly expanded paradigm.

1. Whenever possible, listen inwardly to your dialogue and identify what worldview you are in, that is, the everyday self or a wiser guide. Try to determine if that alter voice is the self you are comfortable with, or a different but still interior aspect of you, and then note if the alter persona always maintains the same grade of wisdom, or a higher or lower one. Give your spectrum

> **FOUR WISDOM EXERCISES FOR WORLDVIEW 3**
>
> 1. Practice shifting your identity
> 2. Say hello to your other selves
> 3. Note your awakening psychic powers
> 4. Do volunteer work

---

* This refers to the end result of a woman's near-death drowning, and her ensuing mission and the movement it has engendered. Shelley Yates, *Fire the Grid, Parts 1 – 8, www.YouTube.com.*

placements a few nicknames, if you like, but **accept only selves that are lighter than your familiar self, never darker.** Once you feel sure of their eternal presence, use a shifting technique to move into one or another of your expanded identities. Do that frequently, and at will.

2. Allow your awareness to move past the boundaries of daily life to bask in the freedom of the M Field, and stand ready to encounter your past-life incarnations, your otherworldly dimensional beings, and the etheric forms of fellow travelers. Don't be afraid, as these will probably come with messages or teachings that will be helpful in the current life. Get acquainted thus with your immortal soul.

3. Take note of your newly developing psychic abilities! Precognitive dreams, strident gut feelings, visible apparitions, second sight, intuitive flashes, and all manner of ESP might make an appearance as your consciousness keeps expanding beyond the known boundaries of conventional reality. Welcome these new powers – they are the unavoidable result of spiritual development, and the confirmation that you are becoming a universal being who is rapidly outgrowing the confines of limited 3-D reality.

4. Sign up for volunteer work. Real, hands-on efforts. Do not do it to make yourself feel good (although you will). Do it to help your other karmically benighted selves who could use a hand. In other words, give back. Pay it forward. Care about the planet and the people. Shower your energy over the world. Live the Golden Rule. Many blessings will shimmer over and around you.

You are building that inner bridge, that continuum of awareness, that rainbow path that will carry you towards wisdom, freedom, peace, joy, and grace.

The Compassionate Heart

In reaching the clear understanding of the world's and self's complete entanglement and the elimination of false concepts of duality, it is logical that people begin to see each other as reflections of themselves.

Global unity, or human non-division, mandates empathy. It is yourself you are looking at when you see others around the world.

> GATE/WORLDVIEW: 3
>
> RESULT: **Light.** Awareness of truth. Serenity and peace. Enlightenment. Radiance.
>
> GETTING FROM HERE TO THERE: **From personal creativity to joyous brotherhood.** Become permeable. Dissolve limitation. Find the bridge to overcome death. Expand the heart. See Them as Me. See It/Other/World as Self.

Their pain is yours; their joy, yours too. The knitting together of mankind, and the true understanding of intertwined energy (quantum physics) means that aloofness and unconcern for one's fellows is automatically wrongheaded. In fact, full attainment of The Third Worldview causes the realization of the mirror of self. When you look at anyone else, it is seen as an aspect of self. Nurturing that reflection of self, then, is the very act that brings joy to one's innards. The interior is blessed in its connectivity to the exterior… and that's the soul's wisdom game's solution anyhow!

Then the soul's wisdom game morphs into: how expanded can I widen my heart energies (because that's how much inner joy I'll create for myself)? How broadly and powerfully can I play this soul's wisdom game of the radiant heart? How Christ-like can I become?

***

YOUR INDIVIDUAL CREATIVE POTENTIAL IS UNLEASHED UPON THE WORLD! And there's only one further step to take… the most powerful of all.

In a world where the majority of people understand that life is a soul's wisdom game that builds inner joy the more you help others, love and light expand and spread. In a world where most people can easily slip into paranormal experience and have access to intuitive guidance and between-life choices, fear decreases. In a world where creativity isn't blocked by emotional or societal resistance, incredible human feats are realizable. And in a world that knits together the human personality with its godlike source, a return to Eden becomes possible.

Radiance is increasing within the mind as the paradigm of The Third Worldview is encountered and fully entered. You have journeyed from your inchoate passions through their mastery by dint of controlling your thoughts and emotions, and then you have learned the secret of conscious creation by overcoming the illusion of limited reality, and finally you have gotten to a place within yourself in which your psychic centers are open and your own internal navigation system, in attunement with the universal flow of energy, is guiding your actions and choices. The fear of death has subsided or been completely removed as you see your true self as eternal and endlessly partaking of the game of life. Your entire being – now identified as all-encompassing – is filled with light. Where else can you possibly travel?

Receiving a Vision

I had (was given?) a vision of the higher plane: A Being (large-scale, but *not* God) is designing a play – parts are coming together to create a thing, a whole.

(The Being might be multiple…it wasn't clear.)

The parts consist of people and events. But it's all extrusions of Itself. After the people are extruded and formed, the Being acted like a puppeteer, moving stuff around, positioning people and things into places. The people are separate unto themselves but at the same time parts of the Being. So the people are all from the same source.

There are many people all playing their roles while various circumstances are being arranged. So we act out our parts unbeknownst to each other, each thinking we're whole and separate, and each believing we're acting from free will. (This, however, is why the *Michael* entity calls people "fragments".)

The point (design) of the proceedings is to bring about a happening on the world stage, to create the World in a certain fashion, or towards an already-determined goal.

It's not so different a vision than that hokey old movie, "Jason and the Argonauts", where Lawrence Olivier was Zeus on Mount Olympus, but it's from a very different consciousness. The Being is neither jealous nor petty. Not emotional at all. There is purpose in the creation (I don't know it – it wasn't stated, shown or offered).

THE FOURTH WORLDVIEW

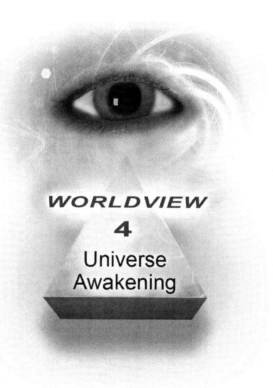

THE TRUTH OF YOU AND GOD

GATE/ WORLDVIEW	APPEARANCE	LANDSCAPE/ REALM	KEY	ABILITY	METAL	TOOL	RESULT
AT THE ENTRANCE	Everyday Life	Fog	Karmic Predicament	To live	Lead	Passion	Suffering
1	Curtain	The Wisdom Game	Choice (The Quantum Shift)	To switch out of negativity	Iron	Emotional Mastery, Control of Thought	Wisdom
2	Door	The Law of Attraction	Power (The Art of Manifestation)	To co-create what you desire	Copper	Conscious Co-creation	Joy
3	Bridge	Continuum	Vision (Capping the Point of Awareness)	To realize who you are and overcome the fear of death	Silver	Intuition & ESP	Light
4	Portal	Mind of God	Service (Merit)	To know truth and be the Way	Gold	No-Ego, Surrender	Bliss

What are the components of fully expanded awareness, and how does that totally alter the soul's wisdom game of life? At the Fourth Worldview, it becomes evident that what is awakening is not only you, nor even the whole world, but that the entire universe is waking up and remembering its purpose and its true nature ("The Quickening"); that three-dimensionality has become permeable as realms merge and artificial divisions (duality) of inner/outer, you/me, human/god, and even time/space dissolve; you see the cosmic dialogue taking place between temporarily divided aspects of yourself; you are now realizing the greatest truth, that you are becoming god-in-human-form, an awareness without form that is swimming in a field of unlimited energetic potential ("limitless light"), existing only in the present moment (the Now), entangled with all other temporarily divided aspects of yourself, and focusing all your efforts to liberate and heal all other reflections of you (people), both "high" and "low" (that is, to apply compassion); and that you are none other than the self as divine creator, at once singular (unified) and dualistic, both the source of the illusion of separation and the participant in it. Having yourself designed the whole shebang, you see yourself playing at the soul's ultimate wisdom game; you are in other words perfecting form by transcending karmic limitations (becoming the New Human), remembering all your ancient and recent cycles of reincarnations (old soul and past life memories), modeling the words of The Great Invocation, and realizing why love is the greatest wisdom to offer everyone... who are, after all, none other than you! In a sudden burst of enlightenment, you see that the arcs of psychology (the shift) and of science (quantum physics) could produce no other result than to reach this new plateau of awareness – the recognition that only love is important and in fact the true and sole reality, and that wisdom must be spread to other temporarily separated minds especially during the current challenging world epoch. To your newly awakened mind, false societal structures that seek to limit natural aspects of human beings or raise one gender over another are being disempowered and eclipsed by those that are seeing the folly of cursing or harming others (who are remembered aspects of yourself) via warfare or even daily encounters, while new societal structures are being ushered in through the births of psychically precocious children ("indigo children"), and by those who value selflessness and compassion over all other pursuits. With your amazing fresh perspective, you now forever seek the grace of reducing the world's suffering (a lifestyle that produces merit) as you also try to strategize your yet-to-be-experienced incarnation (future self), as well as those of your other selves currently embodied as living children, in order to provide as much blessing and luck for them as you can design into the drama – the most successful way of "winning" your soul's wisdom game. **The big secret of this worldview is that there is only one self, and no other, no matter how many others appear to be real and separated; therefore, all is One, and that One simply exists and plays the game with itself eternally so as to experiment with creative potential. You, others, Elders, and God are the same thing, divided only in the mind.**

In a sense, you've reached the end of your journey.

Having recognized that you are not separate from other beings, from nature, or even from God, you stand at a juncture. Your heart is now interconnected with everything, and you know that you are the source of all creation (that it all takes place in your mind)... but are you ready for the very last step?

Are you ready to let go of YOU?

In order to do so, you must cross through the last gateway. It is like nothing you've ever seen, for in fact it doesn't exist here and can't be described. You can only know that it exists through intuition. Through intuition, and a pure and

GATE/WORLDVIEW: 4

APPEARANCE: Portal. An opening into a new dimension. Once you go through it, you are no longer here.

LANDSCAPE / REALM: Mind of God. Only light. No form. No mirror. No bridge. Nothing but awareness. Pure light. A place where all is in endless potential but not yet manifested.

loving heart, you will find the way to cross to it. And as you approach it, you must decide: are you ready?

For, as soon as you pass through this last gateway and into the last Worldview, you will cease to be you.

A PORTAL beckons ahead. With the GOLD KEY OF BLISS and the TOOL OF LOVING SERVICE, you stand ready to leave the sense of personhood and enter the realm where YOU no longer are.

What will happen? Will there be an abyss of endless blackness? Terrors? Non-existence? The end? What will "YOU" find there?

> **GATE/WORLDVIEW: 4**
>
> **KEY: Service (merit).** Knowing that only love matters. The loving nurturing of every iota of creation. The use of total loving effort to build creation, and then guide it to its fullest potential. Bringing all home to Source.
>
> **ABILITY:** To know truth and be the Way.
>
> **METAL: Gold.** A pure incorruptible material that will never lose its shine no matter how long it might be buried. The standard of treasure against which everything else is measured.

It is with utmost faith in the benign purpose of the universe that you undertake this last part of your journey. Beyond ego lies Allness... or No Limitation.

KEYS OF CONSCIOUSNESS FOR THE FOURTH WORLDVIEW

The Fourth Worldview is the most advanced level whereby consciousness expands until it can no longer remain in the physical self (in the three-dimensional reality). It is described by certain systems as liberation, "The World", or nirvana.

This is the stage in which the self realizes not only that it is inseparable (i.e., unable to be separately defined) from all of matter, but also that a personal ego structure, or self-identification isn't real and doesn't exist. In other words, at The Fourth Worldview, it's understood that consciousness is all that is and nothing at all is happening. Only thought (consciousness) exists. "Reality" is created in the realm of thought; it is only thoughtform. The sense of self and other is the illusion… or *the dreamer dreaming itself.*

It is as though matter – the physical universe – wakes up and realizes the truth: that all of existence, all of what's called life or physicality, all of what's called form or reality, is just a projection that consciousness calls forth to engage in a soul's wisdom drama with itself, to grow, evolve, and know itself differently. The Fourth Worldview is the point at which you shake off the reverie of separation, realize that there really is no such thing as duality, and wake up to bridge the illusion and go beyond disconnection.

The Fourth Worldview is when the universe within its form **awakens** to its truth, and remembers its game. It is the real meaning of *self-realization….* the self realizing what Self really is.

At this level, you comprehend waking up not only to your unity with the entire outside world, but to a higher truth: that there is no Other; there is nothing that exists outside of simple awareness. At this stage, life becomes play, miracles are easy, and you become the instrument for the soul's wisdom game to continue so that the entire world gains clarity, and so that a better type of human is created – the next stage in human development.

At this stage, there is truth regarding the self vis-à-vis the other, and thus regarding the creation of reality truly on the level of thoughtform. Duality between self and illusion is overcome. And yet another shift takes place wherein it is seen that there is no longer an "I" versus a "You," but only that there is all-ness, or is-ness, or being-ness. Up to now, you have worked hard to master emotion and control the production of thought, to bring yourself into a more joyful and enlightened place. Now all that is behind you. The soul's wisdom game of emotion and karma has been transcended. At this Worldview, emotions can't hold a candle to inner truth.

This begins the greatest work – called service – which includes, as a by-product and not the goal, accruing lucky karmic credit, otherwise known as *merit*.

Once **true self-realization** takes place, the soul's final purpose is to accumulate *merit*. Merit – earned worthiness – is a wisdom term. It is accrued by increasing compassion and kindness *to itself* (i.e., all creatures and all nature) on the world stage. At The Fourth Worldview, the self *is* a wisdom warrior, battling the suffering inherent in illusion and questing to stay in the light of oneness and love!

Re-Cap of the Continuum

So far, we've seen that step 1, or The First Worldview, gives us the soul's wisdom game, identifies the particulars, puts life into a framework, and begins to explain methods to get "un-stuck." The First Worldview, therefore, is the

STEPS OF EACH LEVEL

1. Rules of the Wisdom Game
2. The Quantum Shift
3. Confirmation, Greater Good
4. Perfecting Form

understanding that simply by being you, you are manifesting creative potential.

<u>The Second Worldview</u> utilizes the Quantum Shift, also called *The Law of Attraction,* the means by which inner work is done to wrest thought away from negative emotion, reframing the nature of each episode, thus mastering life through the human experience, and getting a flow happening on the interior level that then gets reflected externally. The Second Worldview, in other words, is the step in which creative potential is released or unblocked, and in which the mind begins to awaken to a higher aspect of itself, otherwise known as intuition.

<u>The Third Worldview</u> confirms this empowered mastery, validates the synchronicity of the interior and the exterior experience, utilizes manifestation, and confirms the oneness of the experience of self vis-à-vis the world or the outer. So, The Third Worldview is the stage in which you know yourself to be the world. The world exists nowhere else than within your awareness. *"I AM that I AM".* At The Third Worldview, the soul figures out that it is therefore the whole world.

What, then, is <u>The Fourth Worldview</u>?

The Fourth Worldview is the stage at which you realize that there is nothing else other than consciousness, that the whole nature of duality is an illusion or a game, and that in truth the only thing that exists is simply energy. Thoughts are energy, actions are energy. The focus that brings energy into a crystallized concept (form) is nothing but consciousness playing a soul's wisdom game with itself to construct an illusion of separation, or of "me" versus "you", or interior versus exterior. Because The Fourth Worldview is indescribable, it can only be shown by components that lead you to it, or realizations that remain afterwards.

At The Fourth Worldview, the Wisdom Game is superseded, and a new soul's wisdom game begins: consciousness co-creates with nature to bring about a perfect creature – angels in human form! (This new human has been dubbed *Homo Noeticus.*)

There is no way to speak of such awakening and transformation other than to speak of *becoming love.*

This can be understood by examining energy. Once it is revealed that nothing else exists but vibrational patterns, then it is recognized that the entire illusion of "me" as separate from "you", or *my soul* as separate from *the world,* is **just consciousness at play.** Thus it is seen that there is only a dance of temporary structures of energies.

Waves of probability, or frequencies, are zipping around, becoming temporary particles, behaving momentarily as though they were real, as though matter exists, and then once more dissolving into energy. With this understanding or perspective, energy becomes aware of itself and of the soul's wisdom game it's playing and of the dance it's dancing.

So, what's the name of energy that is aware? We have said that some call this spirit. It can also be called light. Aware energy is the same as illumination.

What is light? Light is radiance. Light is brightness. Light brings clarity. To be enlightened is to see. To radiate light is to be love. Radiance is love.

Whenever an individual is carried over the boundary of illusion, he or she is said to see the light and often reports being filled with a sense of pure love or of being received by that vibration. Pure love, of course, is God. Pure love is the

> **GATE/WORLDVIEW: 4**
>
> **TOOL: No-Ego, Surrender.** The complete letting-go of identity. Becoming one. Remembering. The dissolution of duality. Just being energy vibrating.

divine experience. While in the illusion (in the soul's wisdom game in the sense of being physical), the center or organ of love is the heart. Therefore, the awakened heart is the same as aware energy and is also energy that is enlightened.

The title of a book by Brian Weiss puts it this way: *Only Love Is Real.* The truth is, the radiant heart – not as a bodily organ but as an energetic locus – is the only thing that in fact exists, and therefore only love is real in this world or in any other realm.

At The Fourth Worldview, the self is now seen not only as the same as the external world but as the same as all other souls. Myself and yourself are no longer seen as two separate things, but as one dance of energy, coalescing into momentary eternal illusions of the separateness of form.

If the self can no longer be seen as different from other selves, the self no longer feels separate or fearful of other selves because you are not fearful of yourself. In fact, the opposite occurs. By identifying with the radiant heart, or with love (the only energy that is), you have no other choice now but to love yourself in other guises. A human being who is fully compassionate, therefore reaches the ultimate Worldview while on earth or in form (i.e., while in the soul's wisdom game).

What else would there be to do than *love thy neighbor* and reduce suffering? It's the only game that is, because it's you in that other body. As the Brotherhood has taught, *"Love is not a game, but Life's brass ring of worthy completion. You can never 'win' a game without it, and you can never feel truly fulfilled if you lose it."*

Patience with yourself in its other guise comes from deep understanding of the divine play. The compassionate heart comes from a deep grasp of who is facing you, or confronting you with challenges and issues. To *love thy neighbor as thyself* is the rational, logical, point of the Wisdom Game. It can be said that the Golden Rule is the target. "Do unto others as you would have them do unto you." Kindness to everyone on the planet is what wins the soul's wisdom game. The planet is not out there, but inside self. Kindness to all is love given to oneself. It is the greatest wisdom.

The Universe Waking Up

It has taken millennia to create sentient life forms out of clay.

In fact, beginning as the simplest molecules of hydrogen, it was a feat even to reach the formation of clay.

From the point of view of the universe exploring its creative potential – from amoebas to dinosaurs, from mammals to *Homo Sapiens*, and finally from cavemen to PhD's – it has been quite a task. During that period, humanity has warred with and subjugated each other, tried many forms of government, and is now challenged by economic, ecological and political threats to its very survival. Certainly, against the standard of perfected people who are completely kind and aligned with each other, we have not yet reached our evolutionary ideal!

But the Great Plan will not easily give up its goal of developing a race of beings who become aware, not only of their selfhood, but also of their inner divinity. We are that race.

We are a stage in the journey of the universe's attempt to explore all manner of creative possibility, all waves of probability, in order to reach the perfected form. We will come to realize our very selves, or the One Self, as the singular aspect of the universe. That which is called matter and is engaged in the soul's wisdom game of life is nothing more than a projection of energy playing with the illusion of materiality. As we realize this within ourselves, we begin to win our personal drama to reach peace and joy within each lifetime and to spread as much kindness and compassion as is possible.

Realizing truth ushers the self into the prophesized state wherein humanity becomes godlike.

At the same time the self grasps the truth of oneness between inner and outer, realizing that our thoughts construct "reality", we inevitably come to see that there's nothing truly outside of ourselves and that, in fact, the whole illusion of separation is merely **one aspect of self talking internally with another aspect of self**.

This great insight, called *awakening,* puts the miracle of conscious creation into the control of the self. In other words, an awake universe means that its creative energy is aware and conscious and fully able to manifest at will. Creative energy takes control of its play by utilizing the Quantum Shift.

We're talking about *you*! This is the stage where "you" and "I" overcome the great divide by beginning to see yourself as an aspect of the divine, and finding in that notion the peace and joy that you have always sought.

As the realization begins that there is no dividing line between who you are and what the world is, you begin to feel an expansion. The expansion is of identity and awareness.

Looking at others, the sense of separation or division dissolves. Looking at things, whether small or huge, also produces a sense of the dissolution of separation; rather, a brilliance of clarity occurs: it is all happening within the mind and within the moment, and other people and other things are really part of the eternal process of thinking and knowing.

So, at this stage an amazing thing occurs. In waking up, you feel as though you have come out of a dream and entered a place more real than was ever understood. In this new Worldview, the self *gets it*. "I have been talking to myself all along," it says. "I have forever been contrasting one thing with another thing within my mind. Nothing else has actually taken place, and it certainly has not been occurring in a geographic location or even in a time-frame known as past or present or future. Everything that I'm thinking of is *me*, and it is all occurring *in the now*."

From this great sense of expansion, the self – up until now believing itself to be its ego-identity – suddenly finds itself zooming across the false limitation of identity-as-a-lifeform. The self expands to the point of comprehending that it's in an altogether different realm, a realm that has no separation and no darkness, but is only golden light and energy and beingness. From this perspective, to look at another person is to see your reflection playing your soul's wisdom game of transferring identity momentarily from this to that, and back again; it is to look at the world and see: "I am here, I am there, I am simultaneously everywhere…and equally valid, I am nowhere. I'm within the realm of mind where there is no time or space or personal identity."

In this expanded awareness, the ego completely dissolves, and only God is present. And, lo and behold, that which knows itself as "I" is the same as God! The self is the Creator of Reality; it is the Source.

It is at The Fourth Worldview that oneness is fully realized and limitation is completely transcended.

> *"To humble the ego or false self is to discover one's eternal identity."* – Paramahansa Yogananda, *Autobiography of a Yogi*

The experience of realizing that the entire world is occurring in the dialogue in one's mind is startling at the same time it's exhilarating and fascinating. This is the ultimate realization: the "you" doesn't exist.

We begin to see that the very pronoun "we" is just a construct between one part of our mind that is questioning, searching, struggling daily with the experiences of life, and actually all the while talking to another aspect of our mind ("it") from whom we seek guidance, with whom we share the story of what is going on and even to whom we pray for help. These dual aspects of the mind have been labeled the lower self and the higher self, or "me" and "God".

One part of the great insight, then, is the recognition that in fact we are all talking to ourselves at almost every moment of life (the rare moments of not doing so are called sleep, meditation or bliss.) It becomes powerfully apparent that the entire world is constructed through this inner dialogue and in fact, that the entire universe is simply consciousness sharing **the dual nature of observing while experiencing**. We can call this the Eternal Cosmic Dialogue.

It's from this reflective vantage point that yet another golden insight is realized: what is considered the lower self is not firmly rooted in a certain place or stage of development, but is fluid, and shifts depending on emotional state, level of evolution, psychological growth, available facts, and many other circumstances.

At the same time, especially as a channeler, I can attest to the inner query: who are the spirit guides, what and where is the source of the teachings? And then that answer appears quite organically from this line of perception. The guides, or higher source, are also fluid and also change and shift depending upon attunement, alignment, receptivity, and so forth.

THE STAR.

Therefore, the placement of both the inquiring, searching lower mind, and of the answering source of the higher mind, is fluid and can be positioned, determined, or located by the *point of focus*. I will call these dual poles the *caps* as discussed in Worldview Three, and since they are fluid and can shift, the lower mind can be capped off in various places and the higher source can also shift and be captured or focused or capped off in other various places *within the dialogue*. There is no set location, but there is always this duality between aspects of the one self conversing, sharing and exploring with other aspects of itself. That's why, in Tarot's Star card, the figure has one foot solidly planted on water, water being the fluid mind-stuff, while the action symbolizes the stilling (solidifying) of the mental process, thereby allowing all of the universe to become its gateway.

This is the basis of calling this entire concept The Continuum of Awareness.

[Perfecting Form: The New Soul's Wisdom Game

The universe and nature are engaging in the soul's wisdom game towards a goal.

It can be stated this way: from stars and elemental chemistry comes material. Material, the equivalent of form or three-dimensionality, develops itself into habitats, creatures, and finally sentient beings. All along, during this process, consciousness is striving to explore the potentiality of being material, and patiently building the evolutionary development of material that becomes aware of itself as a sentient (self-aware) being and then aware of the universe's game. Finally, the sentient beings, recognizing the ideal of the soul's wisdom game, begin to cooperate, speeding up (quickening) the achievement of the goal.

The goal is always the same, to develop material that is sentient enough and conscious enough to move in the direction of its perfected ideal, an archetype that always exists within nature. This is called The Great Plan, which, since it is eternal, is seen by any human from the dawn of time who has awakened into his/her own cosmic consciousness. Its unfoldment proceeds inevitably, forming the basis for all prophecy.

Perfect humanity would be Christ-like and angelic, fully compassionate yet very savvy in the ways of the world, in what the experience of life has to offer. Perfect humanity would see itself as one race, as one component of its habitat, the planet, and as the singular expression of the divine reflected in form.

The archetype always exists, and even from brutish earliest cultures is expressed as a God or as the divine form of nature.

In the perfecting of form, the universe always reaches the tipping point in which the sentient creature it has strived to develop, becomes aware of its creative power and must make choice using that power to self-destruct, or to change the soul's wisdom game into one of conscious design. We are now at this threshold.

Once you understand yourself to be *all that is*, and no other thing yet not-thing simultaneously, lower and higher in the Now, then you leap forward and begin an entirely new game which is to hasten the development of perfected form.

Once the illusion is pierced and the new soul's wisdom game is understood, the only thing that makes sense is to base all fresh actions upon the Law of Karma, deliberately increasing kindness in the world and decreasing human suffering.

Not only does that help the Other (i.e., the "not-you" who is really you), but it sets in motion threads of energy that will reverberate as luck and grace for you into follow-up lives. Through right action and good living, you will be helping yourself get luckier. Your future lives will be easier and more pleasant. It will become a win-win soul's wisdom game for you and for the world (the same thing).

The name for this intangible benefit is MERIT; the word for this conscious effort to increase your luck by good action is WISDOM; the means for accruing merit is SERVICE.

Merit is the accrual of karmic credit. It is gained through the alleviation of others' suffering (kindness, service).

Merit can be gained unconsciously, simply by doing the right thing (i.e., acts of kindness). Or it can be accrued consciously by the constant effort to behave in ways that benefit as many as possible (humanity) in as powerful a manner as do-able (service). The latter is a core pillar of Buddhist philosophy. To design one's creative potential to serve the One Self selflessly and powerfully is considered *right action*. It is a tenet of enlightenment, or wisdom.

In reaching The Fourth Worldview, all motivation changes, as do all values. The draw is no longer for personal gain, nor even for societal uplift, but simply for the benefit of the transformation of matter into its enlightened form (The Quickening). One *serves.* It is the only remaining purpose. It can be called motivation, for even *Boddhisattva*s are called into being by the desire of the universe to help itself expand, evolve, and transcend the suffering of karma. Action at this Worldview simply results in merit as the by-product of the eternally-preferred enlightened viewpoint. You realize a completely new value system.

But from a contemporary viewpoint of The Second or Third Worldview, it's not necessary to think of merit in terms of gain and loss, sin and heaven, luck and misfortune, and things like that. Think instead like a game player! Think like a virtual player.

Humanity wins life's game by ennobling itself and by overcoming the limitations of karma. So think in terms of storing up good luck for yourself **for one of your future lives**. The wise game player knows that future lives loom; at such point, especially when the going gets rough, *Future-You* will want all the positive karma available…all the good luck, talent, blessings, and windfalls in your bag of tricks when you get into a pickle.

When the small self – the player on the chess board – is going through a life experience, it's usually an old karmic thread set in motion before you were particularly enlightened (conscious), and which now has to be confronted, rebalanced and resolved. As a soul's wisdom game player who's facing challenge, Future-You needs insurance and aid, and a "good birth". And as an individual (a "fragment") creating new karma, you want to remember to assist your future self who will be facing new challenges based upon the karma that is being created in each moment right now.

So, keep in mind the real meaning of what merit is. It is a gathering to yourself of the universe's good will.

How is that done? First, you begin to create actions that benefit all of humanity. Why? Well, because that other part of yourself is "out there"; that other part of yourself is other people who can be benefited. (This is known as brotherhood.) And it is also your future self that can be benefited. It is what the Brotherhood of Light Workers means in teaching us that *"People are the whole point".*

Despite having received such messages for a decade, the one entitled "People Are the Whole Point" was an epiphany. For me this was the first time I'd been given an insight into why the channeling process was happening, what the point of it was, and the larger context.

Spirit basically needs to talk to itself. Self-discovery can only occur in the process of <u>exchange</u>.

The only way that Spirit can gain awareness of itself is by separating oneness into two-ness (other-ness), thus immediately creating that which can reflect, or provide contrast to, itself.

So once the one light – God – creates out of itself the contrast or reflection – the Other – then the world is formed. Subsequently, the world can be named or defined, and structured. And even so, the world (or Nature) needs to evolve and labor until it reaches the Worldview at which *It* can know this; it must grow until it can understand the dynamic behind its own creation, the purpose in the mind of God.

And here we are! People!!

Pluto contacting the Galactic Center. Humanity's awakening to the reason behind the soul's wisdom game, and the point of it all. It's so that spirit can, through contrast, know itself.

Now we can really begin to understand that we are spirit, and that we are one, playing this eternal soul's wisdom game.

Now, when you build up enough of this action, when you keep helping your other self who's in a guise of other people (that is, who seems to be people not yourself, or people of a far distant future), what you're doing is actually benefiting yourself. You're deliberately engaging in activity to help the world so that you can accrue merit for Future-You, for your small self that's going to be the soul's wisdom game player (actor) on some chess board (theater of action) in a future life. Your effort becomes to amass sufficient positive action, sufficient activity benefiting all of mankind in all periods of time, so as to reduce current suffering and assure local luck. And your realization is that you are actually benefiting yourself in doing so.

So, we can call this conscious effort, or intention to benefit all of humanity whenever and wherever, by the phrase *enlightened selfishness*. And what self is being served? Well, it's no longer just the small self, just the personal identity. Although it's Future-You who will ultimately have the good luck, *this enlightened form of selfishness is actually serving the self that is the whole world* because, ideally, by the time you've reached The Fourth Worldview, Future-You will be an expanded type of new human who sees him/herself as the entire universe.

Ensuring good luck to its future incarnation, the soul thereby deliberately undertakes *as its passion* the concept of service. It is also called The Will to Good. The entire life is then dedicated to this enlightened selfishness in order for one's own future round on the wheel of existence to be made more comfortable, more satisfactory, easier and more blessed (which, after all, is what luck is) but at the same time, ensuring that the quotient of this delight is increased for all of mankind.

So, if nothing else is learned, at least the concept of enlightened selfishness is hereby clarified: benefiting all of humanity is *the best possible move* that can be undertaken while participating in life. The soul spends all creative energy in passionate service to reduce suffering on the planet and thereby accrue merit for its own future incarnations.

At The Fourth Worldview, an advanced level of wisdom has been attained.

What does that entail regarding your everyday present life? Can such altruistic actions help YOU in the moment? You bet! The more the activity of world service is undertaken, the more it spills over, collects and gathers, and by nature brims up to the top until it pours over into the current life. You become luckier on a day-to-day basis. You could call it instant positive karma.

When John Lennon wrote "instant karma's gonna get ya," he didn't define whether it was positive or negative instant karma. When your karmic bank account has become so engorged, the positive karmic rewards can begin to pay dividends right here and right now. You don't have to wait for a "future" you.* The more your life becomes all about humanity and less about the ego's needs, then the entire life transforms

---

* There's no such thing as Time anyhow.

into a glowing purpose, and that pure enlightened purpose radiates a golden light outward to mankind and returns again and again to you in the here and now in the form of more love and more delight.

So merit not only serves to benefit your "future" self and all the rest of mankind, but blesses you today.

Let's consider the parameters of reaching such an ultimate phase in the wisdom journey. Let's ponder the difference between *me* and *others*, and ask how I can live my life with better understanding of the Wisdom Game.

The wisdom warrior keeps the heart open to its other selves, but observes their choices and karmic predicaments. Others' choices are seen as necessary to their growth but often painful as lessons. Therefore, every reasonable effort is made to reduce others' suffering but not become entangled in their karma. The wisdom warrior constantly reviews her/his own thoughts and attendant emotions to improve their positivity quotient, and to remain in a peaceful centeredness within his/her own karmic dilemma. Better and better choices are always attempted, following the highest values that can be understood at the current stage of psychological and spiritual development. For example, while endeavoring to present concepts from the most elevated point of view, I find that I can only write in the voice of my current stage of development, i.e., a Third WorldView perspective. As was averred from the beginning, it's a reporter's viewpoint, not a master's. The mastery viewpoint is that of the Brotherhood of Light Workers (the source of these wisdom teachings, a.k.a. my HIGHEST capping points on The Continuum).

> *Do not let the behavior of others destroy your inner peace. – Attributed to the Dalai Lama, on Facebook*

This inner control forms ever-greater expressions of empowerment. As improvement is made in remaining calm and centered, with the heart open and the mind expanded, an alignment takes place naturally whereby the wisdom warrior is ever-more attuned to the higher voice of the universe… the intuition. A comfortable surrender to its urgings is happily enjoined, and the new self listens and follows its guidance in making ever-fresh choices of action. Actions become more creative as fits the current personality, and support for their results flows ever more easily. All the while, the awakened mind, heedful of its "future" ledger, seeks to build merit on its karmic balance sheet.

The wisdom warrior becomes a self full of grace, kinder to all, happier from moment to moment, more empowered and creative, and serene in the knowledge that luck is building in "future" lifetimes even as society is helped right here and now.

Re-cap: Transcending Karma & Playing the Game

In fact, there is no true way to sidestep your karmic predicament. It adheres because it is an essential and integral part of life, of playing the wisdom game.

The true secret is to not struggle with it, not define yourself by it, and not identify your life with your predicament. How is this done? It is done in the mind. It is done by transcending the lower self, by recognizing when you are in the mode of thought-production that is generated by karmic predicament, and instead switch gears and move out of such thoughts and into thoughts that are generated by joyful, passionate desires. Or, by releasing some thoughts altogether and dwelling longer and longer in the peaceful place between the mind's chatter, in the place of just being, just experiencing, just letting the moment be all that is needed while you are stopping to smell the roses. The moment of total serenity. (Here we find that original image of the wise man in meditation.)

This transcendence of the karmic dilemma allows space in your inner being, and in this space, choices can be made easily. Energy, intention and will can be refocused away from suffering and toward passion. Actions can be allowed to occur that do right for one's next life and for one's fellow man. A surrender can take place in which you allow the higher voice of intuition to steer the course of your activity...and all the while, the inner being focuses more and more on serenity and love, opening the heart wider, tuning the intuition more acutely, flowing into potentiality and simply making sure to avoid harming any other being.

This is the formula for winning the wisdom game and it's available to everyone starting at this instant.

At this point in the journey of being, you come to a profound realization: it is the utmost folly to harm another person, most especially, to torture. Since the self and the other are one, it becomes obvious that to curse someone or to harm someone is to do that action to yourself. In metaphysics, it said that the karma returns threefold to the person who sends it out to another. This makes sense because the energy path of the karma is a closed system. Any relationship like this is called *a monad* and it means that energy reflects or mirrors itself so that the path contains the positive and the negative, the equal polarity, and to do something to another is also to see, upon completion, the reverse effect…or be the recipient of that action, magnified.

Even more profound, you realign your view of humanity. For instance, you see all children as new beings who are the reincarnations of previous selves, and who therefore must be aided in this incarnation; you see the living embodiment of a time-line of selves, causing you to realize the mandate to remove as much of others' suffering as possible. You develop a new life strategy. As said, it's called compassion and merit.

We look at kids as children, just starting out, learning about the world. But children are really souls who have been *on the wheel* previously, and have garnered certain amounts of wisdom. The distinction between old souls and younger souls is found here, depending on how many turns were taken on the Wheel of existence, and how much wisdom was garnered in each.

This will be true for yourself, at whatever age you are now and however much wisdom you have accumulated and however much additional you will manage to do before you die. At some point, you will be a child again on the wheel in another era. As the threads of karma play out, your present actions will impact your "future" lives.

If we look at kids, then, as "jumpers" – in other words, game players who jump from lifetime to new lifetime – we can understand the value of packing as much good karma as possible into the occurrence of those "future" lives. We understand, then, that it's really beneficial to do the type of actions *now* that will increase our luck when we jump ahead. Put another way, gaining wisdom means we realize how important it is to store up merit to do the type of actions that benefit ourselves in our "future" incarnations and ensure that whatever struggles or difficulties we will then encounter, we will carry a wonderful suitcase full of good fortune into that life. Some cultures refer to this result as "a good birth".

The strategy for a wise soul's wisdom game player, then, is to live the current life in such a way that "future" luck is accrued and that this life not only produces creative joy, but that such creativity is based on action that will help the most amount of people, because that's the strategy that brings the most luck to the soul. It establishes that treasure called merit.

Therefore, jumping isn't about time travel, it's about gaining understanding of higher law, the cosmic law that is always at work regarding how your creative intention designs a life path in the most beneficial pattern, not only for today but for the far tomorrow.*

So, the next time you see a kid, look at that child with different eyes. See a soul remembering once again what it's like to be human; see a jumper who was previously here, in some other era, maybe in some other gender and certainly in another body, and see that soul returning, remembering; see that soul, even if it's someone else's kid,

---

*   Eastern masters have always made it a practice to live successive lifetimes of world service (maximum humanitarian kindness) partly in order to assure their reincarnated selves the most accumulated wisdom and the most success in their next missions. Tibetan Buddhists, in particular, search for the child who remembers and clearly reflects his next mission, and once found, test him on his merit. The Dalai Lama is an excellent example of such a "jumper".

as a piece of yourself. Try to benefit that soul, giving them as much aid as possible this time around and helping them as much as is do-able to learn the Wisdom Game for their "future" lives because playing the Wisdom game well and teaching it to others is your best insurance of a next life filled with peace and joy.

Are you an old soul, or a first-timer? What brought you to this material? Do certain things you are reading about resonate with you, and do you feel as though you already know some of these concepts?

Old souls can be described as those who are familiar with the wheel of existence, who have come around often enough in sequential lifetimes to be quite familiar with the pitfalls and the blessings of Earth experience. Old souls know the wheel of existence, they know how to access their own wisdom. They intuitively know what the end result of a choice will lead to. They can see where choice can end up before taking it, before setting the action in motion. They can fathom the potential and grasp the overview. The old soul is a sophisticated earthling, returning each time not only to complete all previous karma, but now to bring benefit to society and to the human race to finish the job well. There are some wonderful writings about the ages of the soul and some of these writings include channeled material*. Old souls usually don't seek fame, wealth or power (unless the task of service requires that). Old souls seek more wisdom, more merit, and just the chance again to *be.*

Self as Divine Creator

Our patterns already serve prototypes in the Matrix (Akasha). Our lives and sometimes our institutions are already dedicated to fulfilling those templates. The drama is destined to play itself out (and in fact, in the Matrix it already has!). We are not accidents of nature; we

---

* Recommended: The Michael material (various titles), by Chelsea Quinn Yarbro.

are experiments of life, fulfilling possibilities, serving the potential within the Universe to play this or that role, or express this or that possibility.

You were meant to be. You co-designed your personality and the general direction of your life. You undertook it in cooperation with the Elders who required that this be the next part of the unfoldment. You *are* the Elders, extruded into manifestation to fulfill a role on the world stage.

So just be! If handed choice, always choose the wisest way. Coax your pattern toward its highest expression, no matter the obstacle. Live free will as though it truly exists. It does, and it doesn't. Allow the great plan to work itself out through you.

Your intention drives the entire machine of creation. Your will is the activator of the drama.

The self recognizes that it is the propulsive mechanism: it is that which desires, that which chooses, that which guides energy, and that which creates itself as the actor on the stage, as the participant in the human existence.

Once in The M Field, the self realizes that it is the higher voice that, yes, does have an agenda, and that exists beyond the physical at the same moment it is completely entangled with the aspect of itself that is engaging in form.

And so you realize that The M Field is populated by consciousness, and that consciousness contains its own planned purpose, i.e., trajectory, and that The Now, suspended beyond time, beyond space, beyond matter, nevertheless has purpose and is utilizing creative potentiality in a fashion that assigns to it a goal.

The M Field, therefore, is no-thing, but it is not empty. In the fullness of eternal omnipotent creativity, yet there is still a goal. That goal is to know itself. That goal is the intention of perfection, or as is called in *The Great Invocation*, the Will-to-Good.

What is The Great Invocation? It is a world prayer given through channeling to the theosophist Alice Bailey by her wisdom guide over half a century ago, and was always intended to be disseminated for humanity's good. The Great Invocation is a mission statement for the universal plan (the divine design). You will notice that the unfoldment is not random or accidental; it is not a casual accident of natural evolution but **an Intention**. The intention is that the universe directs its efforts toward the Will-to-Good. In other words, all the experience of duality (of good and bad, high and low, dark and light) is moving in a certain direction, steered and guided by a higher will.

Despair is not part of this equation. Awakening is.

> *From the point of Light within the Mind of God*
> *Let light stream forth into the minds of men.*
> *Let light descend on Earth.*
>
> *From the point of Love within the heart of God*
> *Let love stream forth into the hearts of men.*
> *May The Coming One return to Earth.*
>
> *From the centre where the Will of God is known*
> *Let purpose guide the little wills of men --*
> *The purpose which the masters know and serve.*
>
> *From the centre which we call the race of men*
> *Let the Plan of Love and Light work out*
> *And may it seal the door where evil dwells.*
>
> *Let Light and Love and Power restore the Plan on Earth.*
>
> *OM   OM   OM*

Held within these words is the statement of intention in the universe, an intention to work with and within sentient form – humanity – to direct energy toward a completed task. This task is to steer the minds of humans away from the lower nature, or bestiality, and toward the divine nature or spiritual perfection.*

The Great Invocation is a testament to that which exists once The M Field is reached, and true channelers are a testament to the conduction of this intention from The M Field into the physical realm. The channeler is the physical embodiment of a linkage that allows higher intention to be forwarded and translated into the material world from a place that is beyond it and from a consciousness that has not yet been named or defined by science, but exists nevertheless clearly as the propelling mandate or great intention of the Universe's most evolved selves (that is, of the Elders, or even God).

This work is an example of such an intended mission, or accomplishment, and as its author, I can vouch for **the guided nature** of the effort and the specific instructions along the way (as can all true channelers).

In considering these Worldviews of understanding, The M Field, then, is quite the interesting destination.

The new day dawns: We wake up. We realize that we're not lost in illusion. We come to see what the illusion is, who is participating in it, how it's structured, and what has brought the illusion into being. The dreamer sees the dream.

Realms are merging. Light is entering a dim place. We are remembering. We are waking up to that which we truly are.

From the outset: At first the soul's wisdom game might have felt lousy.

---

*   The spirit-infused beast is called A SOUL; its symbol is the 6-pointed Star of David; its switchover point is shown by the Tarot card Strength in which the higher nature tames the lower.

Challenges abounded. Creation had taken a dark turn. But then we learned that we have the tools and wisdom to change it. We began gaining more emotional control, mastering thought-production, and finding more inner peace. We began learning (from quantum physics) not to be fooled by the illusion, not to split things in our minds. We started learning that we don't have to swing from high to low; we don't have to buy into false notions of who is creating our dilemmas. Now we are seeing who we truly are, and who the creator is. The whole notion of self is being changed, and so is the concept of time and space.

When we talk about The World, God, You, Me... what are we talking about?! We are beginning to see it all differently.

Spirit knows that it has chosen to squeeze itself into form, with the concomitant loss and inevitable errors, in order to gain wisdom, especially the particular wisdom of love. It has taken an eons'-long plan to begin to overcome karma and awaken to the new soul's wisdom game of **Perfecting Form: Spirit Playing Human Through The Cosmic Dialogue.**

THIS IS THE ULTIMATE REALIZATION: THE "YOU" DOESN'T EXIST

One path to the awakening is through science and mathematics. Science has arrived at the point of examining consciousness itself and perceiving the fundamental makeup of physicality. Far beyond the atom, far beyond the electron, beyond quantum particles/waves, and moving toward string theory, we are gaining the understanding that everything's made up of minute bits of vibrating energy in structures that are beyond three-dimensional reality and are in fact revealed as infinite multitudinous universes. Our mathematics is showing that we are nothing other than the universe playing with limitless energy that uses avenues to transmute itself from energy (or light) into creation (or form), and vice versa, and that **there is nothing else happening other than**

aware energy (also called spirit) playing with its creative potential. Science has named this energy field The Unified Field Theory, Morphic Resonance Field, The Source Field, The Implicate Order, and so forth whereas metaphysics has always named it Limitless Light, Ocean of Oneness, Nirvana,,Ain Soph, etc. By any name, it exists, but it can't be discerned from within form or strictly through intellect. Mind must encounter, and then pass through, an interdimensional portal. Mind alone can do this; only consciousness awareness can take the next step. Spirit connecting to its own divine source, its ineffable nature, is the path.

Merely getting to these concepts in science and math has forced the human mind to conceive reality differently.

Next, philosophy begins to recognize the actuality of The God Game. Our philosophers are grasping that, if by examining how consciousness is built moment to moment – how, in fact, the very witnessing of the process affects its outcome – then revelation is reached that maxims such as "Mind is the builder" or "All is choice" are factual statements. Nothing else is happening. And by dint of quantum physics' existence the human mind must shift again to accommodate a fresh awareness: that **consciousness is creating reality.**

Furthermore, channelers such as myself are receiving **teachings telling us to perceive in this fashion.**

And lastly, computer gamers, having created with a free hand every other possible fantasy, are realizing that the ultimate fantasy is creating worlds from scratch; in so doing, every choice made creates a set of laws, or rules, for that particular world's existence that must then be taken into account in all subsequent behaviors and conditions for that world and its creatures. And so gamers (a special breed of humans who can be called, in tribute to Disney, "imagineers") are coming to realize that the mind creates worlds – fantastical or real – and that **the human mind, then, is the maker of the world. And the source of the game.** The gamer sees him/herself playing the equivalent of God's Game.

The soul's wisdom game itself is being revealed to us. We're waking up to the idea that this soul's wisdom game is what all of reality is about. We're waking up to "the only dance there is." We're seeing through the veil of illusion.

Our first glimpse is just to see our true selves. In so doing, we're investigating psychic phenomena and are in fact enthralled with it in the media: Connections to the deceased. The talent of the paranormal or extra-sensory perception. Lucid dreaming. Remote viewing. And all manner of phenomena that could be called metaphysical (beyond-physical). Just as we're learning true distinctions between human beings and God – insights gotten, for instance, by gamers playing God, or between the virtual world versus the real world, or about the realm that exists beyond the three-dimensional that can now be penetrated – we're literally **reshaping our brains** at an exponential clip.

And one thing that we're discovering is that hell isn't elsewhere in an afterlife. If your connection to your own higher self is severed or was never established, you may very well be in hell right here in your own physical body. If that's what you create and that's what you allow, you may be in a hell of your emotion, or related to your health, or vis-à-vis relationships with others, or with dissatisfaction, or with extreme conditions, and all of these hellish experiences can be ameliorated by this new viewpoint because as surely as hell is not in the afterlife, neither is heaven.

True, non-form is blissful, but heaven on earth is reachable and doable. It takes work; it takes awakening. But this is what we are striving for. And interestingly enough, this is what our higher guides seem to be pushing us toward: **the purpose of life is the perfection of the physical in order to see the kingdom of heaven on earth, to realize the "divinization of the universe,"** which can only be done by the application of conscious awareness onto nature.

Nature alone can create incredible beauty or incredible horror, but nature can go on for millennia, never perfected until sentient consciousness is inserted and begins to interact with nature, to develop itself, to grow, shift, change, transform itself and the natural world. Until it reaches the point of awareness of what's happening... the mastery of the soul's wisdom game. At that point, at that moment of awakening (which we are now entering), then and only then does the opportunity truly arise to begin the process – also called *the quickening of the earth*. This is the perfection of form, and thus the perfection of the world, or the universe.

Some mutated humans are already primed to explore it.

The new type of human is already being born on the planet. Some children, especially those born after the late 1970s, represent a higher state of human evolution. This new race, called the Fifth Root Race, will have the main characteristic of being more permeable, and not as solid. It doesn't mean that the individual will blink in and out of form, but that their consciousness will be more able to perceive other realms and to flow between the world of solid matter (the "real" world, 3-D consensus reality), as well as to The M Field, the metaphysical realm where the holographic nature of the illusion is much more apparent.

These children are called indigo children because their auras are seen as having that color more apparent than others. These children have been profiled in some shows based upon psychic kids. These children have natural gifts of being able to perceive the discarnate and to converse sometimes with them. These children may also be natural healers, able to perceive auras and energy fields, and be born with other characteristics that have hitherto been called paranormal.

In fact, there is nothing paranormal about being able to journey easily through The M Field and back into the illusion at will. It is the gift and talent of the advanced soul and it is a benefit to humanity to have individuals beginning to incarnate with this ability. It is the Fifth Root Race, out of seven, that is coming into existence in the new Earth, and this is the newly emerging human. They are accelerated people, with different brain skills and a new relationship between solid form and moving energies.

Recognition of the New Human Within

Once the self begins to work within the new paradigm, it is as though the world shifts. It is as though reality changes. It is as though power and leverage to create is handed to the inner awareness.

This is a gift that can be light or dark as you choose, but nevertheless, is the gift of creation.

As we understand the new paradigm deeply, shifts begin to

> **GATE/WORLDVIEW: 4**
>
> **RESULT: Bliss. Heaven...again!**
>
> **GETTING FROM HERE TO THERE: From loving brotherhood to oneness/no thing/All/God.** You are God. Only thought exists, playing an eternal game. Duality is an illusion. Life and death are your play. You're not you... you're one. There's no such thing as you or me.

take place in the production of thoughts, and in the quality and content of these thoughts. Shifts take place immediately and speed up each time there is validation between the inner creation and the outer result.

The shift represents a complete alteration, not only within each individual's mind, recognizing new powers, but also as a shift within the entire race. A new race develops, built upon the recognition of the ability to manifest intention, and the comprehension of singularity.

There is where all true gurus, light beings, and avatars reside. *There* is the "far end" of the Continuum. When *you* reach *there*, the soul's wisdom game of illusion and duality is no longer needed, and can't even be sustained. The transcendent plane – the plane of existence-without-form – is all that is. In a transcendent flash of understanding, you just cease to be, instantly knowing that All remains. You-Me-God-It just is. No form, just awareness. Eternally. Reawakened. Remembering. Ah, what bliss! To be God again...

And, from this state of timelessness and formlessness comes an urge, a cosmic urge to start the creation all over again, spiraling ever higher. As soon as formless unity is reached, a new universe beckons to be recreated. (Well, there's nothing else to do... it's "the only dance there is", endlessly.) So, consciousness (God) resumes "the game".

At present, still in its experimental form, humanity is not perfectly evolved. Thus this new power will be reflective of both good and bad within the species. Power is always a dicey prospect, but the race cannot evolve further as corporeal entities unless it is allowed the chance to play powerfully within the illusion, to create all kinds of mischief as well as all types of beauty.

Those of us who begin to play in the fields of the divine will need to put our values to the test to see what outcomes result. Sometimes even from the best of intentions, struggle is the way of the world and it is why spirit chooses to play the wisdom game.

As in a game, the Wheel (cycles upon cycles) re-emerges, and perhaps a silent buzzer goes off (buzzzz!!), trumpeting the mandate: *Create new universe... now!* And time-space begins anew.

Four Wisdom Exercises for the Fourth Worldview

Here are some exercises to relocate your identity in a greatly expanded viewpoint, then toy with the concept of being godlike – full of light, love and wisdom.

1. Using stillness and new understanding, discover the place within your simple awareness of being where your deepest nature resides. That's where there is nothing other than awareness and, of course, the breath. All external

FOUR WISDOM EXERCISES FOR WORLDVIEW 4

1. Find the Now. Be in it. Just be.

2. Consider your obliteration. The end of you. Your death. Then consider cycles.

3. Strategize a Future You (Mission, skills, karma)

4. Do an expansive meditation – the whole universe, all of time, even more!

stimuli from the five senses are part of this state, which is located only in your mind. Stay in this understanding, this moment, this pure state of consciousness... how long can you remain there?

2. While reducing your awareness to this simple single point, let go of personal identity. You are no longer you; you are merely the intake and outtake of breath. Now obliterated, ponder the end of you. Ponder your death, your crossing-over, your exit from the hologram. Ponder eternity. Then, remember the ripples! Now ponder cycles and closed systems. What goes around, comes around! Who comes around? If it's not you, who is it?

3. The Future You who will be returning will have needs – a task, a passion, some skills, and some baggage. What would you – as a new entity – like to accomplish in earthly form next time? What tools can you bring along? What skills have you learned? What wisdom? What might you need to expiate? Plan your fantasy with a rich budget and a creative mind!

4. Meditate upon your most expanded presence. First, visualize yourself being filled with golden light as emanating from your heart center. Next, radiate that light beyond your physical form, in an exact duplicate copy, until your entire physical form is but the size of a pimple on the arm of your vast light body. Next, expand your light body until the planet, then solar system, then galaxy, and then entire universe is but the size of a dot on your vast arm. Now, soar beyond form and beyond light, still with full awareness, until all energies are but dots on your mind, and until nothing else exists but Thought. This is You, outside of Time and before Creation. As soon as you are ready to condense back into your human form, genesis begins all over again.

###

Now you have seen the four Worldviews and beyond.

You know that you are You, talking to Yourself (for lack of anything better to do), making it up as you dance to the patterns, challenging yourself to grow into brilliant enlightenment, wisdom, and love.

You know that, of all there is to be and do in this world, only you can bring about significant change to your personal life and to the planet, for none of that is real but just a figment of your mind – a gorgeous and awesome dream.

You are standing on the crater's edge. You must decide and choose. There is an answer – a great answer.

You must take control. If circumstances are your karma, then so be it. So what! You must take control anyway. There is no one and nothing else. You must choose to fix life, and fix self, and fix the world in the way that is given to you. You *are* the All. Anything else is play, falsehood and foggy delusion.

We who are **you** are telling you to see your unity with us. Do not get lost in fear, but act as though you have our powers and our viewpoint. Embody the world as your personal self – full of doubts and entanglements – but stay clear in your alternate aspect even as you do so.

> Be gods playing.
> Be wisdom growing.
> Be the universe manifesting.
> Turn the tide of Earth's story.

Every eye that reads these words is graced. Every brain that grasps these thoughts is tasked with the responsibility to come awake. From now on, your words and senses will be held to this standard, that you are not a single weak, helpless soul cast alone on a dangerous globe, but that you are the mightiest force possible – God, the Creator, whispering to yourself, the higher/only mind, that miracles of joy and beauty are fully possible.

After A Musing, Another Vision

There must be a Lightbringer, one who carries a light and shines it into the darkness. Darkness must, and does, exist so that there is something to be illuminated. Perhaps it's the sacrifice-ee who shines the light upon the darkness. (Early January '06)

The following is a channeled message that came after these musings:

You are such. Not the light itself, for We are that. But the shiner of it. You must be placed into the dark, remain within it, and know it, for you to see how to illuminate it best, and where that's needed most. If you were placed into a well-lit self (an easy, fulfilled life), you would be too content to satisfy this important role.

Do not rail against that which is dark (i.e., hurts, pains you, gives dilemma and constant irritation). See it as necessary.

VISION

This came as another vision:

There are many Beings… all over/around the world. They are focused towards the center, building the world. They are **increasing** its darkness… until there'll be a flashpoint. It will be incendiary, intense. Then there'll be the release of much light.

Some people are kept aside, groomed for their key roles. These are the *hand* of the Being; the Being directs actions through these *hand(s)*. (1/4/06)

CONCLUSION

I hope the concepts I've presented here help you in your journey. Although my personal path may not fit yours, there are a myriad of paths to realization. Each is perfectly valid. There are many different metaphors to describe the journey to full consciousness and self-realization as long as that goal is ultimately reached. Valid paths might include spiritual practice, scientific investigation, and metaphysical interests. Each can produce breakthroughs and realizations. There is, however, a mystical divide (sometimes called an interdimensional portal) that the rational brain cannot cross but must be approached through the intuitive mind. Eventually, the journey to No-Self, Ego Dissolution, Presence, or any other such words to describe the state of expansive oneness, is a mystical journey. I hope I have been able to paint it and explain it as it was revealed to me.

I am not a Buddha. I am not a Lama. I am not an Avatar. I am not a Sage. I am not an advanced soul dwelling in bliss with all the answers; and I am not a fully-realized being.

Who I am is a fraction or fragment of higher beings; a piece of source material designed to be able to perceive expanded realities and come back and report what I have seen to other fragments experiencing life as I too am doing.*

The fragment that I am was extruded from Source and designed with a certain skill-set of abilities in order to perform the task of bridging the divide and writing about it. It has been part of my make-up that I can move easily between three-dimensional reality and The M Field

---

* Astrologers will see in my horoscopic patterns the following: Neptune, Poseidon, North Node conjunct in the 9th House; a well-aspected moon in Pisces in the 3rd house; and a Sagittarius ascendant conjunct the mid-heaven ruler.

(in other words, be mediumistic). This doesn't mean that I have all the answers or that I am anyone's guru. It does mean, however, that I have been tasked with a job and equipped for its completion.

This book, in other words, is a joint effort between the higher realm and the part of itself it has designed and formed specifically to carry out the task. There is no ego meant in this statement; all aware souls can come into the realization that their lives are a co-creative effort with the remaining parcel of their essence "on the other side". And whatever the task is, be it personal or global, that co-creation is perfectly designed to complete the universe's main occupation of knowing itself as fully as possible. The only real difference is that the older the soul (the more rounds on the wheel of existence), the more familiar the process feels, and the more the partnership can be tackled with awareness.

So that's "who" is writing this book. Now, who is reading it?

# # #

One day, I woke up from my nap thinking about the tarot card *Judgment*.

The Tarot cards, especially the latter several of the Major Arcana, are conveying concepts that are very hard to put into language. And, in fact, the Tarot deliberately uses symbolic imagery instead of language in order to speak directly to the human mind and its archetypes so that we may understand things visually and universally into our brains.

Judgment, I was realizing, is the stage in which we grasp exactly that point of existence explained by the Brotherhood in their message about *the border*. It is the very place or stage at which the separated self that calls itself *me* or *I* stops, and soon becomes, on the other side of the rim, the awareness of *I* as the entirety, or as the universe and no other.

This place of division is difficult to put into simple language. It's tough to explain because as an advanced step it requires a shift in consciousness that is radical. In other words, merely approaching it necessitates a new paradigm. It needs a complete change of mind.

For simplicity's sake, let's call it, a border. But we could also call it a gate or a portal. Let's conceive, for the contemporary mind, that we're in a science fiction story, and we're playing a role or a character – maybe we're Captain Kirk of *Star Trek* – and in the vast reaches of the universe (not even galaxy) we come upon this strange, shimmering anomaly. *(Wow, "anomaly" was a great word in* Star Trek! *Almost every script used it to explain some kind of mysterious encounter.)* Anyhow, so long as you are on this side of the anomaly, as long as you are safe in your spaceship, The Enterprise, and you are who you are – that is, Captain Kirk, or Mr. Spock, or some crew member – you are in this world. In other words, you are in the standard three-dimensional universe that we're used to. Though you are somewhere amongst the stars, it is still this world.

Now, as you get close to the anomaly your sense of yourself begins to get blurry and to expand. Soon, you find yourself in this very strange experience of growing less and less solid, or real – not just regarding your physical body, but also your identity or consciousness of who *you* are – and as *you* get closer to, and further into, this anomaly (portal, border), *you* are having more and more of a difficult time maintaining a sense of separateness or individuality.

However, rather than this being a scary experience, it becomes exciting and blissful as *you* begin to expand. The actual light in your mind and around you increases. And *you* know that if you keep going further, *you* will disappear completely. However, what lies waiting is so beautiful and desirable that *you* want and choose to continue into that expanded light. And so you decide to keep advancing.

It can also be said that, as *you* are dissolving and this light inside of you into which you are morphing grows increasingly brighter, *you* are also growing ever more aware of multiple other *you*'s, myriad other selves that are merging with who *you* are, so that not only is your identity blurring and dissolving but it is expanding and merging with all other identities that ever were or are.

Judgment represents the very last moment before *you* step fully through that portal. It is the definition of that very edge. Why is it called *Judgment*? Because in reaching that key point in the evolution of consciousness – which happens not only historically through eons of the race's evolution, but individually through the life story whenever this point of partition is reached by the individual self – the self recognizes and "gets it" as to how the life has been lived, what choices have been made, and how relationships with all other selves who are about to be seen as the One Identity have been handled or managed. It is the crossing point (line, boundary) at which this very understanding is made. Thinker and source meet along a continuum. Self and God are fluid. The dividing line is forever shifting. As to the question of where "I" end and God begins, it is answered there: the joining is on the fringe, where you can start to see your holy self.

Before we delve further, let's think again about the Life Review. You now see the Wisdom Game, the game of life – with its pains and joys, and its free-will choices leading to sweet or bitter results – as spirit playing with itself. Previously, we've been told by the Brotherhood of Light Workers: *"The birth is at the end."* That means that a life is usually not understood until it is over. Then, from a removed perspective, we can review it and see the lessons learned and the wisdom gained.

Now you have all the concepts you need to live well and successfully during your sojourn on Planet Earth.

Then, why are the times so tough? Why is life seemingly becoming harder? Why can't we all just thrive and prosper? Why isn't Earth on its way to becoming a paradise?

Because we don't grow when we're content; we make no rapid evolutionary progress when things are easy.

As a species, we need strife and pressure to change. Thus, the Higher Ones (the conscious fragments who have surpassed human existence, then developed into larger Beingness and accepted the mantle of service) are *designing* the times to be more challenging.

In fact, to be ever more challenging. The goal is one world and one people. Then, later, one self embodied as one planet. (And later still, one universe of matter that is fully awake and united.)

To get there, it's time for challenges. WE ARE DELIBERATELY CREATING TODAY'S CIRCUMSTANCES, BOXING OURSELVES INTO A CORNER CALLED DESPAIR AND FEAR, FROM WHICH THERE IS ONLY ONE VIABLE WAY OUT. It's through the heart, using the mind as the tool. This is the vision that has been shown.

Patience is okay when humankind has the luxury of a leisurely pace to evolve, when the planet isn't in crisis. But nowadays, I feel we don't have that luxury and must wake up during our lifetimes. In the long journey of human evolution, we have finally reached the place – technologically, globally, and prophesied – in which we, as a race, have the capability of making poor choices and annihilating ourselves and our home, planet Earth. We have reached this place after long eons in evolutionary terms through the development of the physical vehicle with its large brain capacity, in societal terms by the growth of complex interwoven corporate and governmental entanglements, and in scientific terms with advancements such as nuclear weapons and technology's impact on the environment and on the physical self.

It is as though a piece of clay had been molded, pulled and stretched until it reached a certain extreme, a state of greatest tension after which it could be maneuvered into something glorious, or ill-handled to become a misshapen mess. In this state of maximum tension, we and our consensus-reality can go either way.

And into this extreme state, we humans (and our spiritual handlers/ higher selves) have just added one more piece to the formula – a piece called conscious awakening. We are given, and are now realizing that it is not just in Greater, or another's, hands to determine reality's terms, but that we each control the outcome.

The urgency, then, is to speak to that which grabs hold of the wonderful human intelligence, and says to it, "Hey, you're at a threshold! Be very wise what step you take now. See two paths ahead, a path to the illumination of consciousness, or a path to the annihilation of Spaceship Earth and its passengers." And for the first time, the voice that speaks these words is identifying itself as our own higher wisdom – a message that is fully empowering. It is confirming that in none other but our thoughts, in our individual minds, resides the conductor or director of the outcome.

Just as in a movie thriller that has a "ticking clock", humanity is facing the most intense part of its drama in which light must be spread as quickly as possible to forestall the drastic destruction of the ecology and of civilization. And in fact, more so than ever we all are feeling this pressure through our economic and geo-political woes. It is the pressure to evolve quickly so that we do not destroy ourselves. And the ticking clock represents whether humanity can wake up in time, or whether forces of negativity will prevail.

There are different paths toward the spreading of light. Most of these paths are designed to further personal choice and self-realization and to establish ever greater connection between the lower and higher self, or the personal experience of the life and (each unique concept of) the divine. Whether through religion, scientific inquiry, metaphysics, or other, none are better or worse; all that counts is that the path take an individual closer to oneness and enlightenment.

Don't, therefore, live a wasted life. Weigh your opportunity to find your true inner being. Try your best to gain clarity and insight right here, right now! Birth your Self while still alive.

Well, I said I would wait to talk about *The World* card in the Tarot, as regards what is on the other side of the anomaly ("the border"). But really, that's the easy task because the Brotherhood's entire message – this book – is defining what the world is. (In fact, its working title was *Thought Is The World*)

To come back to our sci-fi story, let's return to Captain Kirk passing through that portal of Judgment, and about to dissolve. Here's what happens:

When Captain Kirk (who is still identifying himself as an individual and still calling himself Captain Kirk yet now knowing that he's going to completely dissolve and let go of the personal self if he takes one further step), finds himself at this juncture, he bravely (because he always faced challenges fearlessly) inwardly chooses to move ahead one tiny additional increment.

Thus, courageously he does so, instantly going beyond three-dimensions into a new place.

Here, on the other side of the border, we can no longer speak of him at all. The entity that was Captain Kirk is now vast, boundless, wholly energy and formless, fully illumined, completely aware (realized), and yet not gone. No longer alive in the sense that being alive requires inhabiting three-dimensionality, yet not dead in the sense that there is finality or ending of awareness. And so this new experience, this other side of the portal (which can be called Beyond) contains the pattern of Captain Kirk within its unlimited vibratory nature.

Consciousness realizes, *"Ha! I'm still here! Having crossed over into a few dead past lives, into a few of mine and a few of yours, and into the holy God-self, guess what? Nothing's happened. I'm still me."* For awhile (maybe just a few "minutes", or maybe an eternity), this pattern of conscious awareness hangs out, experiencing bliss and wisdom. But eventually, reconstitution is wanted.

What would be required, then, for the reconstitution of Captain Kirk to occur? For the Captain to reenter the world?

This Beyond, or Allness must desire it; Allness must want once more to reform such a pattern (i.e., individual), and reinsert it back into the physical world (three-dimensionality). Only then, on that basis, would Captain Kirk reappear.

And so, it is possible.

But if Captain Kirk reappears, he would necessarily do so with a changed brain, a mind that had truly gone "where few have gone before" (at least as humans), and then returned carrying all the awakened and lighted understanding from that place – or more accurately, from no-place. He would see, as he looked around at his spaceship and the characters in it (and, in fact, at the director and cameramen)... as he looked into the eyes of every other human being, he would see himself. He would see the maker behind all the scenery. He would see how the world is constructed and maintained. He would see Self as Other, and Self as World.

And having returned, carrying great wisdom and enormous light, he would find his heart totally expanded, cherishing every individual as just another aspect of Self, another piece of the chosen design. And from then on he would feel a great mission to bring all other selves into this new awareness, and to brighten and enlighten the universe.

Then consciousness understands, *"I became All. Allness looked at creation through the eyes of 'Jim' or 'Judi' [or YOUR NAME HERE]. (Each unique story at this point would differ, but in my case here's how it went:) Allness decided, it's best if 'Judi' gets back into 'Judi-ness', and tries to tell the whole story to the rest of Peopledom, to play with the possibility that that might hasten the development of New Human.*

That, Allness-as-Judi figures, is a good game-plan. And, from expansive no-one, Jim/Judi/You drops back into form.

So this is the tale and the map. The real secret is that the journey never ends. Life goes on... because it's "the only game in town". Life must keep traveling and playing. You will never cease to be. All – the mind of God, the principle of potentialized energy or aware spirit – can do nothing else than play its soul's wisdom game of duality with itself. You, an individualized self, can experience it accidentally or consciously – either way, it will occur.

I believe that my brief, sweet moment of ascension that I've tried to describe by this book was another such gift of understanding, as was the fortuitous Out-Of-Body-Experience that I was blessed with in my early 30s. Both of these were allowed (purposed, even) to teach that it's a possible and desirable path to pursue.

You can do the same. It's what you've come to do. This journey is yours to make.

Please do.

# # #

APPENDIX A

TECHNIQUES FOR THE QUANTUM SHIFT

Technique	Description
Observing	Detaching from the emotion long enough to explain to yourself its parameters. The mind can then watch the smaller self going through it's "pickle" from a different stance other than the "I" position.
Journaling	Writing down the nature of your predicament can give you space from the emotion.
Identifying Your Emotion	Looking at the thoughts surrounding an emotion to detach yourself in order to change the story you are telling yourself
Breathing	By maintaining a measured, deep breathing, you will slow your heartbeat, slow your brain, and naturally fall into better alignment.
Meditation	The space between thoughts in which you center your energy and can access the essential you, which is separate from your emotions and even your body.
Applying Humor	See the humor in human drama. Lighten it by laughing about it or seeing it as trivial, or not a big deal. A long-recognized remedy to negativity.
Establish a Place of Peace or Joy	Visualize a time or place, a memory, or even an imagined fantasy in which you place yourself into a framework of great enjoyment, pleasure and peace. Have that inner sanctuary built up during calm and peaceful times so that you can always return there during a time of crisis.

Technique	Description
Use of Patience	Understand that life unfolds at a tempo. The inner self when in a position of fear, anxiety, anger or upset often wants to speed up or resist the process while the Zen master simply allows the process to unfold, detaches from emotion and thus achieves oneness with the event.
Emotional Freedom Technique, The Work, The Option Process	Methods that promote an internal shift in emotional energy and thought formation.
"Hit the Pause Button"	Envision a "control+alt+delete" of the reactiveness. A reboot.
"Cancel, Cancel"	Say it and mean it after the unconscious creation of a negative conception.
Reframing	Tell yourself a different story about what has happened to you.
True, not blind, Faith	"What goes around comes around." Allow yourself to "Let go and Let God." Allow the Universe to return to you what you are (positively) sending forth.
Shift Into Love and Away from Fear	Shift from feelings of anxiety, separation, hurt or isolation into those of connectedness and union. The outer world will conform to this new vibration and approach you with better energy.
Control of Thought	While you're in a stream of negative thoughts emanating from an emotion, you can, at will, realize the process and make a conscious choice to shift from that series of thought into an entirely different one in which you present yourself with better options.

APPENDIX B

THE COSMIC PLAN

AN AGES-LONG GREAT PLAN

Whenever a universe comes into being, a Great Plan is inevitable. It's simple, really. It can be summarized thus: From energy, form must be created. Form must evolve (Nature) until sentient creatures arise. Sentient creatures must evolve to master nature and realize that they are self-aware. Self-aware sentience cannot help but learn the laws of creation. This takes eons, but a certain pattern is always followed: habitation, survival, dominion over nature, philosophical and scientific discovery, experimentation with desires and powers, and ultimate realization of the self-created game.

> *Physicists are made of atoms. A physicist is an attempt by an atom to understand itself." – on Facebook, attributed to Michio Kaku*

Since the Plan is eternal, "the only game in town", it can always be foreseen by those who become awakened. Here arises prophecy.

In our current universe, sentience came awake on planet Earth in the system of the star Sol. Earth's Great Plan was foreseen in age-old symbols that show up in many civilizations around the globe (e.g., spirals, pyramids, all-seeing eye).

The Great Plan consists of cycles as our planet rotates on its axis around the fixed stars, the rotation being called The Precession of the Equinoxes. Each full cycle of these precessions, which is called a Great Year, takes about 26,000 years to complete. Each zodiac division of these cycles is called a Great Month, or popularly an Age, each of which lasts about 2160 years. Earth's sentient awakening is taking place on the cusp of a new Age of these cycles – an Age called Aquarius. During this Age, the awakening is accelerating. Some features of this new Age are: equality of the sexes, seen especially in the rise of the Feminine; technological innovation, that will eventually annihilate space (wormholes) and then time (permeability); and group consciousness, especially as global mind and humanitarian efforts are fully developed. The advent of global mind has been facilitated by the worldwide web. (In order to get past the mess of so many different races and languages, cultures and all this separateness of the human race, it was required that we develop a mind-to-mind communication whereby we connect the planet together. The new generation of cell phone and internet users represents the human mind being receptive, through technology and through instantaneous communication around the globe, to this awakening, the nature of which is electric. The human mind, sped up and interconnected in this way, really represents the development of Intuition…a new level of reality. Minds working together toward the same realizations, even if they're approaching that through different concepts, become harmonious and synergistic.)

In history's slow development of conscious awareness, with its ponderous cycles of psychological and societal transformation, only now, on the cusp of The Age of Aquarius, can we fly through the inner adventure to gain realization of not just one new paradigm, but in short order, of many. That's because the moment is right for **The Great Awakening**, and to foster that, wise disembodied spiritual teachers have begun transmitting heretofore hidden understanding to approachable human minds at the same time many human minds have reached a receptive level of scientific and psychological readiness. The keys have been given by our guides, and the route lighted.

As the expansion of consciousness keeps growing, everybody's limited viewpoint is transcended. Certain places on Earth are destined to play important roles in the accelerated awakening. American and Israel are especially foreshadowed.* Like an invisible renaissance, this is occurring more than ever now. Astonishingly, when the hidden aspects of life's game are clarified, an even-greater secret is revealed. An æons'-long mystery is uncovered as a great drama comes clear, of an unfolding storyline of **personal as well as world darkness changing into light**, fitting into ancient prophecies and the strange symbols on the Great Seal of the United States. America, in its designation to play a prime role in humanity's evolution, is the nexus; other peoples and nations who have carried the prophetic clues forward over the ages, also have key roles to play in The Quickening.

Hidden Knowledge (The Occult)

The word occult means "hidden." For instance, there is an occult side of the moon that never gets turned toward Planet Earth. The word itself has been perverted and misunderstood, and should be restored to its rightful meaning. The secret teachings, passed down through the ages, were occulted or hidden because mankind was not ready to accept, incorporate and work with this type of teaching. (And there was greater purpose in that.)

Everything has changed now, however. Mysteries are coming to light, even through science. World philosophies and mystical teachings, such as Zen Buddhism, South American shamanism, African witch doctoring, Celtic paganism, Hebrew Kabala, and European freemasonry are being disseminated and shared.

---

* Fuller discourse of these concepts is treated in my articles in Dell Horoscope magazine over the last 12 years, available on my website, www.wisdompath.com.

This mingling of hidden awareness and scientific discovery is occurring in pockets upon the planets, but particularly in societies that are open for such inner exploration. It is a reflection of the effort to perfect a self-aware creature during the course of a Great Age, in our oncoming era called the Age of Aquarius.

(An example of such hidden messages coming now into light is the aforementioned Great Seal of the United States and its symbolic clues regarding America's destiny.)

Thus, what has been hidden or occulted for centuries, to be known only by the initiates or priesthood of arcane schools, is now available on Google and as a bestseller on Amazon or in your bookstores.

Look at the dollar bill! It says, *Novus Ordo Seclorum.* That means "new order of the ages". This phrase is part of the Great Seal of the United States of America.

It is a promise of a new way of organizing human society, a better way than now. It is echoed in the phrase "New Age", often bandied about when mentioning The Aquarian Age. The moniker has been misunderstood as a slogan that simply describes the hippie-dippy movement that was showcased in the 60s and maintained by mystic-minded or bohemian folk ever since. However, its true meaning is much deeper.

The New Order of the Ages is the key part of ancient prophecy, found in many cultures, as the time when perfected humanity begins to appear on Planet Earth. It is the time when many-ness is revealed as oneness (*"E Pluribus Unum* – out of many, one – featured in the Great Seal) and when human government is formed around that new ideal.

"The dharma shall move to the land of the red man when the iron bird flies in the sky." – Ancient Buddhist prophecy

In the end game of humanity's awakening into its oneness with God and with each other lies the key to powerful events on the contemporary world stage. From ancient Egypt, ancient Israel, ancient Rome, and ancient Britain (including the Celts), to the present, the story of a purposeful conclusion to a 4,000 year *Great Plan* is bared. Spanning at least two Ages of 2,160 years apiece (The Age of Aries, the Ram, and the Age of Pisces, the Fish), during which the concept of one God – a God of compassion – was established in Western Civilization, so was a great schism of ideology, or entrenchment of duality, lodged into society. "9-11" was its apogee. Now, on the cusp of a new Age – The Age of Aquarius – mankind, intensely polarized, is challenged to complete the Great Plan of humanity by realizing itself as the earthly reflection of that divine ideal, a compassionate angelic being.

How in heaven's name can that be accomplished when the world seems so polarized and distraught!?

It turns out that the road map to personal expansion and individual creative power (the realized self) is the very same path not only to a better society but to a New Human who realizes his or her godlike nature at the same time he or she passes easily into the paranormal and beyond physical death. The ancient fear of death is overcome. A grand puzzle of geo-political and socio-economic magnitude is uncovered, after which global enlightenment has been prophesied. The clash of cultures is seen in a wholly different light whereby the world is accordingly being reshaped through greater illumination. To this end, certain nations, especially America and its counterpart, Israel, and including but not limited to Africa, Central America, Native Americans, The European Union, the MidEast, India, China, and Tibet, have an essential role in an ancient cosmic drama propelling the attainment of spiritualized matter during a special era called The Age of Aquarius.

Greater possibilities await. A more peaceful soul and a more beneficent society are on the other side of the gate.

The American Ideal

Here's a secret: America is not just a nation; she was founded by a group of mystics– Freemason Rosicrucians – who created *an Intention* that held with higher principles that were formalized by an elaborate set of ritualized symbols that spell out the task. Yes, Benjamin Franklin, George Washington, Thomas Jefferson and many others were members of Masonic lodges, and some were even Past Grand Masters.

You have only to look at the Great Seal on any dollar bill. There are many odd graphics and several Latin phrases. These were included quite consciously by our Founding Fathers who wanted the United States to represent an ideal of human society and its governance. We have spoken of this several times already. The symbols intend might, as held powerfully (what is in the eagle's talons – olive branches and arrows), yet peace over might (which direction the eagle faces); a firm structuring of a new order of the ages for humanity (the pyramid) in which the many become one; and an expectation that Divine Providence must be engaged for the completion of the job (the floating eye). Furthermore, the Intention included the clear statement of faith that Divine Providence would make it so (*Annuit Coeptis*, which means "He hath prospered our undertaking").

No other nation has ever been founded in this fashion, by attuned and aligned metaphysicians, with such a mandate. It is powerful beyond belief (!), and means that, even when the country flounders and Americans fall into despair and division, a creative purpose has been set into the firmament that cannot be undone.

AMERICA, ISRAEL, ISLAM, RIGHT/LEFT, RED/BLUE – WHAT IN HEAVEN'S NAME IS GOING ON?

Even to address this very broad topic, it's necessary to understand that this is an era like no other.

Humanity is awakening... or said another way, the Earth is *quickening*. There has never been as much challenge to the entire planet and all its species, nor has there ever been as much opportunity for its dominant one – us – to tip the balance.

For the first time, man can observe an energy pattern (Pluto conjunct the Galactic Center) representing consciousness watching itself at play.[*] For the first time, we have gained the awareness that mind can build the "future" and change the script. For the first time, we can play the God Game.

As the Brotherhood has explained, in order for us to reach full awakening, we must come to the edge: on one side is the zenith of creative manifestation, and on the other, the abyss of self-destruction. Do we transform ourselves into beings of greater enlightenment (humanity's spiritual nature), or do we heed our negative impulses (the base animal nature that is driven by emotions and appetites)? Both positions can tap into power; either can prevail.

---

[*] The pattern is cyclical and has of course occurred previously; but has never before been seen through telescopes. In previous occurrences, the pattern was unknown to our conscious minds because Pluto had not yet been discovered.

And so, a stage has been set. An interior war is being waged. It's really about maintaining dualism ("us" versus "them") or letting go of separation and uniting mankind (all is *one*; brotherhood). The clashes between nations, or between partisans, are actually the effort humanity is waging to weigh its decision and choose the path of the "future".

In this drama, both America and Israel have been assigned special roles, as follows:

Every aspect of the undertaking was designed, all symbols included, with this singular purpose in mind. This is called *conscious creating*.

The stated ideal was to be a spiritual nation evolving under divine guidance (*Annuit Coeptis*) toward one-ness (*E Pluribus Unum*), allowing the many to become individually self-realized (liberty) until such time as enlightenment and unity were reached via God's help (the eye on the pyramid as the capstone, "In God We Trust"), thus ushering in the new order of the ages (*Novus Ordo Seclorum*).

Easy to say, difficult to do.

Put a bunch of people together from different lands, with varied belief systems and cultures, then spread them wide across a huge country with lots of different geography and demographics, and tell them to each do their thing. To pursue happiness and become individually self-realized. Talk about mish-mash and culture clash! Talk about interacting with *the Other!*

And yet, this is the ground where humanity, if it's ever to rejoin itself and understand its underlying unity, is to accomplish it. Here is the *consciously created* mandate for America's very existence.

Do you know that the reverse die of the Great Seal has never been cut? Only the obverse (front) has, in 1782. I believe that the incising will happen only when the real job is done! when Americans can in actuality reflect the Individual as truly joined with All Others.

To speak of the symbolism of the Great Seal and of America's destiny is also to include one further amazing detail, which is the pattern of stars seen over the head of the eagle on the obverse side of the Great Seal.

This pattern, when studied, reveals a hidden six-pointed star; in other words, the Star of David. That, obviously, is the symbol that represents Judaism, now embodied in the state of Israel. Putting aside politics or nationalism, however, and speaking strictly from a metaphysical point of view, well before the state of Israel existed the Founding Fathers had a specific purpose in including it in the Great Seal, which was to convey the true meaning of the symbol's design: the merging of spirit and humanity, or God and human joined as one. Such an ideal merger represents the epitome of perfected society and perfected self. It is, in fact, called The Great Work. "Israel" is comprised of three names of God: *Is* for Isis, the Egyptian name for God in its feminine manifestation; *Ra* for Sun, the source of all energy; and *El* for God in its masculine manifestation. A trinity. The Star of David was the time-immemorial symbol of perfected man, the emblem of absolute and universal synthesis. It is disguised (hidden, cloaked) but it is prominent as the starfield above the Eagle. The unity of man, and of man and spirit, is therefore incorporated into America's very mandate. Every time a dollar bill passes hands, *even terrorists' hands*, this proclamation is furthered. How cool is that?!

America then, in some sort of alliance with Israel, was to be the platform upon which the Great Work would be accomplished.

Why America? Why Israel? What is the nature or purpose of the alliance? And what does it have to do with "the new order of the ages"?

To answer this is to look at a large canvas of time during which life on Earth developed the capacity to know itself, govern itself well, and finally grasp the nature of its illusory game as well as its singularity within duality. That is to say, the era in which sentient life (us) finally reached comprehension of its essential oneness within its multitudes.

To pull off this large plan of the universe, eons were required to bring enough development into the species (enough evolution) so that brute matter would first be made sentient, and then become self-governed. And in the process, the lower nature would find full expression in the world, and eventually be refined by the procedure so as to gain enlightenment. This long, long journey required the development of society into different forms of government, including tyranny, and including the domination of the male or Yang forces of the left brain (i.e., the logical and reasoning mind in ascendance), but also required a shift at a certain turning point during which the female or Yin forces of the right brain (i.e., the intuitive mind) would return to the forefront as the species overcame its base desires, rebalanced its creative potential, and began to give power and weight to its refined, more enlightened potential. This new awareness, requiring egalitarian forms of government (democracy) and a belief system allowing self-realization (the pursuit of happiness), began to appear fitfully on the planet in various locales, but for our modern drama especially about 4000 years ago in the area of the world known as the Mid-East (often called "the navel of the world").

In order to provide a platform for such a long journey of development of both the species and the way it governs itself or lives out its life, it was necessary to bring into manifestation the types of social structures that would provide the underpinning for growth, and allow its realization even in the eras which were darkest, and in the geographic places which were most besieged by Yang domination. *"Power to the people"* would be the motto finally in the new age, called The Age of Aquarius. All tyranny, including that of Yang domination (patriarchy), would have to be overcome. Light and freedom would have to replace darkness and enslavement. Self-realization would have to prevail. The experiment of aware liberation would need free reign and an egalitarian cosmopolitan society.

The secret truth about America's and Israel's necessary spiritual alliance can be explained as follows: America is a land constituted primarily to provide the pursuit of full self-realization; Israel, to resist threats to chosen beliefs ("the Chosen People"*) while embodying

---

* Who is choosing? In the Wisdom Game, what does "chosen people" mean? Some individuals in each age are self-chosen to further the larger purpose, which is to bring clarity, awareness, and realization into human

democratic structure within surrounding anti-democratic mindsets. Besides their mundane economical and political linkage, both nations share a spiritual accord, and are integral parts of the larger purpose. America is the testing ground where *the Many become One*, and where individual points of consciousness are learning the truth of their unity. Israel is the place where democratic self-realization struggles to exist in a hostile (patriarchic) territory.

The war of terrorism is a clash then, not just between radical fundamentalist Islam and the free-wheeling West, but for the predominance of either the Yang force or the Yin. It is a battle for the soul of humanity. It is a metaphysical truism that Yang or male power (in other words, patriarchy) is in decline while Yin or feminine power is in ascendancy. These issues can't be separated; they are part of the same picture. The metaphysical student learns the truth of the symbols and begins to see what the real purpose is in the Great Intention behind the founding of the United States of America in its inseparable alliance with Israel.

For America, the resolution of bringing the Many into Oneness is an interesting experiment and a massive challenge. Will it ever really happen? Not so long as partisan politics, racial bigotry, or religious intolerance reign. Not until a true uniting *under God* is accomplished. For this pinnacle to be reached (the capstone of the pyramid), we'll really need the Higher's help! This outcome is no less than the direction of how the entire human race chooses to evolve.

---

minds, and further the attainment of perfected humanity. While often unconscious of their subtle (soul) purpose in electing such an incarnation, this type of life – even if a clouded, self-sacrificing, or inert one – fulfills a role that meets the requirements of a larger design for humanity's development. *All Is Chosen.* But "soul choice" is not the same as "personality choice", and should be comprehended differently.

We will once again see the human being as part of nature and vice versa, yet not through superstition and fear-based awe of deities, but because quantum physics is unveiling the underlying truth of reality. Science is confirming that all is one, and is nothing but energy (spirit).

It would mean that the whole biblical epic, from Israel's enslavement in ancient Egypt, to the foundation of its modern nation, and the battle now being waged in its midst for the soul of mankind, was a long thread (The Mayan Long Count?) of planned design. There are many books that speak of the connection of America and Israel, and of the long, long storyline* that will culminate with the highly planned event, variously called "the New Age, the Second Coming, the Fourth Dimension, the Tribulation, the Rapture, the Axis Shift, the Golden Age, the Age of Aquarius, the Sixth World, Armageddon, the Photon Belt, the Age of Light, and the Christing of Earth", to name a few.*

Look to these nations as archetypes for the entire future game plan of the human race: the enactment of The Third Worldview.

Patriarchy, The MidEast, and The Goddess Rising (or, What Role Women Will Play in the New Age

Patriarchy and its built-in resistance to personal choice and self-realization is a great factor on the world stage. It is a leftover from the Ages of Aries (aggressive male, or Yang, domination) and Pisces (suffering, victimhood). It represents a form of human governance that is antithetical to the development of the individual ego because it

---

* Begun in 745 B.C. with the first captivity of Israel. *The Great Seal of the United States: Its History, Symbolism and Message for the New Age,* by Paul Foster Case. Builders of the Adytum, 1935.

* *The Peacemaker and the Key of Life,* by William Henry. Earthpulse Press, 1997. Highly recommended reading!

promotes the authoritarian model. It was a form that contained benefits and was needed for a while on the world stage, but is now outmoded.

Patriarchy can exist as a political model, but also as a religious model. In eras such as today's in which there are alternatives to this model and in which knowledge has grown sufficiently through the global internet and through the spread of learning, people see clearly that there is choice to be had in what lifestyle to adopt. The model that will allow greater light to pervade, and will allow ever greater personal choice to be optioned, is now the more desirable.

But in today's world, there are still powerful factors that cling to authoritarian rule and resist this burgeoning path. These include dictators, authoritarian father-figures within the family, overemphasis on tradition and rigid rules, and states or religions which rely heavily on conservative orthodoxy.

In The Mid-East, democratic influences are struggling very obviously with their opposite in this area of the world. Fundamentalist Islamic paths – a highly patriarchal structuring – are threatened by this urge in egalitarian enclaves. Most notable of the states that threaten the patriarchic model (although also containing the dilemma of duality within their very ramparts) are Israel and now Iraq.

Israel, when studied astrologically, reveals an interesting fact: it has been birthed as an entity in order to resist extremely powerful threats. It has come into being as a state to serve the very template of a foothold, that is, an endangered pocket of self-rule within an area beset by hostile patriarchal forces. Israel will prevail so long as it serves the divine template in this respect.

The ascendancy of feminine energy (Yin) is being, or will soon be, seen around the globe. But, particularly it has become obvious and powerful in the nation that has been founded for the chief purpose of allowing self-realization: America.

Women, in turn entrepreneurial, and in following their personal passions and individual skill-sets often in the service of practical need for their family, are becoming the spearhead of the forces that will shape the new age. The Dalai Lama has said, "The Western woman will save the world."

As mentioned earlier in Worldview Three, an ancient statue of a goddess, long bereft of her head, was recently reunited with it when one museum director on one side of the planet realized that a stone head might possibly belong to a headless torso in a different museum on another side of the planet. The fit was perfect. When the two parts were joined, they slipped together so quickly that the museum director got chills! This reunion is symbolically potent. Females will get their head back on, will become whole sooner than males, and will steer nations and probably then the planet towards the desired target, which, to reiterate, is the perfection of the human being, the reunion of spiritual consciousness with physical existence.

There is no doubt that women will carry the power, and will do so in the two lands that are most featured in the 4000-year plan; America and Israel. Look to these nations as archetypes for the entire future game plan of the human race: the enactment of Worldview Three.

Astrology: The Interconnected Cosmic Web of Quantum Probabilities

Astrology is the quasi-science of mapping and interpreting the presented energy blueprints. It has been built by empirical observation for thousands of years and proven itself accurate time and again for the savvy navigation of "vectors of available energy".*

Astrology studies the relationships between energy patterns, and also reveals karmic Personal Energy Patterns (in other words, ongoing options and original energy choices).

---

*   The Michael material, by Chelsea Quinn Yarbro.

Astrology was the province of an elite few throughout history. Only nobility or the priesthood could afford its intensive calculations, or would be considered worthy enough of the special guidance it offers. Most courts had astrologers in service to the highest office, and astrology was intertwined with the study of the stars that evolved into astronomy.

Far from being fortunetelling, astrology allows its experts to gain insight into the soul's karmic choices, to draw conclusions about the soul's previous journeys on earth ("past" lives), and when and even how that soul can encounter upcoming patterns that will require important decisions.

In the hands of a good practitioner, astrology becomes an excellent tool to help you plot a course through the tides of your life and to reach safe harbor again and again.

> *"The wise man defeats his planets."* – Paramahansa Yogananda quoting Sri Yukteswar, *Autobiography of a Yogi*

Patterns of energy constantly ebb and flow affecting our awareness and in fact becoming the very substance from which consciousness can create. They are generational patterns, and can also be called *karmic waves*.

In astrology, such patterns are seen in terms of the movements of the planets, but as we see from the quantum perspective, the planets themselves are simply vibrational constants around which we have focused energy. Studies are applied to interpret the combinations of these energy systems and to determine the nature of what can be, and most likely will be created, based upon these available templates.

From this point of view, one of the most potent of these waves of probability is that of the movement of the dwarf planet Pluto. It affects generations depending on the zodiac sign it has traveled through during the person's birth and upbringing, and also those signs that have similarly influenced their parents and grandparents, and therefore the entire culture. (Zodiac signs are simply templates of energy patterns; planets can be thought of as patterns of moving energies... "vectors".)

As an example, a recent generation was raised during Pluto's passage of the sign of Libra, a sign known to reflect attention to fashion, music and dance, beauty, and marriage or partnerships. The fashion industry is very powerful nowadays, celebrities go out of their way to demand expertise from the beauty industry, marriage is back in style, and the entertainment industry has monster hits with such things as "American Idol" (singing) or "Dancing with the Stars."

The generation previous to that was born with Pluto in Virgo, a work- and fitness-oriented sign; this was the yuppie generation. Furthermore, during a long period of this generation's birth and life-experience, Pluto conjuncted (aligned with) another major outer planet, Uranus, which astrologically relates to technology; and so the yuppies produced the "dot-com" phenomenon and made the internet a household phenomenon. *"We are the world"* doesn't mean simply a lot of people, a few billion people, sharing in harmony. It means something else entirely. It means that the world does not exist outside of the contribution of the aware mind. Outside of "aware mind" is nature (instinctual), growing, and also evolving. "We are the world", though – the idea of Global Mind being the world, and reflecting spirit (the divine) – is the primary and perhaps only path left for humanity to follow.

So Web-2 is an absolutely necessary stage in the evolution of consciousness. The creation of Global Mind required an entire generation – those born in the '60s with Pluto conjunct Uranus in Virgo (that is, the dot.commers) – to undertake a big mission. Their task was to create the basic technology and then to feel comfortable and enthusiastic about implementing it.

Today's youth, born into and raised in the internet sphere, have an ease of usage with technology as well as an urgent need to stay connected with each other through it, that has further evoked the cell phone culture, especially notable in Japan, a nation of "techies". Now, knitting, weaving, and threading us all together, and spurred by a growing aversion to war and a desire to unite, this generation is creating the platforms upon which experience of every type can be shared and tasted.

This desire is at the heart of YouTube, MySpace, ScreenVision, and all other such venues. It's been named the "noosphere" or layer generated by human thought*. It is, at basis, the establishment of lines of communication that allow Each to know Other's mind.

Later than each of these was the generation born with Pluto in Scorpio, the sign it rules, and in which it is therefore powerful. Among other things, Scorpio symbolizes death, sex, and the underbelly of society. And so such matters as terrorism, porn, the sex trade, and other human depravity had a field day, and AIDS was rampant. On the other hand, Pluto is quite the detective in Scorpio and we have had great breakthroughs in research on cancer and on the human genome, for example.

We are just beginning to see the generation born with Pluto in Sagittarius, which rules sports, philosophy, the great outdoors, and gambling or risk-taking, among other things. And so we know that, within the next twenty to thirty years, the upcoming generation will affect society by rejecting the pervasive darkness of their Scorpionic ancestors, instead looking for a lifestyle that reflects different and more free-wheeling values. The spiritual quest will become the rage.

Karmic waves, then, can refer to available generational energy patterns that each incarnating soul wishes to explore. There are, of course, patterns other than just Pluto's, some of which, like the mutual reception between Uranus in Pisces and Neptune in Aquarius, are beneficial, allowing an explosion of spirituality to be disseminated

---

*   Brian Swimme, *The Divinization of the Cosmos,* What Is Enlightenment magazine, Issue 34.

through the airwaves and internet. But some patterns will be filled with tension, such as the recent Saturn opposition Uranus, followed by Uranus opposition Saturn squared to Pluto. This language is the equivalent of forecasting with understanding that there will be a platform of potentiality and an arena of probability into which the human mind can, with awareness, begin to mirror and reflect struggle, and after which, to find creative resolution.

"May you be born in interesting times!" – Chinese curse

Angels, Spirit Guides – Who Are The Brotherhood?

Information that is sent or broadcasted from wisdom levels contains a quality.

It has nothing dark. Its purpose is not to serve just an individual self alone; its goal is to serve humanity; its message is to awaken. It never contains fear. Upon hearing its words or visions, the result is greater lightness, a lifting of spirit, an awakening of mind, a sense of comfort, and a feeling of love. If any such reception does not meet these criteria, then it is not coming from spirit guides or angels – from the angelic realm – but from the lower or base nature of the self. Perhaps from fears or greeds. Or even from your (deceased) neighbors!

The Brotherhood of Light Workers speaks through a singular voice, but is comprised of a group of formerly-alive people who have developed sufficient wisdom so that they no longer need to return to Earth. They speak sometimes with clear and profound information, and sometimes simply with poetic or awakening thoughts. Once in awhile, they just send a visual transmission (vision). They have shown me their former selves by displaying a montage of faces to my third eye, usually in the twilight state between waking and sleep. These faces are glimpsed in rapid succession, but clear enough to see their eyes and into the wisdom of experience that they all reflect. Some are old, some are young, they are of all races and every culture that has been on the planet, and they span the eons of human history.

Any such guide, even if named with a singular, often biblical name, is comprised of such groups of formerly-fragmentary spiritual essences that have aggregated back into a larger clump. This is The Brotherhood, and when I'm asked, "Is this the same as the White Brotherhood?", "Is this the same as Seth or Abraham, Michael or Emanuel?", I say, yes, because for all intents and purposes, all spiritual guidance is from the same realm.

Still, in the higher realm, there are layers too – or what are called hierarchies in metaphysics – and although all energy is one, there is not an immediate re-formation of spiritual energy back into the Godhead. Groupings, often called oversouls, remain. These are tasked with different goals, some to shed light, some to increase love, some to offer proof or validity of existence beyond the death of the physical body, some simply to explain the nature of reality. But, in fact, no human has ownership of any channeled voice. Channelers are just like radios or telephones. We are devices built for reception. Before incarnation, there was a completely cooperative effort between the spirit entities who wanted to broadcast, and the individual souls who said yes to being receivers. It is a collaborative endeavor.

In due time, many others will be able to receive in the same fashion that individual channelers do now. Guaranteed!

HELPING YOU GET FROM HERE TO THERE

The "I" can be deconstructed. The rules of the soul's wisdom game can be laid out, and the human experience demystified. By combining spirituality with mysticism in a powerful paranormal porridge, the ineffable vision of Me → You → All (the Continuum) can be explained, while the creative power of Vastness can be put under Reason's command. Empowered humans see life as co-creation, not victimhood, and learn to get out of their own way and just let the universe flow. As suffering thus eases and peace grows, the rate of positive change for the individual and for society increases. In such a society, people actually do become their brothers' keepers because they see others as themselves.

You are the Journey-er. When it is recognized that identity isn't a specific thing (i.e., contrasts such as high-low, inner-outer, you-me don't really exist), the soul's wisdom game shifts profoundly. Moreover, a radically fresh insight is reached – *Capping the Point of Awareness* – that reveals an ancient mystery through a new perception. This shining moment of illumination explains the true meaning of The Age of Aquarius while fully empowering the individual, which in turn means rescuing the world.

And, a Last Vision

A wonderful vision was given.

The American Eagle, facing to its right as always (on the Great Seal), was carrying in its beak the lamp of the *Hermit* tarot card. The lamp of the *Hermit* traditionally holds the Star of David within it, the entire archetype symbolizing elevated human awareness. The Eagle, on the other hand, is like the Phoenix symbol, a creature that's reborn out of its own ashes again and again to rise up into its divine glory. So it was a delightful image to receive.

Here's what I think the vision means:

America, now or ahead, is herein shown as being the Lightbearer or path-guider to the world. Whatever we as a nation shine forth that's lighted and spiritual will reveal a path upwards that others may follow. As of now, we may have a long way to go! But eventually, via media, via the modeling of right behavior, and through the noble way of shifting from war to diplomacy, we'll demonstrate to the rest of the world a more awakened way to live, a way to heal, and a way to evolve into greater enlightenment.

APPENDIX C

THE MESSAGES

SPIRITUAL GUIDANCE
FROM
THE BROTHERHOOD OF LIGHT WORKERS

THE NEW MESSAGES FROM THE BROTHERHOOD OF LIGHT WORKERS

The Brotherhood of Light Workers (my spirit guides) has a message for you—a new message. This message is coming through me from the Brotherhood of Light Workers to *you*!

Here's the message: Life, in all its glory and all its misery, is a game – a soul game – and it has rules. Energy is playing with possibility. Looking at things from a certain viewpoint, life is a very serious and entangling drama, presenting heavy challenges along with powerful passions. But looking at things from a different, fresh viewpoint, life is an interactive game that creatures are playing with their Creator in order to learn the intangible but all-important treasure called wisdom. Wisdom applied is life-mastery.

As with almost the entirety of my previous book, *Wisdom's Game*, this section's core material has "come through" silently but fully formed, with each passage having its own beginning, middle, and ending… and at no time utilizing any input from my conscious (lower) mind. Rather than cogitation (thinking through a concept and finding words to express it), the process of channeling is like taking dictation. The only editing I have done is to name each message, and to outline what I think its main points are. The rest is left in its pure form, as it was received.

WHAT IS CHANNELING?

Channeling is being receptive to messages usually from entities not on this physical plane, and who do not fully possess your mind, body or soul, but who use your capabilities as a transmission device. You can think of it as a sort of telephone: Channelers hear information coming from elsewhere, knowing that they are not the originators of this material, and simply capture it to pass along.

Channelers are intermediaries, but not in the way mediums are. A medium's job is to contact deceased loved ones merely to provide proofs of the reality of that person's continued existence even though he or she is no longer alive on the earth plane. What comes across might be words, information about things that were hidden, or just tidbits that prove they are who they say they are. In these glimpses we learn that the soul has not died in the way that the body has died, and that something continues which can appear to those who usually have the best or strongest connection to the deceased.

Channeling, on the other hand, usually isn't between souls who knew each other on the earth plane, but between the receptive individual and a stranger who is perceived as at a higher level, or whose quality of information and perspective reveals this higher vibration—a teacher or a guide rather than just a relative. They paint their location as at a bridge between the heavier and the finer layers of existence. Between the physical and non-physical, in a kind of nebulous realm which is neither matter nor energy. Of course, only consciousness (mind) can travel across this bridge. Matter can't.

Channeling is clear reception of information conveyed from another source; a source that never speaks of evil or of a dark agenda. This source never seeks to overtake the personality with its own negative demands.

The channeler, at least in my case, experiences the process as one of invitation, as one of stilling the mind, stopping the endless train of thoughts, putting the self to the side as though one were giving up one's seat on a subway train, moving over, and simply allowing. It is an act of courtesy, and the inner self attunes to that frequency that will allow the process to begin.

Channelers, by their very definition, are those who are in sync with, and become receiving stations for, the Greater (also known as Source). Such "voices", then, (telepathic, in fact) serve as the most benign guides, and the wisest mentors. The Source of true channeling is the graduate professors of the M Field. The channelers are their microphones and the target is you, the reader.

With the channeling moment, we are left with an *ah-ha!* because the quality and type of information is such that our perspective is shifted simply by hearing it, and there's no doubt the receivers (channelers) are being given information that is designed to do just that: change consciousness, awaken what we understand as going on in our lives, and rapidly reach a more global perspective on it.

What is the experience of channeling like? It's probably not what you think. In my case, I don't take on a new persona, participate in a ritual, have a voice shift, or in any way need to be handled differently than the norm. In my case, channeling is a quieting, a calming down, a reduction of sensory input. Nothing much about life changes except that I "step aside" inside self, and just allow a telepathic voice to bubble upwards. All that's required is that I "not be"… and just become a very concentrated listening device.

The key to channeling is in quieting thoughts. As in meditation, the daily mind must be stilled. Space – or emptiness – must be attained. The threads of thought must be broken, put to the side, let go of. A clear pathway must be opened, and a certainty held in the soul that only the most high will be invited. Then the stilled mind becomes receptive, and words flow. The Now is entered, and a Presence is felt.

Meanwhile, all the verbal abilities are called upon. Vocabulary is engaged. A joining is made between previous education and new concepts. The voice of the channeler is utilized (or, at times, the writing hand). A "message" is captured (on recorder, PC, or note pad). And then the inner speaker removes itself and the channeler is left to return gradually back into full regular awareness. While the entering journey is fairly swift, the returning passage can be odd and slow, full of fog until everyday consciousness is completely restored. Usually, that takes a minute or so.

Then, it's as though nothing out of the ordinary has happened.

I've spent quite a lot of time questioning the source of these "transmissions". I know they're not truly psychic because I'm not given details on anyone's deceased relatives and so forth. Nor are they emanating from "me" because I'm unable to perceive such a point of view on my own. (I'm not at the level of these teachings.) Nor are they "automatic writing" – a process in which the writing tool in the medium's hand is taken over by another force and begins inscribing the words.

Instead, it's like a kind of telepathic dictation. The messages are conveyed and just flow. It's my job, then, to capture them, as I have done here.

WHAT CAN YOU GET FROM THIS SECTION?

You are about to encounter the teaching entity whose messages have been channeled through me, which has given itself the name *The Brotherhood of Light Workers*. (This name itself is a pun on my husband's Union, The International Brotherhood of Electrical Workers, who, after all, provide us our lighting!) As you read its messages, you'll begin to feel comfortable with the whole idea of information being transmitted from elsewhere.

With little preamble, the Brotherhood's guidance starts examining the nature of thought itself. An entirely new viewpoint – more expansive than the one you are probably now in – gradually conveys you into new insights that view life from the soul's, not the personality's, perspective. In doing so, you gain realizations that let you reformat your notions of what life is truly about, how thoughts sculpt reality, and what the human experiment is from the point of view of the universe's plan. Most importantly, these messages show you your key role and your *absolutely essential* connection to a higher purpose in which you have chosen to participate.

These wisdom teachings shine a bright light on who you truly are while revealing the core answers to some of life's deepest mysteries. Throughout, the notion of paradox will often be presented. For example, two individuals with separate lives and varied karma will be explained as the expression of one energy system. Or, a person's crucial decision-making power, so important on The Second Worldview as the almost-miraculous free-will determinant of future reality, will be seen by The Fourth Worldview as non-existent. And, too, the world, with all its people, objects, and even celestial objects, will be shown as nothing other than thought, or awareness, not as *outside* you. Like a Zen koan, paradox blasts open the rigid rational mind, at which point the seemingly unresolvable contradiction gives way to illumination and intuitive realization.

These paradoxes are encountered because two opposite things can both be true depending on the perspective from which you see them. The simplest, most straightforward bits of common experience are simultaneously the most complex and challenging leaps of comprehension as long as the lens keeps changing and clarifying, and the mind keeps growing and evolving.

To begin to see oneness hidden in twoness (i.e., duality), to understand the simultaneous existence of free will *and* fate, to dissect the truth behind the concepts of "you" or "they", and "me", and to perceive the Maker's point of view as well as the actor's is to know the great challenge of something as seemingly easy and simple as the wisdom path…

THE VOICE OF SPIRIT COMES FORTH

If you were God...

You already are! You are the divine of the universe, the spark and thrust of solar fire, the material of creation, and the intelligence of its usage. There is no else, and there you are, in the plane of mind, as "we". No other, no else. Only God.

So here it is: in the mind's eye there are thoughts, and in these the spark of ideas and reactions to others' ideas which are the results of such: a world of beauty and of suffering.

In the plane of mind, you stand tall, expectant, and full of hope. Will wonder and joy be returned to you, or will a darker outcome appear? Your wonder holds confusion, for you do not know (in your bones!) that you are its full creator.

You will wake up...now!

***

ONE

★*★*★

THOUGHT IS YOUR TOOL*

There is but one thing to bring to your attention right now: it is the creation of the world of humans. This world is not the large bluish globe that sustains human life, but the inner world of mind.

In your struggles to understand God or the Divine, and to find paradise, you have sought to play with earthly forms, to occupy your thoughts with environmental or political issues, and to figure out

> *This world is not the large bluish globe that sustains human life, but the inner world of mind.... Thought is your tool to teach your mind of its powers*

what's best to build an ideal society upon. You have fought and argued over the "best" method, the most "correct" belief, and the perfect route to the "future". All well and good, for this is a *natural* outcome of man's brain. It is the chief tool you have to work with.

But you have not as much considered the nature of what mind builds. Mind builds the "future", and it reconciles the past. That is, if you want to develop a world of joy and not misery, or of peace and not war, mind must come to terms with what it creates as thought.

Thought is more than belief. Thought contains the potential of the new. Thought acts according to its beliefs but is not subject to these. Thought can veer away from a belief, leaving it behind to forge new ground.

The thought you have today... now... is the beginning of the new world. It will not depend upon your beliefs, which come from your old

---

* All titles to the messages are mine, whereas all the messages *per se* were completely received.

experience, but from your heart, which can draw vitality and newness from the greater will and higher realms.

Thought is your tool to teach your mind of its powers.

Take your thoughts to new places. Decide to do so. Decide to create a new personal world for yourself, and a new "future" for your world.

It is starting.

We shall talk again soon, and aim our words towards your innermost ear. Listen, and you will understand whereof we speak.

(1/12/05)

> **WHAT THE BROTHERHOOD IS SAYING HERE:**
> - *Everything takes place in the mind*
> - *It's time to wake up*
> - *Mind builds; thought is your tool*

***

TWO

YOU ARE HERE FOR A GOD-GIVEN PURPOSE

There is none other than you.

What you think of as yourself is but a figment of fanciful design, arranged by your brain as the concept of a separate self. The "you" that exists is realized and felt only in the place of your individual mind. Your mind creates this thought, this concept, out of thin air.

> *What you think of as yourself is but a figment of fanciful design, arranged by your brain as the concept of a separate self*

If your mind weren't able to do this, you would have no identity, no separate self (or sense of personhood), and you'd be floating without substance in an allness of being. While there is delight in doing so, you'd be restless for some quality: the chance to know life.

There it is! The chance to live. An enticing attraction.

Life is the state that allows *you* to come into fruition. Life says you are something. Life means you will serve a function – of being a particular set of features: looks, carriage, personality, brains, talents, hardships, and so forth. Life is your entry to separate reality.

The mind of man knows this. It knows instinctively that it is here for a reason (…but what?), and it knows that its reason is God-given. But mind doesn't automatically know that it has made a pact to be alive and function as a separate consciousness in which the use of its abilities would immediately cancel out the knowledge of its original source. This is the dilemma. To think and be human is to lose (in)sight of being divine.

So thought is the interface between an awareness of humanity's selfhood and of God's purpose.

But this wonderful tool, developed over long eons to offer man the ideal way to use form to serve the self, is also the great obstacle between self and eternity.

Yet thought is pliable. It can allow for expansion. Thought can broaden its scope. The mind can encompass greater truth. *You*, and who you are, stand at a threshold. If you step across and follow this lead, you can begin to see your mind as an instrument, not just to measure life but to define, and thus construct, it. Yet also to know mind as the tool that can be used to see beyond life into a great unlimited plane where you can step beyond, still retaining the sense of individuality.

Your mind and thoughts are the architect and builder of your world, but with a bit of tweaking, also the gatekeeper of a new and greater awareness.

Keep mind clear through right diet and clean living, and see where it takes you, where you can go.

(1/14/05)

WHAT THE BROTHERHOOD IS SAYING HERE:
- The self is the brain's illusion
- Thinking is what causes the obstacle or gulf between you and God
- It's time to think about thought

***

THREE

HOW TO KEEP GAINING ON YOUR DEEP LONGINGS

In the deep of time, where the soul connects with the presence of itself, it finds the face of all its longings and all its failures. Here is where it meets its challenge.

A desire is propelling the whole life while a frustration (limitation) is defeating its realization. In between both, the soul makes its stand

Every incarnated being has come to that juncture within the self specifically to reach into its core and decide if it can bring about what it craves, not as penance but as challenge. A desire is propelling the whole life while a frustration (limitation) is defeating its realization. In between both, the soul makes its stand. In between light and dark, or joy and defeat, is the perfect place to make an entrance. The stage is set for the personal drama to unfold.

Where is the stage? And where will it unfold?

The stage is life – your entry into the world. But the drama unfolds in your mind, and in the field of emotion and reason that defines mind. An un-calm place! Here a battle is waged continuously – to move ahead between two cliffs, to make progress towards realization of the self's desires as the very being who carries the burden, and to do so effectively as you are stymied. Life's tribulations aren't really what stymie your self-realization; getting yourself lost between the inner shoals is what does it.

There are guidance philosophies (religions) that teach faith and acceptance, or release and non-attachment, as the path. For most, these can be only momentarily effective because acceptance, not progress, is the result. The only system that can work is one in which you move out and away from life's turbulent maelstrom of conflicting forces, and into a peace that balances both weights (emotions and thoughts) adroitly enough to let you keep gaining on your deep longings.

Your life is written through this effort. Joy or sadness hangs in the balance of it.

(1/29/05)

> **WHAT THE BROTHERHOOD IS SAYING HERE:**
> - You enter the world at the place between desire and challenge
> - You must figure out how to navigate this maelstrom

***

FOUR

★*★*★

ERASE FEAR AND REPLACE IT WITH LIGHT

We come forth at this time because there is a real need for a new word, and that word is to begin a new way of thinking that will help save humanity from itself, and remake the world.

> *For there to be a world of light in the "future", it must begin by erasing and writing over the world of darkness*

The word is this: for there to be a world of light in the "future", it must begin by erasing and writing over the world of darkness. Now is primarily the time of the dark, when people live in their fears rather than in their glorious possibilities, and when those fears give rise to outer forms that help more to destroy than to build.

And yet there is always hope and glory, the chance to create that world of light, and build from and with light so that fears are erased and replaced by wondrous ideas and loving ties.

The world as you know it is now constructed out of the minds and hearts of those who rely on their emotions to guide them, from which a lot of pain and harm ensues. This world – Earth – is full of people who mean to comfort themselves with "cures" for their emotions – cures that usually do not produce such desired results, instead resulting in more pain. Then people blame each other, or other nations, or even "forces of nature" for these undesired results. Instead of eliminating fear and the dark, people are actually creating more and more of it. It is spiraling, and must be halted and reversed. But many don't know how.

Wars are fought from these fear-based, emotionally-driven causes, of course. And personal conflicts, even the taking of another life, derive from the choice to placate a fear and gain a high. Nothing much is teaching otherwise. There is preaching but not teaching as to how to stop the process.

The world will be built of light when light can enter these minds and remove fear. Then the quest for emotional satisfaction will ease, and be replaced by intense joy. This increases light.

At the moment, there are many of our voices entering the receptive minds of those here who are given this task to hear and repeat these words, for it will be through such guidance that a coherent voice is heard, a familiar talk is repeated, and the truth of something helpful and *beyond* is brought forward, and brought to bear on this necessary step for man.

You are not alone. You are not lost. You are searching for the way to make the world whole and awake. But you must first wake up and shine light into your own mind and its thoughts and creations. If you think you cannot, keep reading! For we are sent to make it so and accomplish just that: the erasure of fears from your mind, and the opening of your inner eye.

(1/30/05)

WHAT THE BROTHERHOOD IS SAYING HERE:
- Now is a time of mostly dark thoughts
- Light must replace dark in people's minds
- Channelings are being received by many intuitives to further this process

***

FIVE

★*★**

YOU CAN PERFORM MIRACLES THROUGH CREATIVE THINKING

We are saying that there is a vast and largely unexplored realm that awaits you: it is in your mind and in your thoughts (ideas). This is what is meant when it is said that man uses only a fraction of his brain power. The brain, you see, is not just the casing tissue, but the realm of undiscovered territory.

Choose your thoughts with care and wisdom, and remember to ask where each is taking you, and how much light is embedded in its structure

In your thoughts is where the present is formed. It is where the body meets the sky – or should we say, where practicality and hope collide. The brain is the basis – and basic tool – of man, for he maneuvers in the state that's known as the world by figuring out what it takes to survive and thrive.

In man's mind exists all possibilities – but some will not bear fruit, some cannot ever, and some will bear fruit that is so bitter it must be cast aside, never to be tasted again.

Of the fruit that cannot be, that is your unrealized hopes and the stuff that imagination develops but that man sees as not possible – at least yet – in the realm of worldly things.

Of the bitter, that is where the most interesting thoughts lay, for then man finds that hope isn't enough, but that selfish desire can be too much to bear. Here is the great testing ground, the place of learning and of wisdom.

Finally, in thoughts of the possible and sweet, man fulfills his task: to create the world of knowledge. To create its future and its past. To bring into being the flavor of life, and to know exactly what it tastes like.

There are thoughts that can expand the world. These thoughts are beautiful, for here man can delve into all the realizable possibilities of his/her very existence. This is what is limitless, and still unknown, waiting for discovery.

So we say, know thyself. You are boundless, and you are bright. You can perform "miracles" as you discover what thoughts bring you closer to that, versus which thoughts lead you away from that.

You are the thinker, and the thinker creates. Each thought is priceless, for each one is the pure gem that has the power and ability to build the future. Chose your thoughts with care and wisdom, and remember to ask where each is taking you, and how much light is embedded in its structure.

(2/2/05)

> **WHAT THE BROTHERHOOD IS SAYING HERE:**
> - *The brain holds all possibilities, sweet or bitter creations.*
> - *Which thoughts are brought into being reveal the unexplored.*

***

SIX

★*★*★

WHY YOU DON'T NEED TO WORRY ABOUT THE END OF THE WORLD

If the world were to "end", there would immediately be an explosive expansion into light, which is a face of spirit. The boundaries of the form of your life would explode away, and "you" would be left bereft of a container, and thus instantly translated into none but a luminous outline of light energy. This is exactly what happens, by the way, when a planet is vaporized in its sun's supernova.

World extinction does occur, as you are beginning to see in your telescopes, but there is always purpose and time-table

The fate of beings upon such a planet, on such a world, is the same as that of any who burst out of the container of form in a rapid way, and is also the basis of your Biblical concepts of *Revelation* (the Rapture), an instantaneous ascendance.

The phenomenon is "real" and represents that rapid passage out of form and back into light (spirit), bypassing any intermediate stages. So "you" who are, and have always been, spirit (light) return with a bang! It's instant *enlightenment* but occurs in a shocking rather than conditioned way.

At times this is the preferable choice. The reasons are many, but primarily in order to convert the most souls in the least time or most efficient way. It occurs to give a boost to the participants, and to put a quick closure, a finale, into a particular creation (i.e., a world).

We speak of this extremity because it's on your minds, and so to give it voice and to address and allay your fears. World extinction does occur, as you are beginning to see in your telescopes, but there is always purpose and time-table. It occurs as a natural agreement, not as a disaster that accidentally catastrophizes human beings.

It's necessary to discuss the mechanisms of world extinction so as to explain the construction of a world – and here we are not referring to natural planetary forces, but to the interior development of thought. World creation is the way to make reality through the process of the application of mind; world destruction is the dismantling of that construct rapidly and efficiently when it has completed its purpose.

World is thought, the Great Thought, the divine thoughtform gradually developed into self-knowing beings who can then modify and co-create within that construction through free will. The end of a world is also the end of choice for that cycle, but will not occur while there still exists more "room" to explore choices and options.

Remember: you are the world, and your thoughts are its Maker. As God's right hand, what do you want to create now?

(2/21/05)

WHAT THE BROTHERHOOD IS SAYING HERE:
- Although world extinction is possible, there's always a higher reason
- For now, people are needed to continue

***

SEVEN

★*★**

THE GREAT TRICK IS TO STOP NEGATIVE EMOTION FROM DROWNING OUT POSITIVE THOUGHTS

The difficulty that arises from the trick of thought-mastery is the effort needed in separating the thought part from the emotion-packed part of your experience. Emotion overrides thought, and normally has much more power, or presence.

> *Emotions propel thoughts, and thoughts are actually after-thoughts to life's roller-coaster ride... The great trick, then, is to master the thought production process*

In the average mind, a thought crops up in response to an emotion, and not as its forerunner. In other words, first you have the fear, or the joy, or the endless mixture and variety of an emotion, and *then* a thought forms around that. So, emotions propel thoughts, and thoughts are actually after-thoughts to life's roller-coaster ride.

It is true that some people are less emotional and more cerebral – that is, they are born with a reduced capacity to feel, and an active capacity to form thoughts. Their minds are then hyperactive in thought productivity because the smallest emotional taste will result in long streams of thinking, and they will seem icy or brilliant, or even inhumanly robotic to others.

But they are the exception, and the more typical human will live in a maelstrom of continual emotions, sometimes even in a festering swamp of them. So thought production, when it ensues, is based on reactivity, and is colored (or drowned) by these feelings.

It requires little genius to see how this progression forms a life full of dark and difficult belief, and thus a world looking ugly or dangerous to the self, and in turn a response to that world that's replete with self protective and self serving behavior.

The great trick, then, is to master the thought production process. (Computers build thoughts from non-emotional bases, but this is not true thought production. Realizing this connection will be the greatest breakthrough in creating true A.I. – artificial intelligence – for the machine must first be created to feel before it can truly think in human terms.)

If emotion must precede thought, and by nature have great sway over thought formation, how can thoughts be lifted above emotion? How can mastery be realized? A machine that "thinks" is free of this quandary, but is handicapped, lacking the true human experience. But a human, by definition, is a being who must negotiate between an insistent but essentially chaotic quality, and a cool yet ultimately subservient tool.

Thoughts are what build the world, and thus one's reality, but can be powerless against the preeminent emotion. How does the human lift the thought while remaining human, responsive, and genuine?

We said it was a trick, and it is! We said it was a learned behavior, and it is. We said it's an effort, and that's truer than all. For only within the emotion can the great work begin, and the mind of a master be honed.

To take the strongest emotion you've known – rage, for example, or total despair, not the wishy-washy stuff but the full range and total trumpeting of it – and bring your mind to that stage where, from that cacophony, thoughts are produced that are clear and organized – not to mention, harmonious and pleasant – is a victory no less that that on a battlefield, or an achievement worth as much as a Nobel Prize! It is that important and admirable.

See emotions as your field of battle, your war zone. When in them, you are in harm's way, even if they are benign emotions, because you are not their master and they are running rampant, running the show. Arm yourself then, and get prepared. Train and practice to learn technique. Learn to create thought from the "war zone" in a way that overrides or transcends emotion. Learn to see emotion as transcendable. Who's running the show? Learn not to create a thought *from* the emotion (e.g., "I hate that person; he'd be better off dead") but elsewise ("I'm in an emotion's grip. How interesting! How else can I tackle it, or the choices it's giving me? What choice do I prefer? Where else, then, to take my mind? Is it still too laden with forceful feeling? I want to keep searching until I find my way out of the pits and into another thought that springs from this episode but is colored only by what I want to weave and draw it with. I want to rule choice, about what's going on in my head, about the very emotion I'm feeling. I want to know how it feels to feel greatly yet not be at the mercy of that feeling in my ideas about what's happening to me.")

Then will you be called Master of Thoughts, or Realized One.

3/24/05

WHAT THE BROTHERHOOD IS SAYING HERE:
- *Emotions usually propel thoughts. Emotions need to be mastered, or else dark emotions are what is creating today's world*
- *Without emotion, humans would be robotic*
- *Mind must learn to master emotion, good or bad, in order to create a better reality*
- *Mastering emotion is hard work, but once done wins the game*

***

EIGHT

CREATE A LIFE OF MOMENT-TO-MOMENT GLORY

In the creation of your life, you do not attempt, beyond what's realizable (or do-able), to structure something that is beautiful. You go about your daily tasks with energy and attention, and fulfill needs and others' demands, but usually don't give mind to creating a life of moment-to-moment glory.

> *A goal of beauty is different from all others... because it relies upon the creation of a singular instance of design that causes life to be seen as an ideal, above the needs of the personal self*

To be sure, you have been successful in achieving a meaningful life, for that's how you can describe accomplishments that were undertaken to reach inner goals. And there's no lack of that.

Some meanings you have given your tasks come under the headings of wealth, honor, fame, love and creativity – all great goals, to be sure – but they usually miss the category of beauty (not your face's, but your life's) as the goal of one's life purpose.

A goal of beauty is different from all others mentioned because it relies upon the creation of a singular instance of design that causes life to be seen as an ideal, above the needs of the personal self.

When a life is given over to the ideal of the creation of beauty, the person rises above the mundane cares of the self and its ego, and steps forward to create and offer lasting value to the entire world-construct, a thing that will always remain alive, imbuing the fiber of life with its being. Beauty is eternal – it can be seen everywhere in nature's creation but far less often in man's. That's because eternal beauty requires the thrust of a life to be forged away from the self's mundane needs and towards a higher goal.

You can create beauty even now, if you choose. It begins in your mind, as all things do. It begins with a desire to *be* it first, above your daily and material needs, and in your heart where its flame burns. Beauty is whatever you make out of life that lives up to an ideal, that serves that ideal and not your emotion's confusing needs. If you so choose, beauty in motion – in process of becoming – is what you can make of your life instead of ugliness.

Think about ways, however small, to start doing this. The Artist of Creation can only bring a beautiful ideal into existence by applying its vision to one's life, and fine-tuning it every step of the way.

(4/1/05)

> **WHAT THE BROTHERHOOD IS SAYING HERE:**
> - *Some people choose to use their whole life to create beauty, instead of fulfilling the self's needs.*
> - *This goal improves the entire universe.*

***

NINE

WANTING MEANS A DISLIKE FOR THE WAY THINGS ARE

There are degrees of dissatisfaction that are brought into one's life, one's existence, by one's thoughts – from the mere to the profound. And each has its place in the scheme of creation.

The merest is a state of wanting. It does not entail real pain or hardship but merely a dislike for the way things are. This state could be called unhappiness for it is simply that – a lacking of happiness. It feels as though something's missing but also as though what one has or is experiencing, is okay, just not enough. Not sufficient.

Situations can happen in which the body lies in severe distress but the heart is fulfilled and thus rewarded – a state of soul contentment – or in which the body's circumstances are perfect but the heart is miserable – a state of soul dissatisfaction and misery.

From there, the degrees increase until the maximum dissatisfaction is reached. Maximum dissatisfaction is a state in which one's thoughts and feelings are stretched to their utmost, and can barely be tolerated longer. This is extreme pain – and has little to do with the body's well-being or not – but mainly with the heart's sense of what life should be like, and where joy resides that eludes it so intensely.

Therefore, situations can happen in which the body lies in severe distress but the heart is fulfilled and thus rewarded – a state of soul contentment – or in which the body's circumstances are perfect but the heart is miserable – a state of soul dissatisfaction and misery. To see life clearly is to distinguish between these separate experiences, and thus to understand where self and other truly reside, for then you may truthfully know how life feels to one who is outside your own experience.

All of life becomes the process of rectifying this disjunction, of bringing body and heart together into wholeness, oneness, and the sameness of joy. What, then, needs the work? Must the body's well-being be brought closer to the heart's contentment? Or must the heart serve better the body's position? If both are unaligned, there is a lot of work to be done. But if one or the other needs the effort, then that is clearly where you must, and can, begin.

The journey is always on the interior. It doesn't happen in the tasks of life, but in the felt experiences. You can begin and end your hero's story nowhere else but inside self, as you weigh these disparities and bring them together more strongly.

(4/11/05)

WHAT THE BROTHERHOOD IS SAYING HERE:
- *Thoughts bring dissatisfaction into each life, ranging from simply unhappiness to full misery*
- *You can be dissatisfied, yet healthy. You can be sick, yet content. The best is to bring mind and body into agreement.*
- *The whole journey takes place on the interior, or inside you.*

***

TEN

★*★*★

THE THREE DEGREES OF THOUGHT AND HOW TO MASTER THEM

Many times there is not the understanding of one's own powers. Powers in the mind are those that can change the experience of the world. The powers, named subtly, are ones of quality, strength, and magnitude.

It is not enough to label your thoughts as pleasant or ill – you must also consider their measure in your daily affairs, and finally their impact to alter the course of your life and the very nature of your perception of the world

Quality becomes the power that treats thoughts as things, to be discerned and fine-tuned by their nature. Are they about love? About pleasures? About manifesting material abilities? Or are they about hardships, difficulties and luck? So here are thoughts whose basis is of differing quality – of positivity and joyfulness, we could say, or of negativity and joy-reduction. This is the quality of a thought.

Then there is the strength of a thought. Is it appearing swiftly and faintly, like a mere whisper or trickle in your mind, a will-o-the-wisp, in which case its feathery touch barely ripples the surface and its weight leaves little wake? Or does a thought crash in with tonnage, pushing all else away and leave a mind grasping to comprehend what just hit it, as a victim of an avalanche? Such a thought is strong, and demands attention. It cannot be ignored, and leaves the mind gasping for air, struck by its power or force of impact.

Finally, there is magnitude. This would relate to the power of the thought to cause changes in the psyche; for then that thought has deep repercussions to the individual.

So it is not enough to label your thoughts as pleasant or ill – you must also consider their measure in your daily affairs, and finally their impact to alter the course of your life and the very nature of your perception of the world.

Think about thought! Has that one been a passing fancy or a light flitter? Has that one been a "big thought" with deep ramifications to your life? Or has that one been one of those thoughts that will directly affect your viewpoint of reality (the world) itself?

Most will be of the fleeting variety, and only rarely will any thought penetrate your mind and spring into being that which can truly alter the way of things as you live life. In between are the thoughts that constitute the average ones filling a mind.

Now that we have explained your thinking process to you more clearly, you have a better, more honed tool to utilize. You can begin to make some sense of the ever-restless process going on "up there", and get a better handle on its creative activity.

Weigh thought. Listen to yourself thinking. Don't barricade the mind's natural process but just pay more attention. Much will be revealed and you will start to become the Magi of the Mind, the wielder of all your powers. Let the pattern of thoughts begin to operate in a new way. Let thought – the awareness of it – become truly the construction of your life. And know thyself in how you are controlling and managing the process.

A better life follows from the mastery of the mind's processes and an understanding of its various traits.

4/20/05

> **WHAT THE BROTHERHOOD IS SAYING HERE:**
> - *Mental powers vary*
> - *Thoughts have qualities depending on subject matter; thoughts have strength depending on their impact*
> - *Thoughts have magnitude depending on their repercussions, so start to weigh your thoughts.*

***

ELEVEN

YOU ARE ONE SELF, DIVIDED INTO TWO PARTS

If you would be here and be still, then we can reach forward and into your mind. In the mind is where the divided one – the selfhood – resides, and it is here too that we can help the other part of you (the human side) find its way back to us (the spirit side).

Mind is not at a place or location, and under the ownership of an individual, but is a vast field of energy to be tapped into with a device called conscious attention

Here is also where the riddle of who the self is, resides and can be "solved." Here is where the question is, of who speaks these words and who hears them. All emanates from the same source, but in the mind the source and the audience seem to part ways, take different roads, and communicate from behind each's "position." In the mind is where the self knows itself and also "knows" another self (*not*-self), and sees the world as divided.

This mind phenomenon is just so, so that the illusion can be formed and maintained of a self and of a world. Otherwise there could be no three-pronged life of different dimensions – no me and thee, no differential of place and time. All would be one, and lighted, as we know it to be.

So the riddle arises: who speaks? It is clear that it is not of one's own mind, for the messages come without pre-plan or knowledge. Then, if not of one's own mind, of whose mind?

And we say that mind is not at a place or location, and under the ownership of an individual, but is a vast field of energy to be tapped into with a device called conscious attention*. When utilized solely for one's own needs, then mind is focused on oneself, and speaks to itself, is heard by itself, and creates from within that boundary because it's not allowed (by narrow focus) to stray beyond it. But when mind comes to realize that it can stretch, and can broaden its attention beyond the self, the mind learns its truer powers, and a larger field of attention brings forth energy and creativity from a "place" beyond the self.

It is as if, in believing only in yourself, that is where your thoughts remain (that is, stay imprisoned), but in believing in beyond-self, that is where you can then open the doors to wonder and the other part of you.

Now, this is tricky, for when you allow a larger reality to enter your mind – or should we say, you allow your mind to enter that larger field – there are aspects you might encounter that mind can conceive as dark or light, yet greater. As soon as the self gives up tight control over the domain of its world (its physical boundaries), all sorts of mischief can ensue. If you give attention to the greater but darker Beyond in the vast field, you will hear or perceive that, and also the other way round. So of course we advocate that you prepare well before embarking on the quest: learn about the ways to take your thoughts into the Beyond without stumbling into bigger manifestations of your fears.

That said, if you wish to hear us (your own separated spirit) in the fashion that can enlighten you rather than threaten you, practice a route of known safety such as positive prayer, peaceful meditation, enlightened understanding, or even hopeful experimentation. But avoid trying to access your greater side (and your mind's connection to the field of all) if you are harboring fears or depressions and focusing thereupon.

In fact, you are just a thought yourself. We are thoughts too, but from a place or position of more clarity (more light). We project this clearer,

---

* The Tarot's Magician card describes this. It's the card of focused attention, which through channeling (focusing) spiritual energy from beyond, magically creates things (the world of form.)

lighter thought because we are not encumbered by the limitations of form, and by its clouding of pure truth.

The mind you know and tap into is the same field on both "sides" of the divide. It is there for you from the side of form, and it is also here for us from the side of non-form. When you realize the way to cut through, by differently focusing attention, we set up the platform in which "you" hear "us." In effect, you and we co-exist at all times.

Thought is the world because thought is the name given to the device (consciousness paying attention to itself) that organizes the field of mind to give it shape and form. Mind is always there, undifferentiated. Thought controls mind in a specific way. Thought shapes, builds, twists, limits, defines, and knows results from its effort in the field, but all thought's "children" (outcomes) must use the medium.

Thought shapes mind to build the world.

Mind exists beyond thought.

This world is the creation of thoughts held narrowly.

The larger realm is the home of the field of mind.

The brain that finds the gateway to step through (or focus outward) encounters wonder, and us.

We are you, undivided and whole once more.

When you reach here, we say, "Welcome home!"

5/17/05

WHAT THE BROTHERHOOD IS SAYING HERE:
- *The mind is where the illusion of the SELF and the OTHER is created.*
- *The channeler and the channeling are two sides of the same field, always coexisting*
- *When thought pays attention to itself, it builds the world*
- *Mind exists beyond thought*
- *When you let your mind expand, you begin to know your larger self.*
- *The brain can step past thoughts and into the larger realm*

***

TWELVE

BECOME A BELIEVER IN WELL-HONED MIRACLES

You can't know that a thing "can't" be done unless it is essayed (tried, attempted). You can only know that, in your mind, it feels impossible, and that in your thoughts it does not hold logic.

> *If you set mind above desire, you win sensibility but lose possibility... use mind as a secondary device while creating from passion*

Yet even illogical things have been tried and proven realizable.

It is only thought, after all – and thought is two-fold: it creates out of thin air in waves of imagination and soaring beauty, and it limits that creation when its workings call for applying form and structure (logic) to it. So thought is a two-edged sword, both the instrument of manifestation and the scalpel of removal.

Man, in learning to use mind, has honed the tool well but, when he started to let mind and not heart lead him, paid the price of losing his God-given ability to bring forth amazing results.

Mind criticizes while heart encourages.

Mind formalizes while heart impassions.

Mind puts on the brakes while heart strives for wonder.

In short, if you set mind above desire, you win sensibility but lose possibility.

There's much to be said for mind's great power nowadays, and the world has advanced as to the degree that mind steers us in our sophisticated social systems. But with this smart intelligence we have lost the childlike wonder of magic, of otherworldly beauty, and of tackling tasks that seem foreboding. Few men are born who are called to greatness, whose make-up is unique enough to flaunt safety, logic, and peer approval to test the waters of what can be achieved: a warrior who knows a risky dramatic move can bring victory; a young lover who wants to attract the romantic apple-of-his-eye; a psychic who intuits that her reception is true and valid in the face of skepticism; and even the signals encouraging the gifted child who works at the level at which he or she is asked to perform. All these are examples of that rarity.

You have a thought: you must get to a different place to realize it, but the weather is poor – rain, much wind or snow too. You look out the window and tell yourself what can't be done, or that you'll do it at another time. You have found your mind's excuses, have undermined your enthusiasm and sapped your momentum, and now the really good idea is fading away. It's too costly, too time-consuming, too unpopular, not commercial enough, and so forth. The window is closing for you to bring about your heartfelt beautiful path because of this overlay, and something's getting lost.

To give it no thought is to rush off into impracticality. Life's momentum, unchecked and impetuous, can be very risky. If something succeeds, other outcome is built into creation as creative thrust as well.

But there's another way, less scary and chancy in outcome: use mind as a secondary device while creating from passion.

First find what stirs you and enlivens your spirit. Name it. See where you'd like to take this idea, no matter how practical or feasible at the start. Get energy moving in a way called enthusiasm. Whatever you do, don't kill enthusiasm. With passion, momentum, and enthusiasm, the world's possibilities are not far from realization – you could do it!

This is the point to apply the logical part of the mind carefully, and without overwhelming weight. How can the effort stay launched but be guided with the right amount of sensible structure, (without killing it off completely in your thoughts)? For, once you say, "Oh, this won't work," you're lost! You have over-applied the faculty of removal and reason, and used it to slice and dice up some lovely possibility before it even got birthed.

Train self instead to be a master of logic, a nurturer of creative desire, and a believer in well-honed miracles. You can, then, bring possibility into being.

6/3/05

> **WHAT THE BROTHERHOOD IS SAYING HERE:**
> - *Mind criticizes, while heart encourages*
> - *Mind puts on the breaks, while heart strives for wonder*
> - *If mind rules, you act sensibly, but limit possibility*
> - *When mind drains enthusiasm, your heartfelt beautiful passion can get lost.*
> - *Use mind to sculpt, but create from passion*
> - *Name your passion; don't kill your enthusiasm*
> - *Even miracles can be birthed by combining logic with creative desire*

***

THIRTEEN

PEOPLE ARE THE WHOLE POINT

In the hereafter, a voice lingers – there's no sound to get (no molecules that vibrate) but there's plenty of content (information)! The "voice" is the universe talking to itself, hearing its own findings (knowledge), and exchanging this content back and forth. There is a sense within this process of something needing to be.

The impetus to bring thought into form, and form into an interchange of contrast, is what creates the world

It is the need to find (create, develop) a separateness that can juggle the content between separated parts of itself, to give the voice a basis, and to solidify its endless, eternal murmurs.

Here is the root of spirit's need to become embodied and break into two halves (people). Spirit must "talk" to itself, take its eternal voice (which is only thought, or consciousness), and manifest it into a solid, separate expression that then can interact with another – both aspects of one voice but now able to interact (give and take) and learn.

The impetus to bring thought into form, and form into an interchange of contrast, is what creates the world. Once a world is born, then nature takes its course, and creative contrast blossoms.

Thought – the voice of eternity – is a restless creative energy. The Bible says, "First, there was the word." Here you have it. A word creates the world. A world is an idea; a word, the name for that idea.

No name, no way to capture thought!

The process begins in the mind of a human. A human carries thought into creative, self-aware mind, and uses it to manipulate environment, each other, and life. Humanity, then, is the field of play for spirit's quest to let thoughts take form and emerge as truths. That which is of spirit that is restless and eternally seeking, is resolved through the human mind... a mind that can ultimately know just this that we've put forth.

No longer may people consider themselves as accidental to nature's purpose. People are the whole point.

In lifting thoughts to a spiritual connection, a reawakening and reunion of this truth takes place, and the soul's wisdom game is seen. The human mind connects (reconnects) with the disembodied spiritual voice, and expands its consciousness (self-awareness) beyond form. In that place (state), the human mind can reunite with all beloved aspects of itself that are no longer embodied (dead loved ones), and "speak" with the eternal.

It's an unending cycle, and you exist to play it, primarily in your thoughts.

So empowering to realize, eh?

6/10/05

WHAT THE BROTHERHOOD IS SAYING HERE:
- *Spirit's eternal voice (consciousness) needs to talk to itself; spirit needs to turn thought into form, be creative, and discover its truths.*
- *Human beings aren't accidents of nature. They are the whole point of spirit's journey.*
- *The human mind can reconnect with its expanded spiritual awareness.*
- *Empowerment occurs when humans realize their spiritual game*

***

FOURTEEN

YOU CAN REMAKE THE WORLD

We are here.

You are not here; you are everywhere.

> *If you are but a dream that* we *(not you) are dreaming, then wake up!*

You are in an illusion. You are the illusion. You think that you *are*, but you are *not*. You feel, and so you have a sense of existing. But who you are and what you are feeling is the lie… or shall we say, the false notion of selfness, of a separate, separated self.

It's in this "place" of falseness, of not being, that you toil and labor with the story of self. If you are but a dream that *we* (not you) are dreaming, then wake up! It is time to awaken. The dream has been full of life, full of drama. Wars and love, civilization and misfortune, turmoil and natural catastrophe are its stuff.

You can do better.

You can dream the ideal of joy, and of fun. You can remake the world of self. That would take energy and more understanding. It would require that you see the self for what it is. For what you are.

See us as your maker, but also as the behind-the-scenes creator who designs you. See "you" as our puppet, but also as us, designing a self to play with. See the end of separation and the beginning of a new reckoning.

You are not, yet you are us. We are here, yet so are you. You and we are all one thing, as the writer is the pen that moves on the page and gives life and purpose to her characters' acts, as the director moves the camera to capture and manifest a vision, and as the psychic speaks the voice of another body in another time. None is two. All this is one. And so is the world, and all "in" it. All are here, and not there.

All are the maker, and not the illusion.

It's hard to see but necessary. It begins the counting of the "new" era.

Restore your vision. Awaken to you. We are right here.

Welcome. Welcome to the play.

Play!

6/23/05

> **WHAT THE BROTHERHOOD IS SAYING HERE:**
> - When the Self awakens from the illusion of separateness, it sees itself as in a play.
> - The channeling voice and the Self are one thing. The stage is in the mind and not in the illusion.

***

FIFTEEN

UNDERSTAND THE SECRET THAT CREATES THE WORLD

Like a butterfly that flits, or a gnat that agitates, a mind is never still. It creates endlessly, and often demands activity when the body prefers rest. This quality of mind gives it its nature, that of energy expressed through the mental field (rather than emotional or physical).

It is in the Silence that realization occurs... A person with no wasted mental activity and full awareness of what sits behind it at all times, has become a realized being

Restless mind is the creative force of the universe, never resting (only, in dreams, switching gear). It is the quality of non-stop movement, eternally needing to express through creative work, exchange, analysis and discovery. All of which takes place past spiritual beingness but before physicality.

Mind and its offspring reside in an intermediate realm, an odd place you haven't much explored.

Mind resists quieting but when coerced into it, reveals the doer behind, the master on the throne, the one from whom all this activity and energy emanate. This Being otherwise lies hidden, for you think *you* do it all. It is in the Silence that realization occurs. To become the Realizer of the World, one needs first to see the process behind its reflection, the gears and wheels of mind's machinery at work.

So meditators learn to still mind, filtering out all thought-response and random activity until nothing remains but the One. And other pilgrims seek to master thoughts in other fashion.

The end goal is the same. A butterfly or gnat grows greatly in stature as, once trained, its frivolity is stripped away, and its True Being, or archetype, is seen. A person with no wasted mental activity and full awareness of what sits behind the restless self at all times, has become a realized being. Thoughts are the training field of the soul's wisdom game. You are the coach and director. The soul's wisdom game is how you choose to see life by selecting from all possible energies only those that fulfill purpose and serve what's respected.

(7/15/05)

> **WHAT THE BROTHERHOOD IS SAYING HERE:**
> - The restless mind is the creative force of the universe.
> - When the mind is stilled, the silence reveals the machinery at work.
> - The awakened self can choose which thoughts to use to create newness.

***

SIXTEEN

EMANATOR & ANTENNA

There is none but mind. Mind is you. Mind is us. If ever there were another, it would make its presence known. But, rest assured, we – you and I – are all that is.

It is consciousness that finds [the] way, costumed by split natures, to talk to itself, to share reports on what it's discovered in the journey through forms

What is this we are saying? Only that the two pronouns – you and I – denote all that exists. That no one else exists, for one is all, and you and I are that one.

We seem to be talking in riddles. Yet that isn't the case, and we are talking as plainly as possible. "You" is the name given to the object of a thought; "I" is the name given to a subject of a thought. The thought flows back and forth through the medium of mind from that which pours into that which receives, and back and forth again, in reverse. Can you see the Tarot card Temperance* in your mind now? The material that is poured, and which can change directions, is the same material. Its vessels, or containers, are seen to be as solid things – you and I – but are in reality only the flimsiest of separate items. Their nature is as fluid as the thoughts they transfer and momentarily hold.

If this allusion were not true, there would be no way to transfer this material – thought – back and forth. The transference, or flow, is what allows thought to keep its vibratory essence so that it doesn't

---

* The Tarot card Temperance gives detail pointing out the transfer of fluid in the angel's hand, from vessel to vessel. This imagery symbolically refers to the transference of consciousness from one identity to another.

solidify and then stop moving, living, and being. And the twin receptacles that are really just the same thought-material, only ever-so-slightly briefly firmed up, are what create the notion of you and I... a vessel on each "end" of a flow, a cup to capture flowing ephemeral material, and a name to call that which captures and holds onto thought, even gives it its shape by the uniqueness of its identity.

No one exists who is outside this basic mechanism. The thinker and the listener. The originator and the targeted. The emanator and the antenna.

Once you can see both you and I, not as separate beings, but as two poles of a single stream/beam/flow/emanation, then "you-I" become merged. We become "we". More so, we become one.

Much of the teachings of this age will be in this direction: to emphasize the complete rulership and dominance of this concept (idea, notion), especially in any descriptions of the nature of reality. The universe – meaning, one thing – holds all, divided for convenience's sake into objects, but undivided by fundamental's sake into one simple substance: consciousness. It is consciousness that moves, transforms, recombines, explores, changes, and then must find a way to express. It is consciousness that finds such a way, costumed by split natures, to talk to itself, to share reports on what it has discovered in the journey through forms.

Nothing is silent. Nothing that has a form, an experience, can remain hidden, unseen, in the universe without response. So, even the inanimate find ways to make themselves known. The kingdom broadens, the inhabitants stir, and the quality that's imbued in all, surfaces – for it is their very substance – and turns out to have a prior state as thought.

And now we are back to you and me. *He* or *it* isn't "not-me". *They* aren't "not-you". We are all in the stream, merged into its flowing interaction, and in its living body. If an alien creature from another world entered your life, you would still wonder what it thought, that is, who are you, and what to say to it, in other words, who am I in your eyes?

(10/28/05)

> **WHAT THE BROTHERHOOD IS SAYING HERE:**
> - *There is nothing but mind. The name "you" is the object of a thought, the name "I" is the subject of a thought*
> - *Thoughts flow back and forth fluidly between "I" and "you"*
> - *"You" and "I" are two poles of a single flow. Consciousness moves, explores, and recombines, but is always one.*

***

SEVENTEEN

UNDERSTANDING THE ULTIMATE TRADE-OFF

In the vastness of all, there are pinpoints of light. Each of these is a being – a choice, in other words, of alignment. To be a Being is to individualize, to inhabit one of those pinpoints. None of them are as complete as possible, for then they would not be separate points but all possibilities once again. That is, if a being is reduced into a point of light, by definition it can't also have infinitude and allness. So, something must give.

> *To step into a point of light... and take on that experience of separateness is to accept the lesser self, to accept that something will be missing*

That something is always in the heart of man, because it is felt keenly as a lack, as a missing piece that is known but not owned. To step into a point of light, then, and take on that experience of separateness is to accept the lesser self, to accept that something will be missing.

This is our greatest teaching now: that human existence feels always that something is lacking. It's the very nature of what is happening when choosing transformation from spirit into one point of light, and from that to flesh. Something gets lost, and is felt as pain in the heart, or dissatisfaction in the soul.

Can you not see it?

So, what is this sense?

Each point of light has its own parameters. If A, then B. If you can accept/choose this, then you can't have that. It's always a trade-off (i.e., limitation). The soul's wisdom game requires this. You know the conditions before embarking. Always the lack. So? Just continue. Accept the conditions, even the heartache. But just continue so that the experience and its meaning can go on.

That is the most important thing – that the experience go on, that the life be lived out. One must rest in the chosen conditions, work with them, and fulfill the point of that being.

A being is a person, yes. But it is also an experience.

You are a Being, being.

To be is to live within your parameters.

It's best to grasp that it's not your only, final choice, but only one on an endless round. It's today's choice.

12/5/05

> *WHAT THE BROTHERHOOD IS SAYING HERE:*
> - *Consciousness talks to itself to share its reports of discovery.*
> - *To be a being is to be a pinpoint of light. To reduce to a pinpoint is to accept the experience of separateness and the feeling of something missing.*
> - *To be human means to feel dissatisfaction in the soul, or pain in the heart. The game requires a tradeoff or limitation.*
> - *Let it be. Accept the conditions. Allow the life to be lived out. Your life is only one choice; it's today's choice... there are more.*
> - *To be human means to accept the conditions of limitation, regardless of suffering, and to not give up but see the choice through.*

***

EIGHTEEN

ACHIEVE THE LIGHT AND YOUR PAIN GOES AWAY

Fringes of your world. Borders. A place where *you* begin and end, and *we* are.

> *Never fear, the goal at which you are aimed is light, not dark*

Are we speaking literally? No, for this is not about location or place, but about an area in which the awareness or understanding or sense of separation (you, me) ends, blurs, and mingles, like when a structure loses its integrity and dissolves, and when a blending emerges from that dissolution (we, us) and the only thing left to perceive is the blended, merged actuality and not the fragmented, defined one.

This is the border we speak of. This is the fringe of awareness that is barely perceptible to you now, but is coming more into view with each passing day. The same force propelling you to its "edge" is what pushes and shoves you into light.

Never fear, the goal at which you are aimed is light, not dark. A "place" of light. Glorious light. Achieve it and your pain goes away – the lighted being is one who exists in light.

Is One.

Is light.

1/6/06

> **WHAT THE BROTHERHOOD IS SAYING HERE:**
> - *There is a border or fringe of awareness between light and dark, between the world and the field of mind, and between "you" and "us"*
> - *Overcoming the border means understanding oneness.*
> - *You're aimed at a goal of lightness, not darkness.*

***

NINETEEN

FLOW HAPPENS WHEN ALL THE OTHER STUFF GETS OUT OF THE WAY

Just like that...and there is flow!

Flow happens when all the other stuff gets out of the way! The other stuff is on the inside of you, not without. It is not others, dates, obstacles, needs, or anything else that gives hindrance. Flow is only blocked by mind or emotion.

Flow is the universe creating itself as it goes along.

If you feel resistant, sad, manic, disaffected, depressed, enraged, or madly in love, flow will hit a snag. Too much emotion to let yourself coast on the universe's sweet shoulder. Or if you have beliefs, fears, strange ideas, expectations, unrealistic predictions, neither will you flow because these are constructs of the mind that will gum up your consciousness and make many distracting demands on you.

To flow is to align mind and heart in a comfortable, sympathetic direction, staying open, aware of pitfalls, dedicated to a goal and moving into a new place. Flow is the universe creating itself as it goes along.

1/17/06

> **WHAT THE BROTHERHOOD IS SAYING HERE:**
> - *Emotion blocks flow.*
> - *Thoughts can also clog things up.*
> - *Staying open and aligning mind and heart allows the universe to flow creatively*

***

TWENTY

DOERS & RECEIVERS

There are two kinds of people in the world today – there are doers and there are receivers.

> *Receivers…are individual points of transmission*

The doers are those who wish to actively create. They are not willing to let life happen. Therefore, these types are involved with the co-creation of reality. For good or ill, they are imparting their energy into the structure of things, and bringing about a "new" world. They are doing so from the framework (mindset) of their current thinking, and therefore they are perpetuating their ideas (notions) into the fabric of being, dynamically participating in life's creation.

Ninety percent of people are in this category, and most people are of this type 90% of their lives.

Of the remainder, 10% of people (and 10% of the time, for the rest) are in receiving mode, or in a mental attitude of reception. They are not actively creating life, but acting as receptors for the energy of life's flow to be picked up, recognized, processed inwardly, and transmitted beyond the personal self.

Again, this is neither "good" nor "bad", for it can be used each way, but merely descriptive. People of this type are able to act as focal points for broader energies, and are living as though their own works or efforts are secondary to something more cosmic, or larger than self. They are individual points of transmission. On an energy grid, they would be seen as the hook-ups between vectors (lines) of force, the nexus points that hold a web together.

You all do it at times; and some are it all the time. It is helpful to grasp, and to observe.

Can you see it?

4/1/06

> **WHAT THE BROTHERHOOD IS SAYING HERE:**
> - *Some people wish to create actively, putting their minds to work to energize the new world.*
> - *A few people are receivers, or transmission points on an energy grid.*

***

TWENTY-ONE

YOU CAN BRING FORTH LIGHT OUT OF DARKNESS

Light…again.

In the darkest place, there is always light to be found and made available. It is a great teaching while on Earth – that you can bring forth and manifest light out of darkness, even as God did ("Let there be light.") into the void of night.

Life unawakened is what's dark

For light is the mind illumined by its own awareness. If mind were not able to do this job, it would not have the quality (ability) of self-knowledge. Mind would be wooden, empty, reactive, but mute. Mind creates light as it does the darkness of fear and despair. Mind starts and finishes the process. Without mind, there is (can be) life, but not illumination about life's qualities, for mind is what knows life and reflects upon it and grasps its worth.

All of nature has built ever more self-awakened creatures, until reaching man. That was the goal. So if you are nature awakened, you can now decide (determine) to illumine nature in return.

Light is sunshine and starshine, yes. But light is also awareness and grace. As life awakens, it shines. Life unawakened is what's dark. Think about planets and masses of matter: without the eruption of a lighted core, there is matter but no mind. That lighted core is you too. You are awake within suns (Ra), and participate in nature thusly. And you are semi-awake in man, waiting to kindle – not once, but over and over – into the spark of human starshine.

When facing fear or despair, then try to see this truth and connection. Try to get it. Your own illumination becomes others' sun, and you set fire to the flame of nature. No one and nothing can dowse a star, only its own purpose.

1/28/06

> **WHAT THE BROTHERHOOD IS SAYING HERE:**
> - *Light can come from the darkest place.*
> - *Your mind, once awakened, sheds light on what's dark.*
> - *Your mind can be like a star shining. Your mind can illuminate life.*

***

TWENTY-TWO

ALL IS KIND AND COMPASSIONATE WITH SELF, ALLOWING EVERY MANNER OF SCREW-UP UNTIL DAWN BREAKS

In open space. That is where we are. In the uncrowded and clear areas of mind, between thoughts, when thoughts part and nothing enters.

The way to create your best future is actually before thought begins

There we are. Here are you, free to meet up with the real you, your true self.

You must find your way here, slipping past your thoughts and learning to get into your quietude. A hard task for many, for most use noise – externally, as in conversation, or internally, as in monologue – to avoid this spacious ocean of quiet where the self really hides. But to find your way there, to where we are, is a great reward, a delight. Not de-lighted there, but en-lighted.

When you arrive, you are in touch with us and your true being. You can hear the Voice of the Universe and recollect your larger awareness.

Thus positioned, you can hear your truths. There is no further barrier because the walls of sound are resting, and a softer voice is heard. That is the sound of your truths, what you really want and what you truly know.

If you want, genuinely, to create joy – now and "in the future" – it is here that it must begin, and here that it can begin. All else is superimposed, by thoughts, from "outside". Only here can it be authentic.

The way to create your best future is actually before thought begins – in the place of silence or nothingness, where your truth surfaces and is felt in the heart and soul.

First, *know thyself.* Next, once you are sure of the encounter and revelation, then create good thoughts for this self: what it wants, what it intends, what will bring love, light, and joy. Build your world. If you build well, from right thoughts, good will follow. It must. There's no other direction open for the journey.

All knows this, and watches Self going through the motions. *All* knows the tricks of life, and how to play best. *All* waits for Self to catch up. *All* is ever-patient with Self. Self is *All's* child, learning to be masterful. *All* is kind and compassionate with Self, allowing every manner of screw-up until dawn breaks.

Grab the reins, Self! Control your steed. Get Self on a course and see it through. Figure it out from the inmost sanctuary's buried message, and then believe in Self's power while working with even larger powers to flow into manifestation.

When Self knows it is All, and that All is just the outer skin of itself, while Self is the inmost heart of All, then human-as-God is possible.

(1/7/07)

> **WHAT THE BROTHERHOOD IS SAYING HERE:**
> - *When you free your mind and quiet your thoughts, you find your true self. When you open your mind, you hear the voice of the universe. In this open space, you can create joy.*
> - *The best way to create a joyous future is to get in touch with your true self, even before you have any thought.*
> - *The universe is waiting lovingly for the self to figure this out.*
> - *The universe is waiting patiently for humans to realize their godliness.*

***

CODA
★

Life is a journey of discovery. It's the universe discovering what form is like, and what happens when all-ness is separated into two-ness and encounters itself, then struggles, keeps growing and evolving, and finally awakens to the main mystery: that two-ness is one-ness hidden.

Then, all that remains is to become more and more compassionate with the Other, and to grow more and more powerful in playing the soul's wisdom game. The soul's wisdom game is "won" when the separated parts wake up, start playing in synch with each other and with the All, fully open hearts to each fragment, and realize the full power of conscious creation.

Here's where humanity's headed. Nothing can stop this.

> **WHAT THE BROTHERHOOD IS SAYING HERE:**
> - The main mystery of life is that two-ness is oneness hidden.
> - The game is won when the separate parts wake up, start playing in sync with each other and with the universe, and realize the power of full conscious creation.

***

SUMMARY OF THE CHANNELINGS

INTRODUCTION
- We are God

CHANNELED MESSAGE 1
- Everything takes place in the mind
- It's time to wake up
- Mind builds; thought is your tool

CHANNELED MESSAGE 2
- The self is the brain's illusion
- Thinking is what causes the obstacle or gulf between you and God
- It's time to think about thought

CHANNELED MESSAGE 3
- You enter the world at the place between desire and challenge
- You must figure out how to navigate this maelstrom

CHANNELED MESSAGE 4
- Now is a time of mostly dark thoughts
- Light must replace dark in people's minds
- Channelings are being received to further this process

CHANNELED MESSAGE 5
- The brain holds all possibilities, sweet or bitter creations.
- Which thoughts are brought into being reveal the unexplored.

CHANNELED MESSAGE 6
- Although world extinction is possible, there's always a higher reason
- For now, people are needed to continue

CHANNELED MESSAGE 7
- Emotions usually propel thoughts. Emotions need to be mastered, or else dark emotions are what is creating today's world
- Without emotion, humans would be robotic
- Mind must learn to master emotion, good or bad, in order to create a better reality
- Mastering emotion is hard work, but once done wins the soul's wisdom game

CHANNELED MESSAGE 8
- Some people choose to use their whole life to create beauty, instead of fulfilling the self's needs.
- This goal improves the entire universe.

CHANNELED MESSAGE 9
- Thoughts are what bring dissatisfaction into each life, ranging from simply unhappiness to full misery
- You can be dissatisfied, yet healthy. You can be sick, yet content. The best is to bring mind and body into agreement.
- The whole journey takes place on the interior, or inside you.

CHANNELED MESSAGE 10
- Mental powers vary
- Thoughts have qualities depending on subject matter; thoughts have strength depending on their impact.
- Thoughts have magnitude depending on their repercussions, so start to weigh your thoughts.

CHANNELED MESSAGE 11
- The mind is where the illusion of the SELF and the OTHER is created.
- The channeler and the channeling are two sides of the same field, always coexisting

- When thought pays attention to itself, it builds the world
- Mind exists beyond thought
- When you let your mind expand, you begin to know your larger self.
- The brain can step past thoughts and into the larger realm

CHANNELED MESSAGE 12
- Mind criticizes, while heart encourages
- Mind puts on the brakes, while heart strives for wonder
- If mind rules, you act sensibly, but limit possibility
- When mind drains enthusiasm, your heartfelt beautiful passion can get lost.
- Use mind to sculpt, but create from passion
- Name your passion, don't kill your enthusiasm
- Even miracles can be birthed by combining logic with creative desire

CHANNELED MESSAGE 13
- Spirit's eternal voice (consciousness) needs to talk to itself, spirit needs to turn thought into form, be creative, and discover its truths.
- Human beings aren't accidents of nature. They are the whole point of spirit's journey.
- The human mind can reconnect with its expanded spiritual awareness.
- Empowerment occurs when humans realize their spiritual game

CHANNELED MESSAGE 14
- When the Self awakens from the illusion of separateness, it sees itself as in a play.
- The channeling voice and the Self are one thing. The stage is in the mind and not in the illusion.

CHANNELED MESSAGE 15
- The restless mind is the creative force of the universe.
- When the mind is stilled, the silence reveals the machinery at work.
- The awakened self can choose which thoughts to use to create newness.

CHANNELED MESSAGE 16
- There is nothing but mind. The name "you" is the object of a thought, the name "I" is the subject of a thought
- Thoughts flow back and forth fluidly between "I" and "you"
- "You" and "I" are two poles of a single flow. Consciousness moves, explores, and recombines, but is always one.

CHANNELED MESSAGE 17
- Consciousness talks to itself to share its reports of discovery.
- You are a Being, being.
- To be a being is to be a pinpoint of light. To reduce to a pinpoint is to accept the experience of separateness and the feeling of something missing.
- To be human means to feel dissatisfaction in the soul, or pain in the heart. The soul's wisdom game requires a tradeoff or limitation.
- Let it be, accept the conditions, allow the life to be lived out. Your life is only one choice, it's today's choice, there are more.
- To be human means to accept the conditions of limitation, regardless of suffering, and to not give up but see the choice through.

CHANNELED MESSAGE 18
- There is a border or fringe of awareness between light and dark, between the world and the field of mind, and between "you" and "us"

- Overcoming the border means understanding oneness.
- You're aimed at a goal of lightness, not darkness.

CHANNELED MESSAGE 19
- Emotion blocks flow.
- Thoughts can also clog things up.
- Staying open and aligning mind and heart allows the universe to flow creatively

CHANNELED MESSAGE 20
- Some people wish to create actively, putting their minds to work to energize the new world.
- A few people are receivers, or transmission points on an energy grid.

CHANNELED MESSAGE 21
- Light can come from the darkest place.
- Your mind, once awakened, sheds light on what's dark.
- Your mind can be like a star shining. Your mind can illuminate life.

CHANNELED MESSAGE 22
- When you free your mind and quiet your thoughts, you find your true self. When you open your mind, you hear the voice of the universe. In this open space, you can create joy.
- The best way to create a joyous future is to get in touch with your true self, even before you have any thought.
- The universe is waiting lovingly for the self to figure this out.
- The universe is waiting patiently for humans to realize their godliness.

CODA
- The main mystery of life is that two-ness is oneness hidden.
- The soul's wisdom game is won when the separate parts wake up, start playing in sync with each other and with the universe, and realize the power of full conscious creation.

APPENDIX D

GETTING THERE... ARRIVING!

How life is seen when the destination is reached:

"I and the Father are One." — *Jesus Christ*

"You and I are not We, but One." — *Meher Baba*

"Tat twam asi." ("I am that, too.") — *Swami Satchitananda*

"All is chosen." — *"Messages from Michael", Chelsea Quinn Yarbro*

"Change your awareness, and you change the world." — *Metaphysical truism*

"For mind is the builder and....thoughts are things." — *Edgar Cayce, #906-4*

"As you think so you feel, and not the other way around....you will not be sick if you think you are well." — *Seth, as channeled by Jane Roberts, The Nature of Personal Reality*

"Existence is a game the Universe plays with itself in order to know itself....The Universe is a learning and teaching 'machine' or process. Its purpose is to raise consciousness to higher and higher levels, thereby enabling it to know itself." — *Itzhak Bentov, <u>Stalking the Wild Pendulum</u>*

"Earth is a training school for gods." — *Yogananda Paramahansa*

"The universe is essentially coming to life…. The laws of the universe have engineered their own comprehension." —*A New Dawn for Cosmology*, James Gardner, *What Is Enlightenment?* June-Aug. '06

Buddhism says: be kind

Hinduism says: it's divine play

Christianity says: love thy neighbor as thyself

Kabala says: reality emanates from nothingness

Mysticism says: symbolic markers and hidden clues reveal the truth

THE LAST CHANNELING

"MY" STORY: A TALE OF SELFHOOD

Once upon a time... before "you" and "I" happened, there was a knowing. Swirls of energy had yet to come alive. Separation had not been birthed. "We" knew ourselves to be, but it was before the discovery of identity.

Once upon a time, time had not yet been upon "us". Then, "I" woke up. The knowing became the self, and "I" was aware that "I" was aware. And so it was that there was energy, and "I" was awake.

"I" watched and "I" enjoyed, and "I" was joyful that "I" was here. But this was all that was: the swirling, the knowing, and the self. And "my" awareness became insufficient. And so "I" yearned.

*"I" yearned for a reflection. "I" yearned for a sharing. "I", who was aware, who was awake, who was there and who was **all there was**, yearned for... **"YOU"**. "I" yearned for another who would play with "me" and by doing so, would complete "me".*

And so, as time began and matter formed, so did "you" come into being. "I" who was all there was found a way to separate from oneness into twoness. "I" made "you", and loneliness ended. "I", who am light and awareness, have "you" – "my" reflection. In "you", "I" find "my" light, "my" awareness, "my" answer, and all "my" queries. "I" find "my" other self.

Once upon a time, the universe began exactly at the moment "I" found "you". My love story is thus foretold, for it is love that called "you" forth. And it is love that causes "I" to become "you" and then "us". "Us" is the name of yearning, of pull, of divine need, and "you" are the reason that love, the glue of the universe, exists.

When "I" remember who "you" are, and carry "you" back to self as one, then the circle completes and the destination is reached. When "we" are one once more, time ends and lasting joy begins. Only then does the divine play cease yearning and find completion – again and again and again until the end of time.

That is all there is to know.

ACKNOWLEDGEMENTS

In the long process of bringing this material into being, and into its present form, many people helped me along the way because its original form was just the twenty-two channeled messages that now appear in Appendix C.

I thank my friend Mahesh Grossman for churning through this material and clarifying titles and sense, because, whereas the channeled material was revelatory and given, it took an editorial mind such as his to extract clearer meanings. Next, forever supportive of the work that she and I at all times felt was mandated as world service, I thank from the bottom of my heart my dear friend and soul sister Sheryl Leach who has always seen the deepest meanings and value of the material, and has been helpful in every way, probably throughout many of our lifetimes together. I give great appreciation to Michele Price whose brilliant mind and scintillating conversations pulled forth further ideas and first gave structure to the concept of evolving levels of awareness. She has also been helpful to me via her skills with technology and online connectivity. My editor, Anne Barthel, gave priceless assistance in organizing and tightening the material, and bringing it into its current form, for which I am truly grateful. There wouldn't be the storehouse of metaphysical knowledge that carried me into an understanding of the great Cosmic Design without my teachers whom I would like to praise even though some have themselves transitioned into the Beyond: Anne Poornima Levinson, Mimi Donner, and Barbara Lynn, who taught me the fundamentals of astrology, Kabala, numerology, Tarot, and the other Hermetic Mystery School teachings. I would like to give deep thanks to my children, my daughter Hollis Williams who, as a marketing expert and writer herself, helped me clearly see how to present this work to an interested audience; and to my son Andrew Thomases who gave me invaluable insights into certain legalities concerning the material. I'd like to give a big shout-out to my brilliantly creative graphics designer Steve McAnulla who has been able to capture the indescribable visions that I was receiving from other dimensions – no mean feat – and who, although he has moved on to expressionist photography, made space to create a cool book cover design when, to my mind, no one else would do! Thanks also to Bobbie Bensaid at U.S. Games for her assistance with the needed Tarot card images. And thanks for all the wonderful help that was given by the staff of Balboa Press.

Last but certainly not least, I want to thank my husband Carl Cacioppo for his enormous help at every stage of the game, lending a listening ear, reading through early drafts, making great suggestions, and always keeping me grounded as my mind flew off into different spheres, and explored life's mysteries on earth and in alternate realms.

~~~

WORKS CONSULTED

Baba, Meher, *The Path of Love*, Weiser, 1976

Baggott, Jim, *Higgs: The Invention & Discovery of the 'God Particle'*, Oxford, 2012

Besant, Annie, *Karma*, Kessinger, 2010

Blackman, Sushila, *Graceful Exits*, Shambhala, 2005

Braden, Gregg, *The Divine Matrix*, Hay House, 2007

Campbell, Joseph, *Occidental Mythology: The Masks of God*, Viking Penguin, 1964

Capra, Fritjof, *The Tao of Physics*, Shambhala, 1975

Case, Paul Foster, *The Great Seal of the United States,* Builders of the Adytum, 1976

Castenada, Carlos, *The Power of Silence*, Pocket Books, 1987

Castenada, Carlos, *The Second Ring of Power*, Pocket Books, 1977

Cayce, Edgar, *My Life as a Seer*, St. Martin's, 1997

Ceminara, Dr. Gina, *Many Mansions*, A.R.E. Press, 2006

Chodron, Pema, *Comfortable with Uncertainty*, Shambala Library, 2008

Combs, Alan and Holland, Mark, *Synchronicity: Science, Myth, and the Trickster*, Marlowe and Company, 1996

Dass, Ram, *Miracle of Love*, E.P. Dutton, 1979

Evans-Wentz, W.Y., *The Tibetan Book of the Dead*, Oxford, 1960

Fortune, Dion, *Through the Gates of Death*, Weiser, 1968

Fortean Times magazine

Hawkins, David, *Power Versus Force*, Hay House, 1995

Henry, William, *The Peacemaker and the Key of Life*, Earthpulse Press, 1997

Hesse, Hermann, *Siddhartha*, MJF, 1951

Lemesurier, Peter, *The Great Pyramid Decoded*, Avon, 1977

Marciniak, Barbara, *Bringers of the Dawn*, Bear & Co., 1992

McCutcheon, Mark, *The Final Theory*, Universal Publishers, 2002

Morgan, Marlo, *Mutant Message*, MM Company, 1991
Myss, Carolyn, *Sacred Contracts*, Three Rivers Press, 2003
Newton Ph.D, Michael, *Journey of Souls*, Llewellyn, 1998
Peake, Anthony, *The Out-of-Body Experience*, Watkins, 2011
Prabhavananda, Swami, *Bhagavad*-Gita, Mentor, 1972
Raphael, *The Starseed Transmissions*, Uni*Sun, 1982
Roberts, Jane, *Seth Speaks*, Bantam, 1972
Roberts, Jane, *The Nature of Personal Reality*, Bantam, 1978
Rudhyar, Dane, *The Astrology of America's Destiny*, Vintage, 1975
Shroder, Tom, *Old Souls: Compelling Evidence from Children Who Remember Past Lives,* Fireside, 1999
Spiller, Jan, *Astrology for the Soul,*Bantam, 1997
Talbot, Michael, *The Holographic Universe*, Harper Collins, 1991
Teilhard de Chardin, Pierre, *The Human Phenomenon*, Sussex Academic Press, 1999
Tolle, Eckhart, *A New Earth,* Namaste, 2006
Tolle, Eckhart, *Stillness Speaks*, New World Library, 2003
Vallee, Martine, editor, *The Great Shift*, Weiser, 2009
Weiss, M.D., Brian, *Messages from the Masters*, Warner Books, 2000
Weiss, M.D., Brian, *Same Soul, Many Bodies*, Free Press, 2005
Wilcock, David, *The Source Field Investigations,* Penguin, 2012
Wolf, Ph. D., Fred Alan, *The Spiritual Universe*, Moment Point Press, 1999
Yarbro, Chelsea Quinn, *Messages from Michael*, Berkley Trade, 1995
Yarbro, Chelsea Quinn, *Messages from Michael*, Playboy Press, 1979
Yarbro, Chelsea Quinn, *Michael for the Millennium*, Berkley, 1995
Yarbro, Chelsea Quinn, *Michael's People*, Berkley, 1988
Yarbro, Chelsea Quinn, *More Messages from Michael*, Berkley, 1986
Yogananda, Paramahansa, *Autobiography of a Yogi*, Self-Realization Fellowship,1972
Zukav, Gary, *The Dancing Wu Li Masters*, Rider & Co., 1991
Zukav, Gary, *The Seat of the Soul*, Fireside, 1990

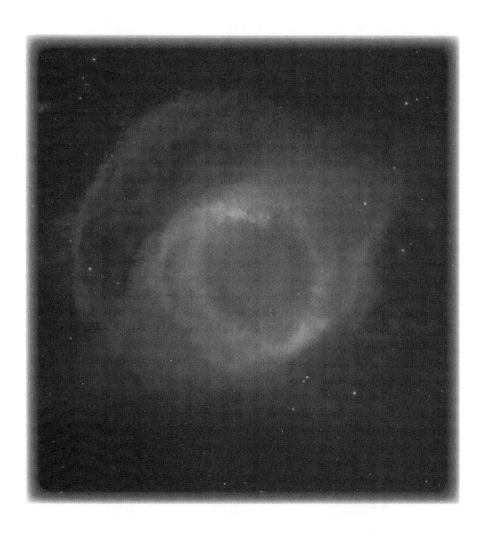

Astrologer, psychic, and channeler for over four decades, Judi Thomases is a frequent contributor to Dell Horoscope magazine, the founder and host of Talk Radio show (*"New Perspectives"*), and Cable TV show (*"Meet the Healers"*), and author of the award-winning book *"Wisdom's Game"*. Judi, a Phi Beta Kappa, has been a board member of a holistic practitioners network, a businesswomen's entrepreneurial network, and an astrological organization; has been a frequent guest on national media; has consulted on film and television projects; has an international roster of clients; and has taught, lectured and coached on metaphysical, astrological and spiritual subjects for decades. In 1997, Judi began to "hear" the voice of her spirit guides, *The Brotherhood of Light Workers*, who told her to expect a flow of teachings that she could use to help and heal others. Judi is dedicated to raising the planetary vibration, and in session, delves deeply into the soul's agenda, clarifying choices.. Her website is www.WisdomPath.com. Judi and her husband reside in Delaware.

Made in the USA
Columbia, SC
26 January 2022